The Program Management Office

Establishing, Managing and
Growing the Value of a PMO

The Program Management Office

Establishing, Managing and Growing the Value of a PMO

Craig J. Letavec, PMP

ISBN 1-932159-59-2

Printed and bound in the U.S.A. Printed on acid-free paper
10 9 8 7 6 5 4 3 2

Library of Congress Cataloging-in-Publication Data

Letavec, Craig J., 1970-
    The program management office : establishing, managing and growing the value of a
PMO / by Craig J. Letavec.
        p. cm.
    Includes index.
    ISBN-13: 978-1-932159-59-2 (hardcover : alk. paper)
    ISBN-10: 1-932159-59-2 (hardcover : alk. paper)
    1. Project management. I. Title.
    HD62.15.K467 2006
    658.4′04--dc22   2006020735

Phone: (954) 727-9333
Fax: (561) 892-0700
Web: www.jrosspub.com

To my parents

TABLE OF CONTENTS

PREFACE

As the role of project management in the modern organization has grown, many organizations have identified a need to formalize the practice of project management and to develop centers of coordination and excellence for project management. A program management office (PMO) is often viewed as a vehicle to achieve coordination, standardization, optimization, and management of the practice of project management. Although the concept of a PMO is appealing, many organizations often struggle with both the strategic and the practical aspects of establishing and managing a PMO. An inability to create a clear and compelling business case for the PMO, struggling with the issues of designing, structuring, and implementing the PMO, and an inability to clearly demonstrate the value provided by the PMO once operational are a few of the typical areas of concern that face management, PMO implementation teams, and PMO staff alike. This book addresses these and other challenges. It provides practical guidance for those considering implementing a PMO as well as those who already work in a functioning PMO.

In the first three chapters, topics of special interest to those who are considering implementing a PMO as well as those who have already been chartered to implement a PMO or who are considering expanding the role of a PMO in their organization are provided. These topics include conducting assessments to identify important project management challenges and PMO opportunities, developing a base business case to present to management that clearly outlines the unique challenges and PMO opportunities within an organization, and conducting a more detailed analysis and implementation planning process that leads to the development and presentation of a detailed business case to formally request permission to proceed with implementation. Following the discussions in the first three chapters, Chapter 4 focuses on implementation execution and PMO start-up, including practical guidance for marketing the PMO to the organization, selecting and training PMO staff, and ensuring a successful PMO start-up.

Subsequent chapters then focus on the PMO in operation. Practical operational aspects such as working to achieve benefit in the PMO's areas of focus are discussed along with planning for the future strategic direction for the PMO. Additionally, three distinct areas of focus for the PMO—knowledge, standards, and consulting—are presented in detail. Discussion of these topics includes the role that each plays in advancing the practice of project management within the organization and in providing value to the organization. From a knowledge perspective, developing a project management knowledgebase and the role of the PMO in education and training are discussed. The focus of the standards discussion includes developing, managing, and growing organizational project management standards. The consulting focus includes the role of the PMO in project consulting, mentoring, and actively managing projects.

Throughout the book, practical guidance is provided to aid the reader in successfully establishing the knowledge, standards, and consulting roles in a PMO. A reader who already has an operational PMO will find these chapters particularly valuable. The material that is presented is largely relevant for those who are establishing a new PMO as well as those who are seeking to expand the focus or grow the value of an existing PMO.

A PMO has the potential to provide significant benefits. Critical components of establishing and maintaining a successful PMO include understanding the role of the PMO and knowing how to effectively "sell" a PMO to management, how to effectively implement a PMO in an organization, and how to establish and grow the value of a PMO over time. The PMO journey is a journey well worth undertaking. This book will be a guide.

ABOUT THE AUTHOR

CRAIG LETAVEC

Craig Letavec is a student of project management. He has led information technology projects in a diverse range of companies including Procter & Gamble, Hewlett-Packard, and Siemens Business Services. He has served as an active speaker and author on a range of topics, including implementing effective change management, establishing and growing project management maturity within organizations, and establishing, managing, and building the value of the program management office in organizations.

Throughout his professional career, he has studied the role of project management in organizations, the process of formalizing project management in organizations, and the many challenges that face organizations and project managers alike. This practical analysis, combined with academic research in the field, has led him to a number of conclusions regarding how organizations can best exploit project management to improve business results.

Mr. Letavec holds a Bachelor of Science from the University of Dayton (Go Flyers!) and a Master of Science in Project Management from George Washington University. He has achieved the Project Management Professional (PMP®) certification from the Project Management Institute. As an active teacher who enjoys educating future project managers and business professionals, he has served as an adjunct lecturer in project management in the Master of Business Administration program at Wright State University in Dayton, Ohio and as an adjunct instructor at the University of Dayton. He welcomes questions, comments, and feedback via electronic mail at craig@gotpmo.com.

Web
Added
Value™

At J. Ross Publishing we are committed to providing today's professional with practical, hands-on tools that enhance the learning experience and give readers an opportunity to apply what they have learned. That is why we offer free ancillary materials available for download on this book and all participating Web Added Value™ publications. These online resources may include interactive versions of material that appears in the book or supplemental templates, worksheets, models, plans, case studies, proposals, spreadsheets and assessment tools, among other things. Whenever you see the WAV™ symbol in any of our publications it means bonus materials accompany the book and are available from the Web Added Value™ Download Resource Center at www.jrosspub.com.

Downloads for *The Program Management Office: Establishing, Managing and Growing the Value of a PMO* consist of a toolkit and templates of easy-to-adapt resources for several of the key functions of a PMO.

INTRODUCTION TO THE PMO

INTRODUCTION

Chapter 1 will introduce several concepts related to the program management office (PMO) and will provide an overview of the potential opportunity areas in which the PMO can provide value to an organization. Chapter 1 will then focus on the process of assessing the organization from a project management perspective, documenting current challenges and improvement opportunities in the organization and developing a PMO base business case. The base business case can then be presented to management for the purposes of informing management about the opportunities that the PMO can provide and requesting authorization to proceed with development of a detailed business case and a roadmap for establishing a PMO in the organization. "Organization" may represent an entire company, a division within a company, a specific region, or another subunit within a larger entity that the PMO will serve. Even if the scope of the PMO is relatively small, certain benefits provided by the PMO may be extended beyond its primary constituents and thereby provide value to a broader segment of the overall organization. Whether the PMO is intended to serve the organization as a whole or to serve only one department within the organization, understanding the key project and program management challenges and documenting how the PMO can address these challenges is a critical first step toward achieving an effective PMO.

THE PROJECT AND PROGRAM CONTEXT

The Project Management Institute's *A Guide to the Project Management Body of Knowledge* defines a *project* as "a temporary endeavor undertaken to create a unique product, service or result."[1] Projects are typically authorized with a defined duration and cost and with a defined scope and set of performance criteria in place that set boundaries for the project effort. Once the performance criteria are met, the project is considered complete and the resources assigned to this project are typically assigned to other efforts within the organization. Depending on the effort to be undertaken, projects can range in duration from a few weeks to multiple years and can represent specific unique *task-force-type* efforts that address specific needs or larger efforts that represent core business opportunities for the organization. In many organizations, projects and project teams are formed within functional groups such as finance, information systems, or engineering. In other organizations, a centralized project management organization that houses project management resources is dedicated to project efforts. Regardless of the specific structure, the goal of undertaking and completing project efforts for the benefit of the organization remains the same.

For many projects of reasonable size and duration, a *single* project team led by a project manager is sufficient to undertake and complete the required work. However, in larger efforts, such as building a jet or undertaking a multiple-year effort to replace an organization's central supply chain infrastructure, typically there are *multiple*, related efforts and each one requires an individual team. In these cases, a number of unique projects may be defined (each with its own project team) and managed under a single *program*—a grouping of multiple projects that enables consolidated management and reporting. Figure 1.1 depicts a common program structure.

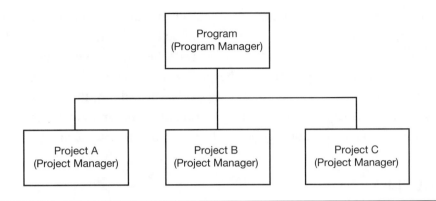

Figure 1.1 Projects and programs.

Within a program, multiple projects may exist and be executed simultaneously. Each of these individual projects will be managed by a project manager with specific responsibility for that project. Therefore, logical divisions of work can be managed and led by teams specifically devoted to that work. Additionally, a single program manager or program management team is often assigned to coordinate efforts across all of the projects within the program, to serve as a central point of contact for the program, and to assist with addressing issues that affect more than one of the component projects within the program. This structure facilitates faster decision making for situations in which only one area of the program is affected because the individual project manager for that program component assumes responsibility for decision making at the project level. For broader issues, the program manager can consult with each of the individual project managers and make decisions that can quickly be disseminated to all affected teams.

Furthermore, the program structure permits simpler management reporting and cost and schedule tracking. In large projects, budget and schedule tracking can be a significant effort due to the number of work items to be managed. The program structure facilitates decentralized management of these functions while still providing for aggregation and consolidated reporting and management across the program. Although a consolidated project schedule and budget are still necessary, individual projects can be managed at the project level with project budgets and schedules that are delegated to the individual project managers for oversight. When individual project efforts are running within the expected budget and schedule, budget and schedule updates can be fed to the program budget and schedule through software tools or via regular meetings between the program manager and the individual project managers. When significant variances are realized, the project manager can bring these variances to the attention of the program manager so that the impact to the overall program can be assessed, understood, and managed.

THE PMO

Defining the PMO

As the importance of project management has grown, many organizations have identified the need for a central center of organizational project knowledge, one with expertise-related project management practices, techniques, and standards. Whether called the Program Management Office, Project Office, or another term, these centers of knowledge and expertise serve many important functions within organizations that are conducting projects. One role, the role of a *consulting* organization, may involve executing projects, rescuing troubled projects, mentoring project managers, or providing consulting on project management best practices to functional organizations within an enterprise. Another role, the role of a *knowledge* organization, involves capturing and organizing project artifacts, creating and delivering training related to project management topics, and helping to grow a project management culture within the organization. Still another role, the role of a *standards* organization, involves establishing and maintaining project-related standards, processes, procedures, and templates that may be implemented to help drive standardization of project management practices throughout the organization.

In this book, the term Program Management Office (PMO) will be used to describe the organization responsible for executing the many functions associated with the central management of project and program administration within an organization. Although the definition of program may vary across businesses and industries, this general concept can be used to define a number of projects that are logically grouped together for the purposes of achieving some business goal. A very complex final deliverable such as designing and building a jet may potentially involve hundreds of unique project efforts, yet it may be desirable to identify a single point of responsibility and reporting for the effort overall. Thus, many projects could be rolled up into a single program under the guidance of a PMO. An organization may have multiple PMOs that are divided along functional or some other organizational boundaries. Regardless of number, the goal remains the same—to develop and deliver an organization that can effectively set standards, provide management and consulting, and build and maintain organizational knowledge as it relates to the function of managing project efforts.

There is no one single central theme that underlies the reasons why organizations establish PMOs. For some organizations, the need to gain control over their project efforts (often due to one or a series of major project disasters) drives them to establish the PMO as a central point of control and oversight for projects. For others, the desire to establish and maintain a set of project management best practices that are applied broadly throughout the organization, but that are managed centrally, is the primary driver. These standards, evolved and improved over time, grow the level of project and program management process maturity within the organization, helping to ensure better project outcomes over time. This maturity concept, representing an evolving state of improved conformance to proven processes that are continuously improved over time, is one of the most common reasons organizations consider the implementation of a PMO. For still other organizations, the desire to establish a project management culture and a central home for project managers is the key driver. If project management is a disparate function within the organization with no level of central management or coordination, project managers may feel that they have been left to fend for themselves to achieve acceptable project outcomes. Developing a project management culture centered on a PMO may be a first step toward bringing project managers together and ensuring that an appropriate system to support project managers in the field is available.

The decision to create and maintain a PMO is not one to be undertaken lightly. An effective PMO requires long-term commitments of human resources, money, and time. If a viable business case and a statement of value to the organization are not thoroughly investigated, documented, and communicated, the likelihood of the PMO failing or not fully achieving its goals increases significantly. If an organization can clearly articulate *what* it expects the PMO to provide in terms of services to the organization and *how* the PMO will improve project results before beginning to establish the PMO, the likelihood of achieving success increases dramatically. Furthermore, defining a scope of work and the overall goals for the PMO up front helps to facilitate making the right decisions about how to structure, staff, and implement the PMO in the organization.

Not all PMOs are created "equal." In some organizations, the PMO will be staffed by expert project managers who report directly to a PMO manager and who have significant responsibility for delivering projects. In other organizations, the PMO will serve primarily in the role of a consultancy, with PMO staff possibly devoting only a portion of their time to mentoring, training, and establishing standards while still having responsibility within a functional group for delivery of projects or programs. In still other organizations, the PMO may serve in an oversight function, executing administrative project functions, such as consolidated reporting, creating and supporting project management tools, and creating and evangelizing standards throughout the functional organization. There are many other possible combinations of roles as well. The first important step in establishing a PMO involves defining what role the PMO will play in the organization and understanding what PMO structure will best support the organization (at a cost acceptable to the organization).

Basic Structural Models of the PMO

One of the first important considerations that must be addressed by any organization considering the implementation of a PMO is the basic structural model that will be used within the organization. The specific scope or reach of the PMO will be of interest to management as it considers chartering the PMO. Having an idea of the intended scope of the PMO in mind as initial investigation into the use of the PMO in the organization is undertaken will help guide the process of investigating the potential benefits of the PMO to the organization and documenting the base business case for the PMO.

Several basic PMO structural models are of interest. At a high level, a PMO may be either internally facing or externally facing. The internally facing PMO exists to serve one or more divisions, groups, or geographies within

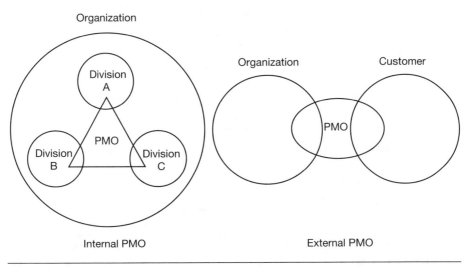

Figure 1.2 Internally versus externally facing model of a PMO.

the organization (or potentially the entire organization itself). It provides program coordination, consulting, education, standards setting, or other functions exclusively within the organization. The externally facing PMO provides a link between the organization and one or more of its customers. It acts in a customer relationship management capacity as well as in a coordination capacity to ensure customer needs are being met and that internal groups within the organization are aligned to deliver the project, program, or other deliverables that the PMO coordinates.

As Figure 1.2 depicts, the externally facing PMO spans both the organization and the organization's customers and may act as an internal coordinator of efforts and a single point of contact for one or more external customers, ensuring that customers have access to the organization and its resources via a single, dedicated group that works to ensure that customer needs are being met. The advantages of this external PMO model can be significant in terms of customer satisfaction and delivery of customer-facing projects, but the externally facing PMO also faces significant challenges in terms of potentially coordinating many internal groups, vendors, and other parties to deliver customer projects.

The existence of internally facing PMOs and externally facing PMOs in an organization is not mutually exclusive nor is there any implied assumption

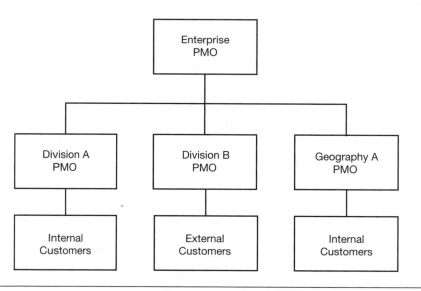

Figure 1.3 Coordinated enterprise PMO model.

that there must be only one internally facing PMO or externally facing PMO (or both) within an organization. As Figure 1.3 depicts, an organization might have multiple PMOs within the organization itself, each coordinating efforts for a particular division, group, or geography.

A *central* enterprise PMO may be included to provide overall organizational PMO coordination, to facilitate organization-wide project reporting, or to maintain certain sets of key standards to be used by the entire organization. Even within this model, externally facing PMOs may exist as well to coordinate with one or more of the internally facing PMOs or with the central enterprise PMO to ensure delivery of customer projects. Other *blended* models may exist to meet the unique needs of a particular organization.

An additional structural model is relevant for the purposes of this discussion. A project or program PMO model exists in some organizations to manage a specific effort or set of efforts. In this model, the PMO often exists only for the lifetime of the project or program and then the PMO team is disbanded to work on other project or program efforts. Thus, the PMO is a temporary entity in the organization that is established and maintained for the purposes of ensuring the success of some particular effort or group of efforts rather than as a permanent entity in the organization that looks at project, program, and portfolio management from a broad perspective. (*Note*: For the purposes of this text, the operation of the project or program PMO will follow the general context of the PMO, but the focus will be more targeted on the operational aspects of project management than on the standards and knowledge aspects.) The project or program PMO is best coordinated through the efforts of a supervisory PMO, such as those operating in the other models previously described, which will ensure coordination and standardization across potentially many project or program PMOs that may exsist in the organization to support certain efforts.

These models represent a set of possible end states for the organization that will be adapted as required to meet the unique needs of the organization. As a point of general guidance, introducing the PMO concept into the organization, regardless of the model chosen, is best accomplished using a phased approach. This approach may involve piloting the PMO concept in one division, group, or geography within the organization to gather knowledge and experience that can be leveraged to implement the PMO concept more broadly over time. Alternatively, if a single organization-wide PMO is being considered, implementing the PMO with a small set of initial goals and expanding the role of the PMO in the organization over time is often the most practical approach. An implementation model that allows the PMO concept to *sell itself* to management through a successful smaller-scale initial implementation is most appropriate in cases in which the benefits to the organization and the business case for the PMO must be proven. Even in those cases in which management's support for the PMO is strong, the desire to aggressively implement the PMO concept with broad scope in order to achieve benefits more quickly should be weighed against the potential impact on the organization of changing business processes and practices to achieve the PMO's intended goals. The PMO, with its many benefits, also creates the potential for some degree of initial organizational upheaval as affected members of the organization adjust to interacting with the PMO and as the PMO fine tunes its operational model to best meet the needs of the organization. Proceeding with due caution initially as the base structural model of the PMO is determined helps to mitigate this risk and ensure a successful start-up.

Benefits of the PMO Concept

Specific benefits of a PMO will vary depending on the structure and design of the PMO within an organization. However, there are several key categories of benefits that can be achieved through establishing a PMO. At the conceptual level, the PMO concept serves as a fundamental unifier for project and program activities in the organization. Whether the PMO actively manages projects directly or serves as a standards and consulting organization, the PMO, as a central home for project management (whether in a department, division, or across the enterprise), can provide significant value. Members of the organization will know where they can seek guidance and obtain answers to project management questions. Additionally, the PMO concept provides a formalization of project and program management oversight in an organization and creates a visible "face" for project and program management that is recognized beyond just the project management staff, signifying a broad organizational commitment to the practice of project management.

From a corporate management perspective, the PMO may serve as the central oversight organization responsible for providing key project status information to management. As such, the PMO may collect project status data and provide management with an ability to have a single view of the project landscape within the organization and to receive consolidated information regarding projects undertaken in the organization as needed. When the PMO serves as a central repository for project data across the organization, data collected enables powerful management reporting and trend analysis that would be otherwise difficult in organizations with no central project reporting standards and processes. Corporate management may also utilize the PMO to manage oversight of project chartering, to consolidate risk profiling and management, and other similar governance activities that ensure an appropriate level of control over the projects undertaken in the organization.

From a process perspective, the PMO can play a key role in providing governance, oversight, and standards setting for the project processes within an organization. Especially in large organizations, ensuring that consistent project management best practices are followed can be difficult. Establishing a PMO with a responsibility for creating and maintaining project standards can provide a focus on researching and setting best practices standards within the organization that cannot be uniformly achieved through the efforts of individual project managers. Whether these standards are based on recognized external standards or developed through documenting and reusing best practices within the organization, the PMO concept is well suited for centralizing the establishment, dissemination, and maintenance of project management best practices. By standardizing common project management practices across the organization, expectations are uniform. Project managers, project team members, and stakeholders gain confidence that regardless of the project, a certain set of fundamental approaches to project management will be consistently in place to help ensure project success.

The benefits of the PMO to individual project managers cannot be overlooked. The PMO may serve as the central home for project managers—a place to turn to for advice, organizational standards, and support as individual project managers manage their project efforts. The PMO may also serve as a central training organization and provide professional development activities that allow individual project managers and project team members to grow their skills and expertise. Additionally, project managers may find a role in the PMO as a possible career path option within their organization. The organization may also use PMO roles as a way to attract and retain project management talent as well as a vehicle for mentoring project team members and junior project managers who wish to learn from members of the organization who have significant knowledge and expertise in the project management field.

Obstacles Facing Organizations Establishing PMOs

Several common obstacles may present challenges to an organization seeking to establish a PMO. Initially, a lack of understanding of the role of a PMO in the organization by management and, perhaps more importantly, a lack of understanding of the value proposition that the PMO provides are common. Often the concept of a PMO is very new to organizations, and management may not understand the specific roles and benefits of a PMO. Defining a clear mission for the PMO and presenting a detailed description of the intended roles of a PMO in the organization and a rationalization of the intended benefits of the PMO may help to alleviate some of these concerns.

A perception among the project management community that the PMO will serve as an obstacle to the timely accomplishment of project management goals may also exist initially. The PMO may create new processes and procedures during its lifetime that can in some cases result in either modifying the way project managers and project team members work and/or creating additional work for project managers and project team members. However, the benefits of standardization, consolidated reporting, increased organizational project knowledge, and other areas of process improvement typically outweigh the incremental costs of implementing and using revised processes. Early and consistent communication and involvement of project managers within the organization in the PMO establishment process are essential to overcoming concern regarding the role of the PMO in establishing standards as a way of bringing simplification and standardization to the organization. Early involvement also helps to ensure that the PMO, when operational, meets the needs of one of its primary constituents.

Concern from management regarding initial funding and ongoing operational costs to the organization is also common. The initial investment in a PMO must be viewed as such—an investment. The initial success of a PMO is largely dependent upon having sufficient monetary and human resources available to allow the PMO to commence operations at a level sufficient to meet its intended goals and to do so within a reasonable time frame. This does not necessarily mean in all cases that large amounts of time and effort are needed. Many PMOs begin as a small organization with a limited scope and expand over time. However, the required investment and intended payback will most certainly be a topic that must be addressed with management. Having a solid plan, well-defined resource needs, and a business case for success will go a long way toward ensuring that management understands the benefits of the PMO and realizes the required investment and intended return.

THE PMO START-UP ROADMAP

The process of establishing a PMO and commencing operations is best undertaken in a manner similar to how projects are undertaken—via a series of defined phases with intended goals and deliverables. Having a consolidated

Assess

Define

Sell

Implement

Operate
and
Improve

Figure 1.4 PMO start-up roadmap.

plan of action that guides the processes of defining the organization's needs, defining the value that the PMO concept can provide, securing approval to proceed with implementation of a PMO, and developing and implementing the PMO ensures that due diligence is undertaken prior to expending significant amounts of the organization's time and money. An action plan also creates a foundation for success by ensuring that a set of agreed-to plans is in place to guide the PMO development and implementation effort. In this book, the concept of a PMO start-up roadmap will be discussed. A roadmap is used to guide the PMO development and implementation process. It includes a number of important processes that help to facilitate a thoughtful and successful PMO investigation and implementation. Figure 1.4 depicts the key phases of a PMO start-up roadmap.

The roadmap begins with assessing the organization's project management needs. A gap analysis or some other identification of current project management challenges facing the organization often serves as a basis for this analysis. After this phase, a definition of and a vision for how the PMO will address some or all of these needs is established and is used as the basis for creating the *sell* for the PMO. The selling process involves presenting the PMO plan to management, addressing issues, and securing approval to proceed with establishing the PMO. Assuming that the selling process is successful, the next step is to undertake several key foundational activities that are required in order to implement the PMO successfully. These activities include tasks such as choosing a PMO manager, establishing the physical PMO, defining the initial goals for the PMO and a time line for the initial initiatives that will provide value (ideally within the first 90 days of operation), and so forth. Once the foundation is built, the PMO is launched and it enters a phase of sustained operations and continuous improvement. Each of these phases is critical to the success of the PMO. No phase should be skipped.

The PMO Team—The First Critical Step

A PMO start-up roadmap does not create itself. In fact, reality is that the process of investigating the PMO concept, identifying opportunities for a PMO in the organization, gaining management commitment to implement a PMO (even if on a trial basis), and creating and delivering a successful PMO implementation and start-up represents a significant amount of work. The ongoing activities of the PMO represent work as well, requiring resources beyond implementation and start-up. As a first important step in the PMO process, one or more members of the organization must be tasked with investigating the PMO concept and completing the first phases of the PMO start-up roadmap, including all of the preliminary steps that lead to the final *sell* and, hopefully, approval to implement the PMO.

Assigning one or more members of the organization as PMO investigation team resources or PMO champions and authorizing work on investigating the PMO concept and benefits to the organization must be part of the first management undertakings. Initially, only one resource may be required. Over time, more resources may be added as needed to support detailed development and implementation efforts as well as to fill full-time PMO staff roles in the operating PMO. (The recruitment and selection of these resources will be discussed in Chapter 4.) For the initial PMO investigation and PMO start-up roadmap process-related work, the resource or resources assigned to investigate the PMO concept and to report to management should ideally have sufficient experience with project management and the organizational culture to allow them to take a broad look at the state of project management in the organization and to objectively assess the current project management challenges and the potential benefits that the PMO can provide. If more than one resource will be assigned, a single individual should be appointed to lead the effort and coordinate the efforts of the entire team. If a single resource will be assigned to this task, this resource will lead the PMO investigation. A senior project manager or other organizational leader, supported by other individuals with project management experience, is an appropriate choice for the lead role. Although prior experience as a member of a PMO or as a project manager in an organization with a functioning PMO (perhaps through previous employment in another organization) is certainly desirable, it is not a requirement. With an appropriate amount of research and guidance from resources such as this text, an understanding of the functions of the PMO and specific implementation considerations that are sufficient to allow the team to identify PMO opportunities and plan for a successful implementation can be obtained. This learning and investigation process will not occur overnight. Therefore, ensure the availability of sufficient resources for potentially a number of months so that appropriate attention is given to thoroughly reviewing current operations and preparing recommendations.

Supporting the PMO Team

In addition to establishing one or more members of the organization as the leaders of the PMO investigation effort, it is important to formally establish management oversight for this function. This oversight might include appointment of a member of the organization's management team to the role of PMO sponsor. Alternatively, oversight could involve establishment of a PMO steering committee that includes several members of management who represent different PMO stakeholder groups within the organization. Establishing a PMO sponsor or a PMO steering committee role ensures that the PMO team is supported and demonstrates management's commitment to investigating the potential role of the PMO in the organization. The PMO sponsor or PMO steering committee member role should be staffed by individuals who are empowered to make decisions regarding the PMO implementation and ongoing activities, are authorized to commit funds and resources to support the PMO effort, and are committed to ensuring that the PMO provides value to the organization.

Initially the PMO sponsor or PMO steering committee will receive reports from the PMO team on the progress of the investigation effort and will receive the final management reports that provide the basis for approval of the implementation of the PMO. Once the PMO is in operation, the PMO sponsor or PMO steering committee will provide management oversight, assist with resolving issues as they arise, ensure that the PMO is reaching its intended goals, and validate that the PMO remains aligned with the organization's goals and priorities. Although the commitment of time and effort required may vary, there is no expectation that the PMO sponsor or PMO steering committee roles will represent full-time roles. However, the PMO sponsor or PMO steering committee members must be committed to providing an appropriate level of ongoing oversight, including attending regularly scheduled status meetings, providing guidance as needed, and assisting with the resolution of key issues that may be limiting the success of the PMO effort.

A NOTE ABOUT USING THIS TEXT

This book can be divided into two sections. In the first section (Chapters 1 through 5), issues related to the establishment of a PMO within an organization will be addressed. Topics that will be examined include structuring of a PMO, effectively marketing the PMO concept to an organization's leadership, selecting a PMO manager and PMO team, and creating the essential plan and deliverables required to start-up a PMO. Guidance will be provided to allow the reader to take the first steps toward establishing an effective PMO and managing the implementation and early life of the PMO.

The second section (Chapters 6 through 8) will address the role of the PMO as a consulting, knowledge, and standards organization in greater detail. For each of these important functions, guidance on the selection and implementation of appropriate aspects of these functions based on the needs of the organization will be addressed. For readers operating in an organization that already has a well-established PMO, this section will provide insight into how to foster and grow these three critical roles of a PMO.

Those who are establishing a PMO should start with the first section and proceed in order through the phases required to successfully start-up a PMO. Those who are working in an established PMO that is already in the "sustain and improve" phase may prefer to proceed directly to the second section of the text. The second section focuses on a more-detailed discussion of the three key roles of a PMO in project organization:

- The PMO as a *consulting* organization
- The PMO as a *knowledge* organization
- The PMO as a *standards* organization

Although these three key roles will be discussed at a high level in the first section, the second section will provide a more-detailed discussion of how to exploit each of these roles. The second section would be appropriate as a starting point for those who do not need a detailed understanding of the process of establishing a PMO.

DEFINING AND SELLING THE PMO

This section will provide guidance through the first phases of the PMO start-up roadmap:

- Assess the project environment
- Determine project management needs
- Establish a mission for transformation
- Sell the PMO concept

The first critical steps in the process of establishing a PMO include determining the needs of the organization from a project management perspective, defining the intended vision and goals of the PMO, and gaining organizational commitment to invest the necessary human and capital resources to start up and sustain the PMO in the organization. Without a clear vision of the purpose and goals for the PMO, the ability to sell the PMO concept to management will be severely limited. Additionally, establishing a clear vision for the initial role of the PMO in the organization will help to avoid PMO scope creep. This situation can cause the PMO to attempt to initially address too many issues and thus dilute its capability rather than focusing on establishing a firm footing in several key areas and expanding in terms of role and scope over time.

It is critical to define the organization's needs from a project management perspective, to determine how to translate these needs into a concise mission and set of initial goals for the PMO, and to determine how to sell this vision to management. These activities form the fundamental foundation upon which a successful PMO is built. Without management buy-in, a PMO will be doomed to failure. By showing the organization that a solid vision exists and that management concurs with the vision, organizational resistance to the PMO concept may be reduced and the likelihood of long-term success is increased.

ASSESSING THE PROJECT ENVIRONMENT

The first process in establishing the foundation for organizing a PMO is to survey the current project environment. The purpose of this activity is to identify the current state of project management in the organization and to begin the process of identifying the opportunity areas within a project management context in which a PMO can potentially provide value. This activity will examine the state of project management in the context of several key areas:

- People (organizational assessment)
- Processes (process assessment)
- Project outcomes (delivery assessment)

In the following sections, the indicators that should be examined within each of these areas will be explained. The order in which these assessments are completed is not critical, but the results of each of these assessments create key inputs to the PMO design process.

Upon completion of the assessments, an assessment summary document will be prepared that encompasses the key findings from the organizational, process, and delivery assessments. This document will be used as a key input to developing an appropriate business case to justify organizational investment in the PMO. Beyond approval and implementation of the PMO itself, the assessment summary may be used throughout the life of the PMO to identify additional areas of PMO focus (recognizing that it will not be possible to solve all of the organization's project management challenges through the initial implementation of the PMO) and may be updated from time to time, based on future assessments, to gauge progress in addressing the organization's challenges or to reflect improvement that is realized over time.

There are many possible formats for capturing the information obtained while conducting an assessment. For smaller organizations in which a limited number of projects are conducted or in organizations that have a limited number of groups within the organization that typically undertake projects, simply documenting important findings in a simple table format or as one summary document per assessment area may be sufficient. In larger organizations, it may be necessary to conduct the assessments within individual groups or geographies and to produce several sets of documents segmented along some organizational or geographic boundary. Alternately, it may be possible to use a single document, but to note specific divisional or geographic differences within the document. For larger organizations, it may also be beneficial to assemble a small team to conduct the assessment if the size and scope of the organization precludes obtaining information in a timely fashion using only one or two resources. When a team approach is used, some minimal level of training should be provided to ensure consistency in how the assessment is conducted and how the findings are reported.

The goal of conducting an assessment is to determine what processes are in place today and the extent to which these processes are standardized across the organization. For now, focusing the assessment on what is in place today rather than what should be changed as work is done to implement the PMO is important. If appropriate, additional assessment areas may be addressed as well, depending on the current needs and challenges facing the organization. The assessment areas outlined are not intended to be an exhaustive list, but rather to be a summary of the core areas that should be addressed prior to considering the possible business benefits of establishing a PMO.

Table 1.1   Project Resource Inventory

Resource	Current Project and Allocation	Current Role	Skills/Certification
Resource A	Server upgrade project (100%)	Project Manager	Internal Project Manager certification
Resource B	Server upgrade project (50%)	Server Architect	
Resource C	Business reporting project (25%)	Senior Programmer	
	XYZ data conversion project (50%)	Data Conversion Lead	

Organizational Assessment

The organizational assessment process seeks to identify the current state of the project organization as well as the resources that are assigned to project activities. The deliverables from the organizational assessment should include:

- Project resource demographics
- Project organization charts
- Project management development processes

Project Resource Demographics

The first step in an organizational assessment is to determine who in the organization is currently leading projects as well as who in the organization is providing support to project leaders. This may be most easily accomplished by developing a simple project resource inventory that includes the names of project resources, currently assigned projects, role(s) on currently assigned projects, and project-specific certification or other skills relevant to the project environment. A basic inventory might take a format similar to Table 1.1.

Other information such as geographic location, division, business unit, or other relevant items may be included as well. Undertaking this exercise can be very time consuming if a mechanism does not already exist to obtain consolidated project resource utilization information, but it yields several key benefits:

- Provides a consolidated view of the resources working on project activities (This view is critical for understanding the work being undertaken and will be an input to later assessment processes.)
- Serves as a basis for identifying project-relevant skill sets and certifications that exist in the organization (This information will be useful for understanding the state of project management skill in the organization as well as for potentially identifying resources to assist with the start-up and management of the PMO.)
- Provides understanding about whether resource commitment to projects is largely distributed (i.e., many resources spend a percentage of their time on several projects) or highly committed (i.e., resources are generally assigned to spend the majority of their time on one or two project efforts only) as well as the extent to which resources devote their time to project efforts versus operational efforts

In large organizations that undertake many projects, completing this exercise for every project resource in the organization may not be practical. In this situation, several possible alternatives will still provide useful results. If the intent of investigating the establishment of a PMO is to determine the benefits of a PMO for only one division (or a few divisions) within a very large organization, only the resources relevant to the projects undertaken in those divisions must be captured. If this information still appears to be too large to capture within a reasonable time frame, a cross-sectional sample of large, medium, and small project efforts could be captured as well. If the intent is to develop an enterprise-wide PMO, capturing only the resources for one division or a few divisions may yield skewed results. In these situations, an alternative methodology may be to capture data on only the resources managing the project efforts in the organization and then conduct interviews with a few of these resources to gauge the general utilization and skill sets of the project resources that report to the project manager being interviewed.

Project Organization Charts

Once the resource inventory has been completed, the next step in the organizational assessment process is to develop an *as is* project organizational chart.

The purpose of this chart is to map the results of the resource inventory to a graphical format that highlights the chain of command in the organization from a project management standpoint. The organizational chart should include the roles of functional managers within the organization, project managers, and project team members. If project team members and project managers are drawn from multiple areas of an organization, it may be necessary to map several functional groups in order to obtain a view of how projects are undertaken in the organization. If formal organization charts exist that show the formal structure of the organization, using these charts as a basis and delineating the associations between members of the functional organization and projects may be appropriate. As resources are mapped to an organizational chart, one of several general patterns may emerge.

Silo. In the silo pattern, projects each have their own individual lines of reporting from the project team to the project manager, but the centralized reporting line beyond the project leads to a single functional manager. This functional manager may represent a division head, vice president, or some other general business function manager. In this model, projects are primarily completed by resources within the division that are under the direct general control of the function head. The function head sets standards for how he or she would like to see project progress reported, validates resource assignments, and may set other policies for his or her division relative to how projects are approved, funded, and executed. Resources assigned to projects in the silo pattern may be full-time project resources or resources that have primarily non-project responsibilities, but spend a portion of their time devoted to project efforts. Figure 1.5 depicts the silo pattern.

Cross-silo. Another pattern that may emerge is the duplication, matrix, or cross-silo pattern. In the cross-silo pattern, projects are still primarily controlled within a single division, but resources assigned to project efforts may either be a mix of resources from multiple divisions that come together to execute a particular project or a combination of resources that span multiple projects across multiple divisions. Each resource has primary reporting responsibility to a particular division head from a management, career path, and performance evaluation standpoint, but may additionally have "soft" or

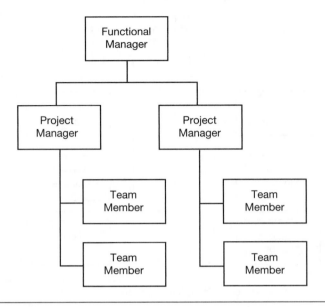

Figure 1.5 Silo pattern organizational structure.

"dotted-line" reporting relationships to project managers in other divisions or to other division heads directly. Figure 1.6 depicts the cross-silo pattern.

As illustrated in Figure 1.6, project resources are shared across divisions as needed to undertake projects. The procurement of resources for a particular effort may be undertaken primarily through negotiation between division heads to ensure that a particular resource is assigned for a certain percentage of his or her time for a particular project effort. The cross-silo pattern usually involves a number of resources who spend only a portion of their time engaged in project efforts in addition to other job responsibilities. Although this model may seem cumbersome, many organizations that prefer strong functional reporting lines or that undertake primarily smaller, limited-duration projects find this mode of operations easier to manage. A potential downside of this model from a project management standpoint is that resource negotiation can be time consuming and can potentially cause split loyalty between the project work and an individual's primary job.

Strong project. A third pattern that may emerge is the strong project pattern. In this pattern, projects are recognized as either primarily *belonging* to one organization or division or potentially *crossing* divisional boundaries to

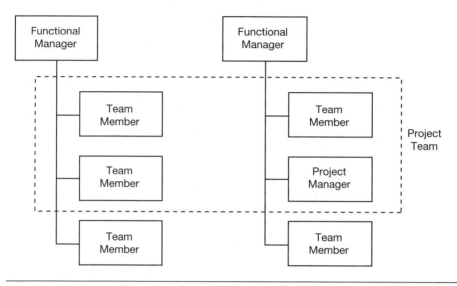

Figure 1.6 Cross-silo pattern organizational structure.

become "enterprise" projects that affect the entire organization. In the strong project pattern, a project manager maintains primary control for the project effort and leads a team that may involve individuals from several different divisions in the organization that are on loan and primarily devoted to the project activities. This pattern ensures that resources are aligned to the project effort and that loyalties are not split between completing project work and ongoing operational activities. Figure 1.7 depicts the strong project pattern.

A strong project pattern has significant advantages in terms of providing the ability for the project manager to direct and manage project resources and in terms of ensuring consistent effort and commitment to project work. However, typically the strong project pattern is the most difficult to sustain given the significant commitment required to ensure that project resources remain committed to project work.

Hybrid. As this step of the organizational assessment progresses, it is possible that none of the general patterns will consistently emerge or that findings will indicate that a hybrid of one of the patterns mentioned may exist. All of these cases are perfectly acceptable. The goal of determining the general project organization is not to attempt to "force fit" a particular organization to a

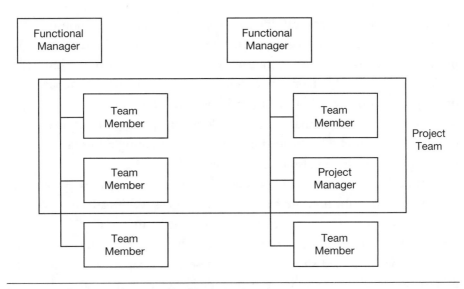

Figure 1.7 Strong project organizational structure.

particular pattern, but to identify the general pattern or patterns that the organization uses to manage projects and resources. Depending on the size and complexity of the organization, it may be possible to assign specific names to specific nodes within a general project organization framework and thus complete a true view of how project resources are currently assigned across projects in the organization. If that exercise is not practical, one may choose to either map only the projects and their associated project managers or to simply create a generalized diagram of how a typical project is staffed and managed in the context of the project organizational chart.

It is important to not overlook this organizational assessment step. This *as is* view of the project organizational chart is a key input to determining the *to be* project organization within the context of a PMO. Without a documented view of the structure that currently exists, an attempt to map how the organization will operate in the future will be extremely difficult.

Project Management Development Processes

Project management development processes include the processes by which the organization trains and certifies project management resources. These processes are not intended to be solely for the benefit of project managers.

Project process awareness training for project team members, sponsor training for key project sponsors and stakeholders, and specialized training for project administrators, finance managers, and others with a vested interest in project processes and outcomes are all part of the overall project management development process. Additionally, training is not the only relevant component of the project management development process. Documentation, resource guides, and other related means of disseminating information about project processes should also be considered.

For project staff such as project and program managers, a review of training opportunities for both new project managers as well as advanced opportunities for experienced project managers should be undertaken. If standard organizational processes exist for project management, the content of training opportunities provided should align to these standards. If the organization follows standardized methodologies provided by external standards organizations, training opportunities should align with these standards and ensure that the standards are placed in the context of the types of projects typically undertaken by the organization. For project team members, the same general principles should apply—training should introduce the role of the project team member in the project process and the expectations of the organization relative to how project team members will conduct their work within the project context.

In addition to training, an understanding of how the organization assesses project manager performance and certifies skills should be obtained. In some organizations, internal staff development programs and internal certification paths are provided to allow project managers to grow their skills and obtain recognition for their level of competence and achievement in project management. In other organizations, external certifications provided by project standards organizations serve as the basis for qualification of project management skill. Regardless of the approach taken, it is important to understand how the organization fosters growth within the project management discipline in the organization, how the organization recognizes proficiency in project management processes, and how the organization tracks and maintains information on the level of skill and proficiency obtained by their project managers relative to the project management standards or training and certification paths or guidelines in place within the organization.

Process Assessment

Process assessment seeks to identify the organizational processes that are in place today from the project selection, initiation, planning, management, and closeout perspectives. These processes may be formal, documented processes that are either created internally or provided by some external provider or ad hoc processes that vary across the organization. Like organizational assessment, the goal of this assessment is to identify the *as is* state of processes. The outputs of a process assessment should include the following:

- Process definitions for project selection and approval
- Process definitions for project management
- Process definitions for project closeout and archiving

These three deliverables require assembling, cataloging, and documenting how the key processes of project management are currently undertaken within the organization. The next three text sections will address the specific types of information that should be considered when gathering definitions for each of these processes. For each process, if formalized methods or documents exist that apply to the entire organization or cross divisional boundaries, copies of the relevant processes should be obtained and cataloged. If consistent, cross-division or enterprise processes do not exist, then any formal processes that exist relative to a single division or group should be obtained and cataloged. If none of these situations apply, individual interviews with project managers in different divisions within the organization will have to be undertaken to determine the types of ad hoc processes that exist. These findings should be documented for use in developing the assessment summary.

Process Definitions for Project Selection and Approval

Project selection and approval processes represent the key processes involved in determining which projects are undertaken by the organization as well as how funds, schedules, resources, and associated project needs are determined and allocated for each project that the organization will undertake. The key process areas and associated processes to be considered include:

- Project selection
  - Determining possible projects to be undertaken by the organization
  - Quantifying the value of potential projects
  - Quantifying the costs associated with potential projects
  - Determining which projects the organization will undertake
- Project initiation
  - Formal chartering and scope determination
  - Assignment of project managers and project teams
  - Determining project oversight

Selection. The selection processes primarily deal with how the organization (or potentially individual divisions within the organization) identifies potential projects and decides which projects should be undertaken. The first step in this process, determining possible projects, may occur largely through informal processes or via some technology-enabled mechanism to capture project needs. In some organizations, an ongoing process may exist in which business units submit projects and subsequent prioritization and scheduling of these projects occurs. In other organizations, a formalized process may be in place that occurs on a regular, scheduled basis for the specific purpose of reviewing project proposals and prioritizing and approving project efforts.

If a formalized review process exists that facilitates managing project requests, the details of this process should be obtained. If methodologies for estimating project effort and quantifying the potential value of projects exist, these should be collected and cataloged as well. In addition to process information, any relevant forms or standardized templates for documenting project goals, cost and schedule estimates, and potential benefits should be captured. If project authorization primarily occurs at the division or business unit level, a review of the parties authorized to charter projects and their scope of authority should be undertaken. The purpose of this exercise is to determine if standardized criteria are established or if formal processes are in place to facilitate prioritizing projects and managing changing priorities.

Initiation. The initiation processes primarily deal with how projects are assigned to project managers and how project oversight occurs. In some organizations, a formal pool of project managers exists and projects are assigned based on capacity, expertise, potential for growth, and other similar factors. In other organizations, project managers are assigned in a more ad hoc fashion based on the scope of the project and availability of resources. If a formal resource group exists, details about the management of that pool should be obtained. If no formal resource group exists, the resource inventory can be used to determine who is participating in project management work, and those individuals can provide input into the processes used to formalize the assignment of project managers and project teams.

In addition to the project team, it is important to understand how project oversight is established. There may be formal processes for assigning a project sponsor, a project steering committee, or a project board to review progress, manage escalation of critical project issues, and address other project needs. Alternatively, there may be single-point oversight by an assigned functional manager who oversees one or more project efforts and who has authority to address significant project issues directly. If a consistent process exists across the organization, the organizational standards for this process should be obtained. If no formal process exists, a representative sample of how project oversight occurs for a variety of project efforts should be obtained and documented.

Process Definitions for Project Management

Project management processes represent the key processes associated with the planning, executing, and monitoring of project activities. Depending on the size and relative sophistication of the project processes in the organization, these processes may be ad hoc, aligned to internally standard processes, or aligned with industry standard processes. Additionally, the processes in place may be established for a particular division or for the entire enterprise. The key process areas and examples of associated processes that should be included in this area of assessment are:

- Project planning
  - Determining detailed project work breakdowns, activity lists, and project schedules
  - Determining project budgets
  - Managing the assignment of resources to project efforts

- Project execution and monitoring
  - Tracking project progress versus schedule and budget
  - Managing variances and taking corrective action
  - Reporting project progress

Planning. The project planning process analysis should focus on the specific tools and techniques used to develop and document project plans as well as the level of consistency in application of these techniques across the organization. These tasks include determining an appropriate breakdown of the project work, scheduling tasks according to precedence and anticipated duration, determining a firm project budget based on the detailed breakdown of project work, assigning resources to execute the project according to the project plan, and other relevant project management activities. If project management software tools, standard templates, or standard process definitions are used to guide these tasks at the division or organization level, these items should be obtained. Planning process analysis should focus on the level of consistency and standardization as well as on the adherence to any relevant internal or external standards if applicable. The planning processes address the development of plans only. The specific monitoring techniques and associated processes for ensuring adherence to plans will be addressed as part of project execution and monitoring analysis.

An important component of project planning analysis is determining how the organization's resource pool is managed. This resource pool may include human resources as well as machines, computers, and other tangible resources required to complete project work. If a standardized assignment and management methodology is in place, its scope and associated processes should be obtained and detailed. If no standardized processes exist, a cursory understanding of the ad hoc methods used in different divisions or groups may be sufficient. If processes exist to forecast resource demand or to track resource utilization across project efforts, these processes should be investigated. The simple goal of this exercise is to understand how supply and demand is managed and whether or not a consistently applied methodology is in place and is effective. In many organizations, detailed resource utilization is not maintained and resources are often "borrowed" from different divisions or working groups in order to accomplish project goals. This mode of operation may be workable and providing relatively consistent results. If so, this should be noted as part of the assessment.

Execution and monitoring. The project execution and monitoring process area focuses on how project tracking and correction occurs. The first stage of this assessment should focus on how individual project progress tracking is accomplished. Some factors to be considered should include the frequency with which data is collected for use in cost and schedule updates, the method of collection (verbal, via spreadsheet, via software tools, etc.), and the manner in which data is summarized and reported. It is important to understand not only how the process works at a project level, but also how data is rolled up for reporting to management on a division, program, or organizational level. If software tools are used to aid in the process of project tracking and reporting, an assessment of the uses of these tools and the level of standardization in the toolsets should be obtained.

It is also important to determine how variances are managed. Typically, project managers are able to manage small variances through work reassignment or reprioritization as long as the overall budget and schedule are not significantly affected. However, in cases in which variances are significant, a process of escalation to management may be in place either via formal processes or ad hoc discussions. If regular project reviews are conducted, representative agendas for those meetings should be obtained to assist in understanding if these reviews are conducted regularly and consistently across the organization. If formal processes for managing variances, consuming project contingency funds, or authorizing additional resources or funds exist, these processes should be documented. If no formal processes exist, a representative sample of how these processes are undertaken within several different areas of the organization is sufficient.

Process Definitions for Project Closeout and Archiving

At the conclusion of a project, one or more deliverables has been provided to the group for which the project has been performed. Upon review and acceptance of these deliverables, the major project effort is considered complete. The process definitions for project closeout and archiving consider the processes that begin with the completion of project deliverables and terminate with complete closure of the project. This assessment should include:

- Project closeout
- Project archiving

Closeout. Project closeout includes the processes associated with completing project documentation, producing final cost and schedule data, formally closing contracts, releasing resources from the project effort, and conducting "lessons learned" sessions to document project outcomes and opportunities for improvement on future projects. In conducting the closeout assessment, it is important to address both the level of adherence to standard project practices (if any) as well as the level of consistency in practices across the organization.

In order to have accurate data regarding project success in any organization, ensure that the reported data on projects will be provided by using standard methodologies so that data integrity will be ensured when the data is rolled up for broader organizational reporting. Typically, the base data that will be captured during the project closeout phase will include some final cost data that can be compared to the project budget as well as some final schedule data that can be compared against the baseline project schedule. (*Note:* If the earned value management technique is employed in the organization, performance indexes may be provided in addition to actual data.) No matter what technique is used in the organization, ensure that project closeout data reporting relies on standard processes, definitions, techniques, and forms because these standardizations tend to better ensure consistency across multiple project efforts.

An often overlooked but critical element of the project closeout phase is the process of conducting lessons-learned sessions to review the project effort and capture opportunities for improvement in the future. These sessions typically include the project team as well as other critical project stakeholders. The lessons-learned session includes reviewing overall project success, discussing the overall planning and execution of the project, capturing data on risks realized during the project, and discussing opportunities for improvement in future projects. If the organization does not conduct lessons-learned sessions, an understanding of how project reviews are conducted should be obtained. If the organization does conduct lessons-learned sessions, the process, associated standard forms and procedures, and the level of consistency across the organization should be considered. Additionally, it is important to understand how outcomes from lessons-learned sessions are distributed for use by the project management community within the organization. Although capturing lessons-learned is an important step in the project process, merely capturing the data is not generally sufficient because lessons-learned data is intended to be broadly shared so that experiences from individual projects can be used as opportunities to improve future projects.

Archiving. The project archiving process includes the processes by which project records are retained once final project closeout is complete. In most projects, a significant amount of documentation is produced over the life cycle of a project effort. This documentation may include pure project management documentation such as schedules, project charters, and project change orders as well as associated project documentation specific to the individual project effort such as design documentation, user interview results, testing plans, and other related project documents. Capturing and maintaining these artifacts of the project effort are important not only to ensure that data is available in case questions arise regarding a particular project in the future, but also to ensure that it will be available as a source of base documentation that can potentially be modified and reused in later project efforts. The primary factors that should be considered include the *means* in which project archives are captured, the level of *consistency* in ensuring that appropriate assets are captured, and the *ease* with which project archives can be accessed and searched. Clearly, capturing relevant assets alone is not enough. It is critical that these assets are cataloged and maintained so that project managers have easy access to this information as they undertake future projects. To the extent possible, determine if a standard taxonomy exists for cataloging information as part of the archiving process. Merely having a shelf full of binders that contain data from past projects does not necessarily imply that a project archiving process is in place.

Delivery Assessment

Delivery assessment involves gathering data on real projects to determine project success within the organization along three critical dimensions:

- Cost
- Time
- Customer satisfaction

In order to accurately assess the relative strength of the organization with respect to project delivery, it is important to gather data for projects of several different sizes, levels of risk, complexity, and cost and, if possible, at levels below merely the project summary level. Small projects (those with planned durations of only a few weeks or months), medium projects (projects with planned durations from a few months to at most 1 year), and large project (projects with a planned duration of over 1 year) should all be included in the assessment. Additionally, projects from several different areas of the organization, if appropriate, should be included. Data may be gathered at the project summary level if this level of data is the only level that is reliably available. If project data is captured at the phase or milestone level, gathering this data may be appropriate as well. The goal is to achieve a representative sample of projects at a fairly consistent level of detail across the various projects captured. The number of projects included from each category will depend on the number of projects undertaken by the organization in each category as well as the level of data available. To the extent possible, projects completed within the past 1 to 2 years provide the best data for assessing the current state of the organization.

When assessing delivery, verifying that the sample of projects is not skewed is important. Selecting only successful projects or only projects that were delivered over budget will not yield the type of data required for this assessment. If the majority of projects delivered by the organization are successful or are over budget, then this data would be appropriate to include, but

Table 1.2 Project Delivery Data Table

Customer Project/Phase (Baseline)	Schedule (Actual)	Schedule (Baseline)	Budget (USD)	Cost (Actual USD)	Customer Satisfaction Score
Simple project/ phase 1	9 weeks	10 weeks	150,000	120,000	9 / 10
Simple project/ phase 2	24 weeks	24 weeks	450,000	490,000	6 / 10
Data center/ implementation	40 weeks	40 weeks	895,000	900,000	9 / 10
Data center/ upgrade	15 weeks	20 weeks	130,000	124,000	8 / 10

it is important to ensure that an appropriate cross section of the organization is sampled and that a variety of different projects are considered.

Cost and time. Measuring performance with respect to cost and time is relatively simple, assuming that data regarding baseline costs and schedules and final costs and schedules are available. If earned value data is used consistently, these measures are appropriate to include and use as a basis for this analysis. If only raw data is available, a simple table of projects, approved costs and schedules, and actual results such as the example provided in Table 1.2 can be developed. If more-detailed data is available or if additional data is deemed relevant, the example in Table 1.2 can be easily expanded to support additional items such as the division in which the project was performed, project manager name, type of project, brief project description, or other relevant items.

As the data is gathered, especially cost and schedule data, keep in mind that there is a distinction between the original project projections for costs and schedules and revised baselines that may be made only after it is determined that the project is significantly off target. For this reason, it is often appropriate to consider the original baseline cost and schedule rather than to measure performance versus a revised baseline alone. However, if a given project was essentially on-time and on-budget, but was revised due to some change requested by a customer or management, late delivery versus the original plan may be considered a success. Because each project has unique dynamics that affect the final outcome, it may be necessary to consult with project managers or members of the project teams (if available) to validate the reasons for any significant variances so that a decision may be made as to how to most fairly represent the final results in the assessment findings. It is perfectly appropriate to include a section for notes so that significant facts for particular projects may be included.

Customer satisfaction. Measuring customer satisfaction has several significant challenges. In many organizations, a project is deemed to be complete once either the customer accepts the final deliverables or the project is deferred or canceled. If a project is deferred or canceled, customer satisfaction data may not exist or the data may be implied to be poor given the lack of delivery. In these cases, an investigation as to the reasons why the project was deferred or canceled may lead to valuable data that can be included with the assessment. In cases in which projects are delivered successfully, determining overall customer satisfaction may still be difficult because quantitative data such as user surveys, post-project follow-up questionnaires, or other methods of gauging customer satisfaction may not exist. The mere delivery of the project itself may indicate some of level of satisfaction in that the project was delivered according to the scope and requirements for the project effort, but further follow-up at some interval post-project (such as 90 days or longer) is often not conducted. In these cases, customer satisfaction data may either have to rely on any facts present at project completion or merely be listed in the assessment as "unable to determine." If quantitative data exists, it is best captured directly and reported. If a qualitative scheme that ranks relative satisfaction along some commonly agreed-to dimensions such as *high, medium, low* can be developed and used consistently as part of the assessment process, this may yield acceptable results as well.

Once the assessment data has been obtained and documented, it may be possible to discern relevant trends. If it appears that one division or department consistently delivers the same general results, be it good or bad, that data can be noted. If project success along the three dimensions discussed is highly varied across projects of different sizes and scopes or across multiple divisions within the organization, this data is helpful to understand and note as it may point to a lack of following consistent processes. The final stage of this assessment involves reviewing the data obtained in aggregate and attempting to discern patterns, trends, or other facts that may point to either areas where quality practices exist (and thus consistent, positive outcomes occur) or to areas where inconsistent or negative outcomes occur more frequently. Depending on the level of data obtained, this data may be relevant only at the project level, or it can be investigated at some lower level within the project.

Assessment Summary

Once an assessment has been completed for each of the assessment areas described (and any others if relevant), the assessment results should be summarized and reviewed with members of the organization in order to ensure that the assessment results fairly represent the state of the organization. This review may be in the form of a formal review with management, a summary document that is distributed within the organization for review and comment, or in the form of a small workshop to review findings with key project managers, project team members, and project stakeholders. The goal of this review is not to formulate an action plan to correct any of the improvement areas identified as part of the assessment, but rather to validate the assessment findings and determine if any additional factors should be included as part of the overall assessment document.

The final assessment findings will serve as a key input to the next process—defining project management needs. Likely the assessment will have highlighted areas of inconsistency or lack of process within the project environment. With a firm understanding of the current state of these processes, it will be much easier to determine the intended *to be* state as well as to begin the process of identifying which processes are candidates for initial improvement as part of the PMO implementation process, which processes are candidates for improvement as part of the longer-term PMO strategy, and which processes are in need of improvement, but are outside the scope of the PMO.

DEFINING THE ORGANIZATION'S PROJECT MANAGEMENT NEEDS

Before considering the technical aspects of establishing, staffing, and starting-up the PMO, take time to consider the challenges the organization faces from a project management perspective. The assessment process serves as a basis for determining areas within the project environment that could be standardized, enhanced, or improved. Yet, additional broader questions may exist that the organization may wish to address. Possible additional questions might include:

- What are the project challenges faced today related to the delivery of projects?
- Is there a real or perceived view by management or other project stakeholders that lack of consistency exists related to project delivery?
- Is management receiving consistent, accurate, and timely information regarding the projects being undertaken in the organization?
- What is the state of the project management culture in the organization? Do project managers think that they have a place to obtain mentoring and support?

Many other questions may also be relevant as the organization considers the primary driving forces behind establishing a PMO. Some of these were likely revealed throughout the assessment process. When considering the challenges faced and the opportunities for change that establishing a functional PMO might provide, certain inherent themes will become evident. This is especially true if analysis is extended beyond just the perceptions of management of the organization and includes the project managers and project team members who are regularly operating in the current project management environment. A PMO will not solve all of the issues that may come forth as this analysis is conducted. However, as key themes emerge, these themes may serve as a basis for determining the few critical roles that the PMO will play in the organization. A PMO can seldom be everything to everyone. Understanding the needs, at a high level, that the PMO will address in the organization will help not only with ensuring a successful PMO in the long run, but also with framing the *sell* for a PMO to management.

Gathering feedback. How this analysis is conducted may vary based on the organization's needs and capabilities. In many cases, if a detailed assessment was conducted, enough data may already exist to begin to document the key challenge areas facing the organization. However, in other organizations, an additional level of survey and analysis may be needed in order to gauge the perceptions of a broader mix of the organization. A survey may be appropriate in organizations in which project managers and team members are widely dispersed or when the reach of the PMO will be large and it was not possible to seek input from a broad range of individuals while completing the assessment process. Focus groups may be appropriate if resources are located in close proximity to a central office location. In some cases, personal interviews may work best.

Regardless of the method used to gather feedback, several considerations must be addressed. Most important is that the individuals providing feedback must be able to provide *candid* information without fear of retribution. Anonymous surveys may address this need if the organization's culture does not address it directly. The initial feedback must also be recorded in a *consistent* manner. A scribe may be employed for live focus group sessions or a single survey format may be used in cases when live feedback is not possible. Additionally, ensure that a broad *cross section* of the organization is considered. In most cases, it would not be appropriate to merely survey the project management community. Beyond project managers and project team members, additional stakeholders such as non-project line management, senior management, user communities, and others have a vested interest in the success of projects. The perceived issues may vary among these groups and some feedback from several different perspectives must be gathered and considered in order to limit the risk of establishing a PMO that only addresses the problems of one or two groups of potentially affected stakeholders.

Using an opportunity matrix. When documenting the challenges and opportunities found during the analysis, using a format similar to the PMO opportunity matrix found in Table 1.3 to capture this high-level data is beneficial. As appropriate, key findings from the assessment process should be translated into this document. This data will serve as an input to discussions with management regarding the purpose and goals of the PMO and should be as complete as possible. Without access to key findings, there is no compass by which to guide further thought and discussion related to the goals of the PMO in the organization. Taking the time to understand the current challenges

Table 1.3 PMO Opportunity Matrix

Current Challenge	PMO Opportunity	Priority
Inability for management to have a consolidated view of project statuses across the organization	Provide consolidated central project reporting; establish project reporting standards; implement project management software	High
Lack of consistent methodology for authorizing projects	Define standards for project initiation; assist with organizing and prioritizing potential projects across business units	Medium
Inability to effectively manage human resource utilization for project efforts	Track and report resource utilization by resource at an organizational level	Low

faced in the organization will facilitate preparing for framing the context of the PMO and the *sell* to management.

A PMO opportunity matrix begins with the current challenges facing the organization at a high level (typically through summarizing recurrent themes in the feedback gathered as part of the needs determination analysis and the assessment process). In some cases, listing broad categories of challenges rather than specific challenges may be appropriate, especially if the number of individual feedback items is large. In either case, do not seek to fully elaborate each of the challenges. That exercise will be completed later as part of the process of further elaborating the opportunities into a value statement and PMO vision.

The next column in the PMO opportunity matrix defines the potential opportunity areas in which implementing a PMO can help to address the current challenges. This section will focus on the specific values that the PMO can provide. In many cases, the challenges facing the organization could be addressed to some extent at an individual project, department, or division level. Yet, the advantages of consistent oversight, uniformity, etc. are often lost through an approach that focuses primarily on limited-scale improvement. Focusing on the specific opportunities that the PMO provides that could not be easily accomplished without a coordinating body is important. Likely the

PMO will not serve as a micromanager of all projects. The objectives should be fairly broad and far-reaching.

Prioritizing opportunities. Because implementing every potential opportunity immediately will not be possible, prioritizing the relative importance of addressing each challenge within the organization at a high level is important. A simple ranking of *high, medium, low* is often most appropriate. Although a more-complex numeric ranking scheme might seem to be a better solution, considering the goal of this exercise is important. The PMO opportunity matrix does not seek to *create* a plan—it seeks to *expose* current challenges in the organization, document them, and elaborate at a high level the areas in which implementation of a PMO could address the challenges. Prioritizing the specific tasks that the PMO will undertake is an exercise that will be undertaken with management once the fundamental decision to implement the PMO has been made. At this stage, framing what is possible rather than what should be done is of primary importance. It is appropriate to identify the areas of greatest need, but inappropriate to attempt to rank order each individual need. Using a *high, medium, low* scheme will help to group the current challenges and to show the areas of greatest relative concern, yet still leave room for further refinement as the process of chartering and starting-up the PMO progresses.

TRANSLATING NEEDS INTO ORGANIZATIONAL VALUE—THE PMO VALUE STATEMENT

Once the opportunity matrix has been developed, a PMO value statement can be developed for the organization. The PMO value statement serves two purposes. It translates the opportunities identified in the opportunity matrix into a set of objectives for the PMO and it frames these objectives in terms of the items that can be implemented quickly (the "quick wins") versus the objectives that will serve as mid- to long-range objectives. For this exercise, a brainstorming session involving project managers, project team members, and members of management is often helpful. The goal is to try to frame what is possible rather than to develop a committed list of firm actions that the PMO will undertake once established. Depending on need and time frame,

Table 1.4 PMO Value Statement

Opportunity	PMO Objectives	Time Frame
Provide consolidated central project status reporting and associated reporting standards	Implement earned value management reporting for all projects over 1 million USD	Short term
	Develop and implement standardized templates for monthly project reporting	Short term
	Establish reports repository for historical reporting and tracking	Medium term
Implement project management software	Implement enterprise project management software for tracking resource utilization	Long term
Formalize the project chartering process	Review and document current processes for project authorization within business units	Short term
	Define workflow and documentation standards for chartering projects and implement in business units	Short term
	Establish project authorization board for all projects over 1 million USD	Medium term

expanding each opportunity in the opportunity matrix may be appropriate. A more concise view of only those opportunities identified as *high* or *medium* in the opportunity matrix may also be appropriate. The format for the value statement document could be similar to Table 1.4.

Several considerations must be addressed as the PMO value statement is developed and refined. First, define the terms "short term," "medium term," and "long term" for the organization. As a guide, "short term" may represent items which can be completed within 6 months of PMO start-up, "medium term" may represent items that can be completed within 2 years of PMO start-up, and "long term" may represent items that would be implemented more than 2 years after start-up. It is acceptable to define different timetables as well. The key is to define those time frames clearly so that no misunderstanding exists as to what the time frames represent. At this stage, it would not be advisable to set individual, firm time frames for each objective. Doing so creates the impression that firm decisions regarding prioritization have already been made. In reality, management review and input will likely drive final prioritization. The time frames that are initially set merely represent a starting point for discussion based on an understanding of the most pressing project management needs in the organization.

Next, determine the level of detail to include in the objectives. The goal of the PMO vision statement is to create a high-level view of proposed values and objectives rather than to create an implementation plan. Depending on the priority agreed for each objective, the critical few items that represent the true short-term objectives of the PMO will be further elaborated as part of the PMO implementation plan. The PMO value statement should be viewed as a management level view. A few sentences defining the essence of each objective should be sufficient.

At a first glance, one significant column may appear to be lacking from the PMO value statement. This column would represent the cost to the organization of operating in the current environment. If data is available to quantify the cost to the organization of not undertaking the opportunities listed in the PMO value statement, that data should be included because it is key data that will help the organization to determine the return on its investment in the PMO. Unfortunately, hard data is often not readily available to quantify the cost of rework, lost efficiency, and other factors that typically drive organizations to consider implementing a PMO. If data regarding historical project success and failure rates is available, that data can be useful in discussions with management regarding the broad objectives of the PMO in terms of better control over projects, but it is often difficult to assign a specific percentage of a particular loss due to project failure to one or two unique opportunities. A compromise could include expanding the challenges in the PMO opportunity matrix to a more-detailed list of current challenges (with supporting data included when available). Table 1.5 shows a revised PMO value statement that includes a column for capturing these current challenges.

Including detailed information about each of the challenges as additional detail in the PMO value statement might be tempting, but fully elaborating challenges is best left to the PMO opportunity matrix or some other document

Table 1.5   Revised PMO Value Statement

Opportunity	Current Challenges	PMO Objectives	Time Frame
Provide consolidated central project status reporting and associated reporting standards	Lack of consistent reporting with standardized measures leads to potentially troubled projects gaining management attention too late to allow for effective response.	Implement earned value management reporting for all projects over 1 million USD	Short term
		Develop and implement standardized templates for monthly project reporting	Short term
	Lack of historical data makes project estimating difficult (estimated 30% of projects exceed project budget by 10% or more due to estimating error).	Establish reports repository for historical reporting and tracking	Medium term
Implement project management software	Inconsistent tracking of large projects leads to inaccurate reporting and schedule misses.	Implement enterprise project management software for tracking resource utilization	Long term
Lack of consistent methodology for authorizing projects	No defined authority for reviewing and authorizing projects occasionally leads to duplicate, similar efforts in different business units.	Review and document current processes for project authorization within business units	Short term
		Define workflow and documentation standards for chartering projects and implement in business units	Short term
	Lack of consistent project review for large projects causes occasional significant misunderstanding regarding project scope and required resources.	Establish project authorization board for all projects over 1 million USD	Medium term

that supports the opportunity matrix. The goal of the vision statement should be to create a very high-level view of challenges and opportunities rather than to create a detailed list of current challenges for the organization. The value statement links the opportunities and objectives to define areas of benefit that the PMO may provide to the organization. Describing how these areas of benefit address the current challenges in the organization can be worthwhile for providing additional detail on why the proposed opportunities and objectives are relevant, but it is not necessary to provide significant detail as long as this detail is documented elsewhere.

CREATING A MISSION FOR PMO TRANSFORMATION

Once the process of defining the PMO value statement is complete, including stating the current challenges facing the organization, the PMO opportunities, and the possible time frames for implementing these opportunities, the next step is to formulate a concise mission statement that summarizes the intent for establishing the PMO. The mission statement is designed to represent a desired *to be* state for the PMO. It is to capture the essence of what the PMO is intended to achieve. The following provides a possible example:

To create a functional Program Management Office that establishes and implements project management best practices for the benefit of the organization in a way that encourages collaboration, standardization, and overall improvement in project results across the organizational landscape

---

The mission statement should be unique to the organization and should summarize the broad mission of the PMO. The mission statement is not designed to list the specific undertakings of the PMO or the specific processes and problems that will be addressed by the PMO. This documentation, along with time lines for implementation, possible costs, and other factors, will be part of the overall presentation to management as part of selling the PMO concept to management. Establishing the PMO mission and agreeing on the desired intent for the PMO prior to initiating the selling process serves an important purpose. The mission statement will help guide the formulation of the PMO marketing strategy.

Important: Note that the mission statement defines a mission for *transformation*—a process of moving from a current state to a new state. A PMO transformational mission is very different from a PMO *operational* mission. An operational mission guides specific activities that the PMO will undertake once it is in operation. A transformational mission guides the establishment process of the PMO. An operational mission ensures that the PMO stays on course throughout its lifetime. Once the PMO goals and activities are approved by management and the PMO is formally chartered, a set of operational goals may be established that will drive the formulation of an operational mission. Yet, initially, the focus should be on the transformational nature of how the PMO will impact and improve the organization.

As the mission statement is formulated, think about the key challenges facing the organization that could be addressed by implementation of a PMO. The PMO opportunity matrix can serve as a source for this information and should be referenced as the mission statement that will be established is considered. The mission statement does not need to be long nor does it need to be an exhaustive list of goals. It serves as a starting a point—as a guiding statement—for creating the marketing and selling plan that will be delivered to management as part of the process for seeking approval to begin work on establishing the PMO. The key is to ensure that it captures the essence of what is intended to be achieved. If the PMO will transform the organization by establishing consistent standards for project management processes, then this should be stated. If the PMO will hire, train, and foster project managers and project management as a profession within the organization, then this may be relevant. The mission statement must be shaped to the organization. Once it is complete, it should stand on its own as a single point of reference for what will be achieved by the PMO implementation. Other documentation, including assessment findings, the PMO opportunity matrix, and other relevant materials will be supplied to management as plans and information to support how the mission will be implemented if the establishment of the PMO is approved.

SELLING THE PMO CONCEPT

With a completed assessment, a PMO opportunity matrix, a value statement and a mission statement in hand, the process of selling the PMO concept to management can begin. Many operational issues relative to the PMO have not yet been addressed. Additionally, the core structure, management, and implementation plan for the PMO have not yet been defined. This is by design. Before tackling the operational aspects of establishing and managing the PMO, it is essential to gain organizational commitment to the concept of the PMO in the organization and to gain approval to perform the detailed work required to make the PMO a reality. Many organizations jump right in and establish a PMO without creating a firm foundation on which to build it. Establishing a base business case for the PMO and selling the PMO concept to key organizational leaders will help to avoid many of the pitfalls associated with establishing a PMO first and then attempting to justify the value and benefits later. Specifically, creating a base business case and selling the PMO concept to the organization will achieve several benefits:

- An awareness of the specific challenges facing the organization relative to project and program processes will be raised, which will serve as a basis for making the business case for the PMO.
- Educating key organizational decision makers on the concept and benefits of the PMO will help to ensure uniform understanding of the role of the PMO in the organization and the specific business benefits.
- Obtaining management's agreement with the base business case and authorizing further detailed design and development of the PMO implementation plan will help ensure organizational commitment to provide the resources required to further drive the PMO implementation.
- Understanding the concerns of key decision makers will provide a basis for molding the structure, design, and implementation of the PMO to address these key concerns.

The process of establishing, formalizing, and gaining alignment to the base business case is not a process that occurs quickly. Taking time to build a solid case and to ensure that there is appropriate data to substantiate the fundamental tenants of the case is critical. Once reviewed with and agreed to by management, the base business case will be a key input to development of a detailed business case, which will be used as the basis for formally chartering the PMO and beginning the PMO implementation process. The following section will provide a simple process for building the base business case and preparing to present it to management.

THE BASE BUSINESS CASE

The base business case will contain an overview of the current state of project and program management in the organization, the challenges facing the current organization, and the fundamental opportunities that will be addressed by the PMO. It will also document the necessary next steps required to fully plan for the creation and operation of a PMO. The base business case will contain four key sections:

- Overview of current project organization
- Key challenges in current project organization
- PMO opportunities
- Key actions and accountabilities—the PMO transformation mission

The base business case is most practically presented as a single document that contains the sections listed above along with supporting documentation or addenda that further elaborate on findings in the business case. The document is intended to be a management report and should be concise, but still provide enough detail to allow management to understand the key issues and opportunities. Most likely, the document will be paired with a presentation in which one or more key members of the team investigating the establishment of the PMO will be able to more fully comment on the contents of the report. If a presentation is not a practical option, complete supporting documentation such as the PMO opportunity matrix, assessment summaries, and associated documents may be included as appendices to the business case document.

At this stage, a case is being built for authorization to create a complete plan for establishing a PMO. Because details of the specific implementation are mostly unknown, the base business case should focus on the key overriding themes discovered during the assessment and opportunity work. It would not be appropriate at this stage to create any firm financial models or other documents that explore possible cost impacts to the organization or possible hard benefits that can be achieved unless specifically required by management. These documents, as required, will be produced later and included as part of the complete implementation plan and charter for the PMO that will be established once agreement has been obtained to proceed with further planning for the implementation of the PMO.

Overview of Current Project Organization

This section will describe the current project organization from both a structural and a procedural standpoint. The purpose of including this section in the base business case is to provide management with a baseline that reflects how projects are undertaken and managed today. This is a factual section that should address the current project environment without explicitly stating the limitations of current operations. From an organizational standpoint, a formal project management organization chart should be provided if a consistent, formal organizational structure exists. If the organization's structure aligns with one of the models discussed earlier in this chapter, a reference to the specific model may be appropriate. If several different structures exist throughout the organization, this should be noted. Additionally, any formal career paths or other forms of organizational alignment to project management as a profession should be discussed. The goal of this discussion is to identify resources currently engaged in project work at a high level as well as to identify how the organization structures projects.

Beyond how the pure project management organization is structured, it is also important to discuss how projects are currently staffed. If a group of dedicated project and project management resources exists, this group should be identified at a high level. If project resources are primarily drawn from functional organizations to support specific project efforts, this should be noted.

From an organizational standpoint, it is important to identify both the structures and processes that are in place to ensure that projects are appropriately managed and staffed. If a highly functional organization is currently in place and project managers are largely "project managers by appointment" rather than "project managers by profession," then the current project organization will most likely closely reflect the functional organization, with members of the functional organization drawn together to perform specific project activities under the guidance of a manager who coordinates the efforts. This may be a perfectly acceptable structure from the organization's perspective, but it is rather limited from a project management competency development perspective. If a formal organizational structure exists, it should be reflected in the base business case document. This structure may represent an opportunity for the PMO to add value by formalizing the process of developing project managers and encouraging project management as a professional career path.

From a procedural standpoint, process assessment data gathered during the assessment process will serve as the basis for this section. An overview of the extent to which the organization has a set of standards for executing the processes associated with project management should be provided. If no single set of standards exists that is representative of the entire organization, a summary of various processes used within divisions or business units within the organization should be provided. These standards may align only to internal processes or best practices or may align with external standards provided by industry groups or project management organizations. Regardless of whether or not the procedures are externally aligned, the extent to which the procedures are documented, practiced, and updated should be discussed at a high level.

In addition to the existence of standards, the discussion should also include the extent to which any standards are consistently followed. If standards are outdated, not regularly updated, or if no mechanism for maintaining a "master set" of standards exists, this situation should be noted. Whenever discussing any form of process, standard, or procedure, it is important that the existence of the standard, process, or procedure is paired with the extent to which the standard, process, or procedure is maintained and consistently followed. If audit processes exist to validate conformance to standards for project standards or processes within the organization, these should be noted as well because they provide important information about how process conformance is managed.

The overview section should also include some of the summary data gathered as part of the delivery assessment portion of the assessment process. Including all data for all projects analyzed during the assessment is not necessary. Instead, either summarized data for various project groupings (large, medium, small projects, projects across different divisions, etc.) or a narrative explanation of the general state of project success in the organization can be provided. If average cost and schedule over-run or under-run data is available and fairly represents most projects (i.e., no significant outliers skew the numbers), then it may be appropriate to provide this data as a general summary. If customer satisfaction data is available, this data may be summarized and provided as well. If no consistent measurement scheme is available to facilitate accurate comparisons across divisions or for the organization as a whole, this should be noted and sample data should be provided for a number of projects to demonstrate the range of project outcomes captured during the assessment.

Key Challenges in Current Project Organization

The second section of a base business case builds on the previous section by addressing key challenges in the current project organization. This section is not designed to be an exhaustive list of all of the challenges facing the organization, but rather a summary of some of the key areas in which the organization is either experiencing undesirable results or other factors are creating inefficiency with respect to project processes, procedures, reporting, and delivery. Findings from the assessment processes as well as the opportunity matrix will likely serve as key inputs to this section. These findings may be presented using the same broad categories as are used in the assessment process—people, processes, and outcomes.

In order to create a full picture of the current challenges, it is often desirable to include with the list of challenges some general statements about the impacts of these challenges on the organization. If quantitative data is available, this type of data is preferable; however, in many cases, only qualitative or "soft" impacts may have been captured. Regardless of the type of data available, including some statement regarding the impact on the organization is important in order to allow management to understand how the current situation within the organization is affecting project results. For example, if one of the challenges facing the organization is that a lack of consistent estimating practices exists, the impact in terms of project outcomes (projects are often late because duration estimates are inaccurate) or processes (inconsistent processes do not implement best practices or align to existing organizational standards) can be addressed as soft impacts or can be discussed using specific project examples in which lack of a consistent estimating process has led to schedule or cost overruns.

In some cases, referencing specific portions of the assessment findings or specific sections of the opportunity matrix (which can be attached as appendices) directly in the review may be appropriate, but, in general, including all of the detail from these documents adds limited benefit in an executive report. A suggested format for this section might include a bulleted-list format such as the following:

- Over the past 2 years, 54% of projects that were delivered late were shown to have used inconsistent or nonstandard project estimating practices, which led to underestimating the required work effort to complete the project. A lack of consistent estimating best practices and guidelines exists in the organization.
- Enterprise-wide views of project performance and projects metrics do not exist. Although divisional reporting on project performance is available in some divisions, inconsistent use of project outcome metrics and inconsistent data gathering leads to an inability to effectively summarize divisional data at the enterprise level.

Whether a list format, a table, or paragraph narrative form is used, keeping several key factors in mind while developing the list of challenges is important:

- Separate the "critical few" key challenges from the list of all current challenges. Present either the critical few key challenge areas or a summary of major challenges by category. Presenting an exhaustive list of challenges is often too detailed for a management report and may lead to an impression that nothing is going well.

- Because addressing every challenge in the organization through implementation of a PMO is impossible, highlight the specific challenges in which implementation of a PMO can provide benefit.

- Ensure that for each challenge presented, sufficient data (either qualitative or quantitative) exists to support the findings presented. Often management will question or challenge the validity of statements that cast a negative light on one or more areas of organizational operation. Ensuring that the challenges have been validated via the assessment process and gathering some relevant facts to support the findings will make addressing questions easier if they are raised.

PMO Opportunities

The PMO opportunities section discusses how challenges faced by the organization might be addressed through establishing a PMO. This section essentially becomes the *sell* for the concept of using a PMO to address the project challenges facing the organization. Like the previous section, this section should be a high-level discussion rather than a detailed explanation of specific action items. Because the purpose of a base business case report is to obtain authorization to develop a complete proposal for implementing a PMO, details on specific action items are not appropriate at this stage. During the PMO implementation planning process, the details of specifically how the PMO will operate, what specific initial targets will be set, and related detailed topics will be addressed in full. The PMO opportunities section should focus on how, at a broad level, the PMO can address the challenges identified in the key challenges section. A format similar to the format used in the key challenges section can be used for the opportunities section. For example:

- Standardize project effort estimating techniques by creating a single, enterprise-wide standard and toolset for project estimating, providing training on project estimating techniques, and gathering data on estimates and actual durations for past projects to create an estimate repository to assist project managers in estimating future similar project efforts.

- Create a single, enterprise-wide project dashboard for conveying all project efforts at an organizational level. Manage data gathering via standard templates and processes and provide reports to management for review and action.

Consider the following points when developing each oportunity statement:

Respond to the challenges. Each of the opportunities should be a response to one or more of the challenges presented in the challenges section. The purpose of the opportunities section is not to list every possible opportunity in which a PMO might play a role. It is designed to identify the *key* opportunities that may be available to address the challenges discussed in the challenges section. If other opportunities exist that do not address any of the current challenges identified, these may be listed separately within the document as potential additional areas of focus or as an appendix to the document. Remaining focused on the opportunities that address the current challenges is important because these opportunities are an important part of the *sell* for the PMO. If management is not clear as to how the opportunities to be pursued will address the challenges that exist in the organization, they will likely question the specific value that the PMO will provide. A significant part of the implementation goal of the PMO is to work to improve the current situation in the organization, not to proceed blindly to address many peripheral challenges.

Provide specific benefits. The focus of the opportunities should be on specific benefits to be achieved rather than on broad categories of opportunities. To state that one opportunity is to "standardize project management processes" is too vague to pinpoint a specific benefit that addresses a particular challenge. Standardization may indeed be a benefit to the organization, but the opportunity at hand is to implement standardization for a specific process that represents a current challenge that the organization is facing. Because it is likely impossible to implement standardization for every project management process at the onset of implementing a PMO, identifying specific areas of benefit helps to set reasonable expectations as to what will be achieved.

Avoid specific dates and targets. Avoid setting specific time frames and specific benefit targets. To state that a benefit will be "decreasing project estimation errors by 30%" or that a time frame will be "implementing standardized reporting for the organization within 1 year" is premature. Having specific time frames and concrete goals is important, but they should be established once a definite plan and time frame for PMO implementation are decided. *Remember*: At this stage the goal is to obtain permission to proceed with developing a detailed plan for implementing the PMO—not to detail the specific time frame and expected outcomes for what the PMO will deliver.

Avoid rank ordering. At this stage, avoid rank ordering of the possible opportunities. The process of determining which one of the available opportunities is the highest priority for the organization should be undertaken after a discussion with management rather than attempting at this stage to determine which opportunity is the most important. Clearly, priority setting will need to occur because the list of available opportunities may or may not align completely with management's view of the role and function of the PMO. Management, if already familiar with the PMO concept, may already have ideas as to what areas the PMO should address first prior to receiving the formal base business case. The opportunities presented in the base business case and the opportunities ultimately explored as part of the PMO establishment process may differ. Aligning these priorities will be part of the process of validating the business case and obtaining permission to proceed with developing a plan for PMO implementation.

Key Actions and Accountabilities—The PMO Transformation Mission

This section ties together the entire document by addressing, in summary form, the opportunities available. It also seeks permission to proceed with developing a more-detailed business case for the PMO. This section should include the following items:

- A statement of the PMO transformation mission
- Deliverables for PMO implementation planning
- Resource requirements for development of a detailed business case

- Milestones and completion targets for development of a detailed business case
- A request for authorization to proceed

Transformation mission statement. The PMO transformation mission statement has already been developed. It should now be restated as the starting point for this discussion. With the key project challenges and PMO opportunities already discussed in previous sections, the transformation mission statement serves to provide management with a concise, understandable statement regarding the intent of moving forward with a PMO. Management may wish to adjust or revise the transformation mission statement, which may, in turn, adjust the planning processes that take place as transformation planning occurs. This is certainly acceptable. Management alignment to a single mission for transformation should be ensured prior to commencing any detailed planning.

Deliverables. The next part of the PMO transformation mission addresses the deliverables that will be presented to management once the planning exercise is complete. Existing organizational standards or policies may guide the types of documentation required. If standardized documentation or policies exist, they should be referenced. At this stage, the transformation planning activities should be treated like a project. A defined set of deliverables should be developed and agreed to with management prior to commencing detailed work. Because the goal of the base business case document is to secure approval to move forward with detailed planning, this section should contain sufficient detail to allow management to see that a plan is in place and to understand what deliverables will be presented at the conclusion of transformation planning. At minimum, the deliverables should include:

- A scope statement defining the role of the PMO in the organization
- A detailed business case documenting the specific challenges to be addressed by the PMO along with specific projected benefits and/or savings
- A PMO organizational structure detailing roles, responsibilities, and accountabilities

- Required resources to commence operation of the PMO and antic-ipated resource needs for ongoing operations

The deliverables contain many of the elements that would be included in a detailed business plan or project charter. Essentially, a detailed business case and the implementation planning process are part of a chartering exercise in the sense that a plan is being created to present to management in order to gain formal approval to commence operation of the PMO. As such, the deliverables presented in the detailed business case will include whatever relevant detail management requires for making a business decision regarding the costs and potential benefits of a PMO. The list of deliverables presented in this section is not intended to be exhaustive. Other deliverables such as return on investment calculations, detailed cost projections, detailed operational plans, and others may be required in order to secure approval to proceed with implementation. If the organization has specific standards in place, any relevant requirements should be included. As part of the base business case review, the deliverables presented in this section will be reviewed with management to ensure that the deliverables presented align with management expectations.

Resource requirements. In addition to the deliverables for the planning work, the resources required to produce the required deliverables should be presented. It is likely that these resources will primarily include human resources, but they may include other categories such as travel and entertainment expense, office supply expense, and others if relevant. From a human resource perspective, the anticipated level of effort as well as a specific resource category should be provided. For example, if a process analyst is needed to assist with documenting existing processes, the process analyst role as well as the expected effort required should be included. If specific resources are required, it is appropriate to state the resource by name along with an expected time commitment. If the organization requires cost data from a human resource perspective, it is appropriate to include this data along with any other anticipated expense costs so that a full picture of the required resource commitment is available.

As is standard with any project effort, a single project manager should be identified as part of the required resources. This resource will guide the implementation planning effort, report to management, and participate in other project management activities. The project manager should be included by name as part of the base business case document so that management is clear as to who will have accountability for carrying out the detailed business case development and implementation planning work.

Time line. Once the required resources have been identified, a time line and anticipated milestones should be presented. For the purposes of this document, a detailed work breakdown structure or task level detail is not necessary. However, an anticipated duration should be provided to assist management in understanding the expected duration of the planning effort. There is no set formula to define the amount of time required to complete the planning activities. Many factors, including the size of the organization, anticipated scope of the PMO, organizational structure, resource availability, level of management support, and numerous others must be considered when establishing the time line. When considering the amount of time required (which likely will, at minimum, span more than a month), looking ahead to Chapters 3 and 4 of this text may be helpful in order to determine, at a high level, the type of planning activities that will be undertaken. At this stage, the purpose of providing an estimate is to set an expectation as to when management can expect to see progress. If management will accept an open-ended estimate, with a commitment to provide regular progress updates (perhaps on a biweekly or monthly basis), setting a firm completion date will not be necessary. However, if a firm completion date is required, the date should include a sufficient allowance for risk and may require developing a detailed set of action steps based on the planning processes presented in this text and associated estimates based on organizational experience with planning and the types of work required.

Authorization. The final part of the document should request authorization to proceed with development of a detailed business case and the implementation plans for the PMO. This authorization should include an authorization to engage resources and an agreement on the detailed business case scope, developmental time line, and deliverables. A formal signature page with approval from management serves as a show of commitment to the project effort and helps to ensure management alignment to the plan. Formal approval of the plan will be requested upon completion of the management presentation on the work completed and a review of the base business case.

Selling the Base Business Case—The Management Presentation

Once the documentation portion of the base business case is complete, it is important to plan a management presentation to provide an overview of the base business case, expand on its content, and address questions and concerns from management. The goal of the presentation, like the base business case document itself, is to secure approval to proceed with further PMO development. The audience for this presentation should be the key business manager or managers who have the authority to authorize resources to further work on the PMO effort. Other key stakeholders may be invited as well, but it is critical that the focus of the presentation is on satisfying the needs of the members of management who will be responsible for authorizing further work.

The agenda for the management presentation should follow the format of the base business case document. A sample agenda might include the following:

1. Introductions
2. Agenda
3. Overview of Work to Date
4. Current Project Management Challenges
5. Program Management Office Opportunities
6. Transformation Planning
7. Discussion/Questions

Ideally the management presentation should be conducted in a face-to-face setting so that participants can formally review and discuss the base business case and the accompanying presentation. If a face-to-face session is not practical, an audio conference with the ability to present slides or other content items remotely is an acceptable compromise. Preparation for the management presentation should include:

- Providing sufficient notice of the date and time of the presentation to allow participants to confirm attendance
- Disseminating the base business case document to the meeting participants prior to the meeting

- Preparing a slide deck or some other summary document that provides relevant highlights from the base business case document
  and serves as the basis for the presentation and discussion
- Providing sufficient time for selection of the presenters and
  rehearsal in advance of the material to be presented

Other practical considerations, such as meeting room set up, availability of audiovisual equipment, catering, and other "administrivia" should be addressed in advance as well.

In order to ensure that participants are prepared to discuss the project management needs and PMO opportunities, it is critical that the base business case document be provided in advance to meeting participants along with a summary page that details the date, time, and location of the management presentation, the proposed agenda, and a request to review the base business case document prior the presentation. Asking participants to come to the management presentation without having advance understanding of the work completed to date and the related outcomes will dramatically reduce the effectiveness of the meeting and may lead to numerous questions that are likely to have already been addressed in the base business case. Additionally, providing the document in advance allows the presenters to focus the presentation on key portions of the base business case document without having to discuss the document in its entirety as part of the presentation.

The presentation should begin with roundtable introductions if the participants are not already acquainted with each other. Next, a review of the agenda should be conducted in order to ensure a uniform understanding of the purpose of the meeting. In addition, the intended outcomes should be addressed so that all participants will understand the goals of the presentation. Then an overview of the work conducted to date should be conducted. This section should include a review of the assessment process, the specific assessments conducted, and how the assessment process findings were used during the process of documenting the base business case. It is not necessary to review the assessment findings in detail, but it is important to demonstrate that a systematic process was followed to arrive at the conclusions that will be presented as part of the sections on current challenges and PMO opportunities. It is also important to demonstrate that the assessment was conducted with input from individuals throughout the organization rather than just the few individuals who worked directly on preparing the assessment findings. This will help reassure management that the findings are representative of a broad cross section of the division or organization.

Following the overview of work to date, a summary of the current project management challenges should be presented. This discussion should not be an exhaustive list of all of the challenges facing the group, division, or organization for which the PMO concept is being proposed, but should highlight the key challenges that face the organization in terms of ability to deliver quality projects within agreed-to time and cost limits. These challenges may be presented as categories or specific challenges, but it is important to avoid referencing specific project efforts if possible. Taking one or more projects and using them as examples of the challenges facing the organization is dangerous. To do so risks offending or alienating key decision makers who may have been involved with the particular projects being discussed. It may be beneficial to research in advance specific project examples and have data available to support the findings in the event a request for a specific example is made. In this case, the research should be conducted and documented in a way that ensures that any examples provided fairly represent the challenge(s) being discussed. This research should also highlight what went well in the project as well as the challenges faced. Taking time to perform this investigation in advance and presenting any requested examples in a concise manner, with a fair treatment of the successes and challenges, will demonstrate to management that a complete and thoughtful investigation was conducted as part of the process of defining and investigating the project management challenges facing the organization.

The next portion of the presentation should focus on key opportunities for addressing the challenges faced by the organization. The PMO concept should be presented here at a high level to ensure a uniform understanding of the purpose of the PMO. The presentation should then focus on how a PMO could be used to address the challenges faced by the organization. Several important points should be made:

Set expectations. Be clear that the PMO itself will not solve all of the organization's project management challenges, but that implementing the PMO as a focal point for driving process improvement and improved project management results can in itself create an environment for broad improvement.

Frame the context. Help management realize how the PMO fits within the broader organizational context. The PMO can have a role as the key focal point for all project activity in the organization, including managing projects directly, or it can serve as a consulting organization that helps to drive standardization and process improvement while still leaving the day-to-day management of projects in the hands of organizational divisions and groups. (*Note*: The level of control over projects and the specific roles of the PMO will be defined in more detail in consultation with management as the PMO implementation process proceeds. Discussing the potential roles at the presentation is important, but not in a manner that prescribes a particular implementation methodology for the organization.)

Link opportunities and challenges. Link the opportunities to the challenges in a way that clearly demonstrates specific areas of potential improvement, but does not tie implementation to a specific set of results. For example, it would be inappropriate to suggest that implementing a PMO would result in a 50% reduction in late projects. Yet, it would be appropriate to indicate that an area of opportunity for the PMO would be addressing the problem of late projects by defining standards and processes for estimating projects so that project managers will be equipped with tools to help them to arrive at better project estimates. Alternately, the PMO could facilitate periodic project reviews to ensure that project scope statements are clear and that any changes in management processes are defined and consistently used to ensure that unapproved changes to projects do not lead to prolonged schedules. The process of defining specific, measurable benefits should be left to the later planning processes. Specific areas of improvement and improvement targets should be defined and aligned with management prior to the start-up of the PMO and, thus, they will be deliverables of the implementation planning process.

The transformation planning section will focus on PMO implementation planning activities and seeking concurrence from management to commence with the planning effort for the PMO. A high-level overview of the required next steps in terms of allocating resources for further investigation and planning for the PMO, specific deliverables of the planning phase, and an approximate time line for completion of the planning activities should be provided. Assuming that the project management challenges and PMO opportunities have been discussed in sufficient detail, the transformation planning discussion need only focus on the plans for moving forward with transformation planning. To the extent possible, the discussion should be focused on what will be achieved by transformation planning and on detailing for management the critical next steps required to ensure that a complete plan is developed. In this section, stress that the activities that are required for PMO planning are focused on defining the specific value of the PMO in the organization and detailing the practical matters required to start-up the PMO. These activities culminate with a fully detailed business case and a start-up roadmap that will be brought back to management for concurrence prior to commencing implementation work. Therefore, approval is being sought to proceed with defining a full plan rather than to commence with PMO implementation activities.

The final portion of the presentation should include a summary discussion of the presentation content and addressing any questions from the meeting participants. To the extent possible, keep the discussion focused on specific items addressed in the presentation rather than on specific details of the PMO operation. If questions arise that address specific plans for implementation, it is reasonable to state that specific implementation planning is a topic to be fully addressed in the next stage of the PMO planning effort and that any feedback from the group on this topic will be recorded and incorporated into the planning process. If questions arise that require a more detailed explanation of items presented during the presentation, a good-faith effort should be made to address these questions fully, relying on data from the assessment and base business case documents as well as from the presenter's experience. If questions cannot be answered directly due to a lack of information, note them as follow-up items to be investigated and communicated at a later date.

At the conclusion of the presentation and discussion, formal approval to proceed with detailed planning, as discussed in the presentation and base business case document, should be obtained. If specific follow-up items are required and if these items must be provided prior to obtaining approval, individuals should be assigned to obtain whatever information is requested and a follow-up meeting should be scheduled as soon as is practical in order to review the follow-up items and gain approval to move forward with PMO planning.

Overcoming Initial Resistance

It is quite likely that one or more participants in the management review session will have concerns about the PMO concept or the specific implementation of the PMO in the organization. These concerns could range from the time, effort, and cost associated with start-up and ongoing operation of the PMO to lack of understanding of the specific benefits of the PMO to the organization to concerns about the level of influence and control that the PMO will have within the organization itself. It is not possible to detail here all of the possible concerns that could be raised nor is it possible to define every possible strategy for addressing these concerns. However, a few general guidelines can help assist in addressing concerns:

Manage expectations. Stress that many specific details of the implementation of the PMO are not yet known. The process of additional investigation, development of a detailed business case, and detailed implantation planning will lead to a more-detailed assessment of the role of the PMO in the organization. This process will include seeking input from management, project managers, project team members, and other PMO stakeholders. This broad feedback will guide the detailed business case development and specific implementation planning details.

Regular reporting. Note that throughout the detailed planning process, regular reports will be provided to management so that progress and challenges will be well understood. The process of providing reports to management will be another vehicle that will help to maintain alignment between management and the PMO planning team. Regular status reports will also serve as a risk mitigation activity, ensuring that if management perceives a lack of alignment or if changes in business conditions necessitate a change in the approach of the PMO, these items will be communicated early so that the PMO planning team can consider them prior to presenting a detailed business case and implementation plan for approval.

Limited investment. State that approval to expend funds and to commit resources to a planning effort does not assume approval for implementation of a PMO. Developing a detailed case will allow management to receive the information needed to make an informed business decision regarding the value of the PMO to the organization. To that end, the cost of developing a plan is a small cost in comparison to doing nothing and allowing the current project management challenges to persist or to immediately charter the PMO, only to later realize that it exists without focus and is not providing a level of benefit to the organization that justifies its existence. Thus, the proposal before management to proceed with detailed planning represents a middle ground between doing nothing and charging forward without a clear charter and plan.

Limited risk. Realize that any process change, organizational transformation, or restructuring effort will involve some level of risk. Defining the potential impacts on the organization, the specific benefits to be achieved, the level of potential disruption, and possible negative outcomes from implementing a PMO are all activities that will be undertaken as part of the detailed planning process. The primary risk to the organization at this stage is the risk of missing a potential opportunity to improve processes, mature the project organization, and create an environment that leads to better project outcomes over time. A PMO is not designed to achieve overnight success. It is designed to assist in growing a project culture that promotes standardization and process improvement over time. The initial PMO rollout, if approved, will likely focus on a few key areas of concern. By limiting the focus initially, organizational impact can be minimized. Cost and time commitments will also be investigated in detail, and the specific cost and resource commitments required will be provided as part of the outcomes of planning. As such, there is minimal risk of creating a significant drain on organizational resources in the planning process.

SUMMARY

The first step in the process of establishing a PMO within an organization is to gain an understanding of the current project management culture, practices, and challenges through an analysis of the organization's project management practices. This analysis serves as the basis for development of a base business case that outlines for management the challenges facing the organization as well as opportunities in which the PMO concept can be put to use to improve project management practices and results within the organization. Once the base business case is reviewed by management and approved, the next step will be to chart a course for successful development of a detailed business case and PMO implementation plan.

Chapter 3 will discuss the process of developing a detailed business case for a PMO and will address a number of practical considerations that must be addressed as part of developing a detailed plan. Chapter 3 will also conclude in a similar manner to Chapter 1, with a detailed presentation to management that focuses on securing approval to commence with PMO start-up and operation, but first, Chapter 2 will describe several essential PMO models and their functions.

REFERENCE

1. *A Guide to the Project Management Body of Knowledge, Third Edition.* 2005. Newtown Square, PA: The Project Management Institute.

ESSENTIAL PMO MODELS AND FUNCTIONS

INTRODUCTION

Chapter 1 focused on the processes involved in analyzing the current state of project management in an organization. It also focused on the processes required to develop a base business case that would be delivered to management for review and to obtain authorization to proceed with developing a detailed business case and the detailed plans for implementing the PMO and initiating PMO operations. Chapter 2 will begin with an overview of several important PMO models and key core operational areas of focus for PMOs. The remainder of Chapter 2 will then focus on determining the scope of the PMO and documenting the intended scope in a single scope statement. Determining and documenting the intended scope of the PMO is the first step in the development of a detailed business case.

ESSENTIAL PMO MODELS

Determining the role of a PMO in an organization is one of the primary initial decisions that must be made as part of any PMO planning exercise. As part of the discussion of the base business case with management, questions may have arisen regarding the specific functions and roles that the PMO will play in the organization. Many different PMO models are in existence today, and the structure and position of a PMO are often unique among organizations. However, a few essential models for the structure of a PMO are helpful to understand and consider as part of the process of defining the specific role and function of a new PMO. In the next three sections, several general categories of PMO models will be presented along with a discussion of the key features, benefits, and potential limitations of each.

The Strong PMO Model

The first model is the strong or managing PMO model. In this model, the PMO serves as the central project and program management body in the organization.

A strong PMO exists with the support and encouragement of management and exerts significant influence over the standards and processes that govern projects in the organization. A strong PMO is often singly accountable to management for setting direction and vision for the practice of project management in the organization. Often a strong PMO also plays the role of a knowledge organization by performing key organizational benchmarking activities, maintaining project libraries and lessons-learned summaries, and building knowledgebases of organizational best practices in the project management area. In addition, a strong PMO often plays the role of portfolio manager—working with management to determine which projects are undertaken by the organization, reporting on the status of all projects in the portfolio, alerting management to potential issues or areas of concern, and consulting with management on potential solutions. A strong PMO may additionally manage projects through a staff of PMO project managers who report to a PMO manager (directly or indirectly) and who are directly responsible for the execution of key projects. Although the primary goals of a PMO do not include actively managing the organization's entire project efforts, a strong PMO may engage in management or oversight of a number of the organization's highest-priority projects to ensure consistent project execution and utilization of a PMO staff's expertise to ensure project success.

The strong PMO model has several distinct benefits. Because the strong PMO model often has significant management support, the PMO is able to exert influence broadly within the organization. This allows the PMO to drive standardization in project management processes across the organization, implement best practices, and support the evolution of mature project management practices over time. Additionally, the strong PMO model fosters a sense of importance and professionalism among project managers. In the strong PMO model, the PMO manager is often a manager at the mid to upper levels of management, holding the title of or reporting to a vice president or other high-level organizational leader. Ideally, this leader is drawn from the ranks of successful project and program managers and can serve as a role model for other project management practitioners in the organization. This role also signifies to the organization the importance of project management as a key driver of business results and as a profession. Other members of the project management community in the organization, whether linked to the PMO directly or not, will feel as though they have a recognized function in the organization that is viewed as important to management.

It is important to note that significant management commitment is required to establish and maintain a PMO in the strong PMO model. A strong PMO is not implemented overnight, but once established, the scope of responsibility is often expanded over time, assuming that the PMO is successful at meeting its goals. In addition to its influence, a strong PMO often receives significant funding and organizational support to maintain its operations. It is often staffed with seasoned, successful project managers from the organization, who are able to build the project culture in the organization, mentor junior staff, and direct or monitor the progress of key organizational projects. Organizations considering implementing a strong PMO model must be willing to make the cultural shift required to align often disparate project management organizations and practices under a single guiding organization that will drive cultural transformation. As previously noted, the organization must be willing to commit significant time and energy to establish the PMO and provide clear direction to the project management community within the organization that the PMO will serve as the focal point for centralized guidance of the project management function within the organization.

In addition to these potential benefits, a strong PMO model also has potential drawbacks. First and foremost, implementing a strong PMO model can require significant organizational realignment. This realignment often includes the addition of PMO oversight in traditionally business-driven functions as well as other areas such as overall project coordination and status reporting. Especially in cases in which the PMO will be responsible for centralized coordination of the organization's project portfolio, initial resistance may exist from business unit or division managers who are used to having single-point oversight and control over the project functions in their organizations. For example, requiring that project managers within the organization report project status to the PMO for inclusion in a project portfolio, which subsequently provides data to the organization's management team, may not only represent an additional recordkeeping task, but may also create greater visibility for off-track projects and unapproved efforts, a benefit at the organizational level, but potentially a concern for those who are responsible for the off-track or unapproved efforts.

Another significant potential drawback is the amount of time required to successfully implement the strong PMO. Organizations looking for "quick wins" to resolve important project management issues or organizations looking to pilot the PMO concept and measure results on a small scale prior to fully implementing a PMO may find that the time and effort required for establishing, staffing, and starting-up a strong PMO exceeds the potential benefits. Organizations already committed to the PMO concept and wanting to establish a PMO on a solid footing and grow the function and responsibility of the PMO on an accelerated time frame may be able to overcome this obstacle because the up-front investment is often easier to justify.

A strong PMO can also become a perceived burden to project management productivity if implementation attempts to drive too much change and realignment too quickly. Especially in organizations in which limited process standardization and best practices utilization exists, an accelerated approach to implementing a PMO to standardize and coordinate project efforts can create chaos and reduced productivity initially. This is especially true if the goals and plans for the PMO are not communicated well in advance or if a solid training plan does not exist to acquaint project management personnel with the initial areas of focus for the PMO and potential changes that may occur in how members of the project management community do their jobs, communicate with management, or deal with day-to-day project issues. In order to mitigate this potential risk, the PMO planning team must validate the PMO opportunities that are identified in terms of organizational need and create a plan that gradually implements changes into the organization and that grows processes and standards over time. The concept of starting small and over time expanding organizational influence, revising standards, and realigning the project management practices may not initially appeal to management if there is an expectation that significant change will be implemented overnight. It is important to manage this expectation and ensure that there is an understanding that implementation of a PMO and then deriving value from a PMO is an evolutionary process. It must strike a balance between "quick wins" that create immediate change and the need to properly plan and gradually implement long-term PMO strategies over time.

The Consulting PMO Model

Another major model is the consulting PMO model. A consulting PMO addresses the project management needs of the organization primarily through mentoring and fostering a sense of project management community in the organization. In this model, the responsibility for day-to-day management of projects and project priority setting rests with the business units or divisions that undertake projects. A consulting PMO may establish standards for project management processes and may serve as a center of expertise, but it seldom has direct responsibility for project efforts. It may play a mentoring role by assisting with troubled projects, providing training and development opportunities for project managers and project staff, or publishing best practices drawn from throughout the organization. In some organizations, the consulting PMO will exist apart from any particular divisional affiliation. However, in many organizations, the consulting PMO either exists within a particular division in the organization or exists as one of several PMOs responsible for the project management function. In this case, several different divisions may each have their own PMO, but share best practices with others and exist in a common community of practice.

The consulting PMO model has several distinct advantages. It can exist within the constructs of the organization's current organizational structure without the need for extensive reorganization. Responsibility for individual project efforts and management of portfolios can still remain within existing divisions or geographies within the organization, with the PMO providing guidance and support. Although day-to-day project management may still lie within the organization, the PMO may support functions such as project management training, consolidated reporting, and gathering and disseminating best practices—areas that typically would be difficult to manage across broad areas of the organization without some amount of centralized management. Additionally, a consulting PMO may provide project support services such as advising on contract management, managing enterprise project management software, or sourcing and managing contract resources to augment staff for certain project efforts. By serving as a centralized representative for these or similar areas, a consulting PMO may be able to take advantage of economies of scale by leveraging the broader organization. It may also be able to reduce the amount of administrative overhead placed on individual project managers for some management functions.

A consulting PMO model also has potential drawbacks. A primary potential drawback is that a PMO operating as a consulting PMO may face difficulty gaining organizational acceptance. Because a consulting PMO does not serve the role of managing resources and key projects or does not have the responsibility for overall standards setting or governance activities, it may be viewed as overhead rather than a real contributor to enhancing project delivery in the organization. Additionally, because a consulting PMO does not directly manage projects, securing resources may be difficult. Project managers who successfully manage projects on behalf of the organization may not want to move from a project management capacity into a consulting PMO staff capacity unless there are significant potential rewards associated with the move. Difficulties may also arise if a consulting PMO role is not viewed by an organization as being part of a career path for project managers because many top project managers in the organization may see limited personal career growth associated with participation in a consulting PMO. Another potential drawback involves the ability of a consulting PMO to penetrate the organization and affect change. A consulting PMO may develop worthwhile best practices, standards, templates, and other deliverables, but if these items cannot be delivered and subsequently be accepted by the organization as standards, then the likelihood of long-term success in implementing change is limited.

In order to overcome these and other potential drawbacks, a strong organizational commitment to the role of the consulting PMO in the organization must be obtained. An organizational commitment must start with management committing to not only deploy the consulting PMO, but to also communicate its intended role, benefits, and values to the organization. There must also be a clear statement that management supports the PMO and encourages members of the organization to embrace its concept and support its goals. Without this statement from management, the role and value of a consulting PMO will be continually questioned, and its prospects for long-term success will be hampered.

The Blended PMO Model

Another general model is the blended PMO. A blended PMO model draws on the components of a strong PMO and a consulting PMO to create a structure that supports project management within the organization at the PMO level and within the divisions or geographies of the organization as a whole. In the blended PMO model, a PMO may have direct responsibility for managing the execution of some projects (such as certain key projects within the organization or large efforts that require the coordination of resources within several different areas of the organization), but day-to-day management of the majority of the projects in the organization still rests with the divisions or geographies of the organization itself. This active project management role is similar to the project management role within a strong PMO model, but it ensures that the majority of management for individual project efforts rests within the organization itself rather than with the PMO. Often in this model, the PMO does not directly seek to manage the entire portfolio management process for the organization. Individual business units or divisions may still primarily manage their own portfolios, but some rollup of those portfolios may be provided by the PMO for use by upper management to view the entire project activity in the organization. In addition to project management activities, a blended PMO provides consulting services, training, and standards-setting activities and is often regarded as a center of expertise for project management in the organization. This role is similar to the primary role of a consulting PMO. It allows the blended PMO to work across organizational boundaries to identify best practices and to implement standards and tools for the benefit of the entire project community.

A blended PMO model offers several potential advantages. Because a blended PMO model supports both management of projects and project support services, this model is well suited for organizations that cannot support a full-time PMO staff in addition to a full complement of project managers. A certain amount of capacity will still need to be retained to allow for consulting, knowledge management, training development, and related activities, but a blended PMO is intended to have flexibility built-in that allows it to serve as both an active project support organization as well as a project management organization. Additionally, the status of the PMO as a key contributor to the project support environment by being a key contributor to delivering project efforts may draw well-qualified project managers within the organization to PMO roles. Assuming a role in a PMO can provide significant opportunities for personal development as well as being a means to help retain talented individuals. Although not every member of the PMO staff will have the time or capacity to lead a large project, the PMO as a whole will likely be actively involved in some aspects of the delivery of large project efforts (e.g., from a project reporting, risk management, or planning standpoint) and thus will offer significant development opportunities for each member of the PMO staff. An additional potential benefit of a blended PMO is that its flexible role allows it to be easily grown over time. By incorporating key features of both the strong and the consulting PMO models, the blended PMO may be implemented as a small project organization first, which undertakes a limited number of activities or projects and then evolves its role over time. Although beginning with a small strong PMO or a small consulting PMO is possible, once the base role is established (i.e., the PMO *will* primarily lead projects or the PMO *will not* lead projects but *will instead* serve as a standards and consulting group) at some point in the future, it may be difficult to convince organizational leaders and the organization as a whole to accept a revised role.

The blended PMO overcomes this potential difficulty by attempting to bridge both functions in a way that provides meaningful value. Evolving this value may start with the PMO focusing initially on a few key trouble areas or planning revised standards or best practices by undertaking projects, analyzing the processes associated with these projects, and determining improvement areas while still delivering immediate value to the organization through managing a certain number of project efforts.

The potential drawbacks of a blended PMO typically relate to how the PMO functions in the broader organization and how the PMO resources are utilized. A blended PMO may have difficulty operating in the broader organizational context, e.g., if a clear distinction between "PMO projects" and "organizational projects" is not defined. A lack of clarity can lead to no common understanding of when the PMO engages in project management activities and when projects are left to individual divisions or groups within the organization to complete. It may be possible to define general guidelines such as ensuring that the PMO is only involved in the management of projects that cross significant divisional boundaries or only involved in projects that fall within certain project cost ranges. If these guidelines are not established and clearly communicated, divisions or groups within the organization may believe that they can request assistance from the PMO to manage projects at any time. They may become dissatisfied if the PMO is unwilling to assume responsibility for certain projects.

A blended PMO may also face issues related to resource utilization. A blended PMO is typically staffed with individuals who are dedicated to PMO activities on a full-time basis. If the PMO varies between a functional project management organization and a consulting organization, there may be a tendency to rely on the PMO more heavily as a project management group when large numbers of projects and limited resources exist in the organization. A *consulting* PMO model seeks to overcome this issue by not directly engaging in project management, thus culturally presenting itself as a standards and consulting organization. A *strong* PMO model overcomes this potential issue by clearly focusing on management-supported portfolio, standards, and best practices activities and on a limited number of key organizational projects.

In a blended PMO model, often there is a less-distinct line drawn between the consulting and project management roles. Therefore, it may be easier to "borrow" resources engaged in consulting and standards roles and move them into project management roles when project manager capacity issues arise. When this occurs, the PMO will spend less time on building and improving processes and as a result will have limited ability to create significant long-term benefits for the organization.

General Considerations for All Models

Regardless of the particular model that seems most appropriate for a particular organization, several key considerations must be taken under advisement as the decision on how to structure the role of the PMO in the organization is undertaken.

Centralization. The organization must consider whether the PMO model will be centralized or decentralized. A centralized PMO exists as a single organizational entity that serves as the program office for the entire organization. A centralized PMO manages all PMO functions for the organization. This model often works well in small- to medium-sized organizations or organizations with limited divisions or geographies because establishing a single point of management and responsibility for project and program processes ensures a certain level of control over the development and implementation of project standards and practices within the organization. It also allows everyone in the organization to understand where they should seek project support. Additionally, it better enables functions such as standardized training, single-point project reporting, and other similar functions in the organization project and program management functions in the organization.

Conversely, a decentralized PMO may have a single-oversight PMO that manages broad organizational initiatives in areas such as project reporting and standards setting, but different divisions within the organization or different business function teams may themselves implement PMOs for their individual divisions or functions. In large organizations, this model often works well because the central PMO can define certain cross-organization standards and procedures and the individual unit- or division-level PMO can implement these standards as well as additional processes and controls that are unique to the division, group, or geography in which the lower-level PMO resides. However, it is critical that the decentralized model includes a single point of overall control for PMO activities. Without overall control, the cross-organization benefits of a PMO are lost. Although divisional- or unit-level PMOs certainly can play a critical role in effectively managing project activities at the divisional or unit level, there must be some means of assuring a level of process uniformity within the organization as a whole in order to ensure that the benefits of standardized processes are realized.

Resource allocation. An additional consideration is the level of resource commitment that must be made in order to implement the model being considered. At minimum, all of the models require a full-time, devoted PMO manager who does not undertake any activities except management and development of the PMO. Implementing a PMO without a designated leader who concentrates fully on ongoing PMO operation and development will significantly lessen the likelihood of PMO success. In addition to the PMO manager, one or more additional PMO staff members will likely be needed to support PMO operations. In models such as the strong PMO model, a full complement of devoted PMO resources may eventually be acquired depending on the scope of work to be undertaken. In a consulting model, several full-time members of the staff may be appointed along with additional effort from part-time resources that spend a portion of their time participating in day-to-day project management activities and a portion of their time devoted to mentoring, consulting, and participating in other PMO activities.

Having 100% of the PMO staff available as full-time resources is certainly ideal, but often this is not practical in smaller organizations with limited resources. Even if unlimited full-time resources were available, following a general principle of starting small and growing the PMO over time would still be advisable. To that end, at the formative stage of the PMO, consideration must be given to the level of resources required to establish a base PMO that can then begin operation toward achieving improvement in several of the key improvement areas that have been identified as part of the base business case. In all cases, this consideration should include appointing a full-time PMO manager. Investing in additional resources may be required as well, on either a full-time or part-time basis as time and resources permit.

Environment. Another important consideration is the cultural environment in which the PMO will operate. The "place" of the PMO within the organization is significant. If the role of the PMO is to give advice and guidance, then the organization must be culturally open to accepting this advice and guidance. If the PMO's role is to set standards, then there must be organizational commitment from management as well as project managers and team members to accept and utilize the standards developed. Nonconformance to standards must be addressed. A strong commitment by management to the benefits of standardization will certainly help ensure that standards can be deployed and universally adopted by the organization, but the PMO must be recognized as the standards-setting organization, operating with input from a variety of stakeholders within the organization, but with final authority to set standards and ensure compliance. If the PMO is to serve as a functional project management organization, the culture of the organization must support the ability of the PMO to obtain and manage resources from within the broader organization and execute projects across organizational boundaries with limited conflict.

These are just a few of the potential organizational issues that must be understood and addressed. Although cultural shifts are certainly possible and some level of initial resistance is likely with many types of change, certain cultural factors may limit the effectiveness of the PMO if they are not understood and addressed as part of the PMO planning effort.

Organizational input. At this stage, an important consideration is the role of the existing project organization in the further definition and development of the PMO. As the discussions progress regarding the base model of operation for the PMO, ensure that feedback is considered from a broad range of individuals within the organization. Whether a centralized or decentralized model is envisioned, how existing project managers do their jobs and how the project organization functions as a whole will be affected. As such, consider feedback not only from management, but also from project managers, project stakeholders, business unit managers, and other affected areas of the organization regarding their vision for how a PMO could fit within the organization. As part of these discussions, providing a general level of background information regarding the PMO concept, specific potential roles of the PMO in the organization, and intended benefits of the PMO model for the organization may be necessary to ensure that the concept and goals of the PMO are well understood. By having the general concept and goals of the PMO in mind, these parties should be able to provide valuable feedback regarding the potential challenges that might be faced when implementing the PMO as well as the potential benefits that they perceive will be realized from operation of the PMO. The findings from these discussions should be used as additional inputs to final discussions regarding the intended model for the PMO within the organization.

A final decision regarding having a centralized or decentralized structure and whether the PMO will operate as a strong PMO, a consulting PMO, a blended PMO, or some hybrid of these models is not necessary at this point, but having a general direction in mind will be of benefit as development of the detailed business case is undertaken.

CORE OPERATIONAL AREAS OF THE PMO

In addition to the PMO models discussed in *Essential PMO Models*, prior to considering the details of building the detailed business case for the PMO, it is important to discuss several key operational areas of a PMO and their role within the project and PMO contexts. By having an understanding of several basic PMO models as well as several potential operational areas for the PMO, building a construct for the implementation of the PMO within the organization will be much easier. The core operational areas of a PMO include three essential functions:

- Consulting
- Knowledge
- Standards

These three functions are the core for the activities undertaken by the PMO. An understanding of the extent to which the PMO is intended to serve as a consulting, knowledge, and standards organization will be important in the development, implementation, and operation of the PMO. The role of the PMO in these areas will evolve over time. Although planning for the same level of involvement in each of these areas from the beginning is not critical, having an understanding of how these areas contribute to an effective PMO as well as understanding the values that they provide to the broader organization are critical. Each of these operational areas will be described in the following sections, along with the major goals of the operational areas and practical PMO responsibilities that fall within each.

The PMO as a Consulting Organization

The consulting role includes the functions associated with providing project consulting and mentoring to the organization as well as the functions associated with managing actual projects, such as in the strong PMO model. As a consulting organization, the PMO will have responsibility for serving as a center of expertise for project management in the organization. Project managers, project team members, and project stakeholders, as well as others with an interest in project management, should be able to rely on the PMO as a source for competent, timely advice on project-related matters. Additionally, as a consulting organization, the PMO should be the first point of contact for questions regarding project management processes, organizational project standards, reporting requirements, and other areas of project work in which defined standards exist (often defined by the PMO as part of its role as a standards organization). If a question arises regarding project management, the PMO in its consulting role should be able to either answer it or to seek feedback from other experts within the organization or externally to provide input to the individual seeking an answer. In order to function effectively in a consulting role, the PMO must have several elements in place.

Staff. The PMO must be staffed with competent, experienced project managers who have broad project experience and, ideally, experience in a consulting capacity. In smaller organizations with small PMOs, the PMO manager may serve as the key project expert and be primarily responsible for serving as the "in-house expert" on project management. The PMO manager may rely on input from other experienced project managers within the organization to provide additional guidance and assistance as needed. In larger centralized PMOs or in decentralized PMOs of varying sizes, there may be a number of members of the PMO staff, each an expert in broad areas of project management, or perhaps a functional expert in a specific area of project management such as risk management or schedule development. Regardless of the number of individuals, the individuals must be credible project managers who are able to provide advice and who understand the organizational context within which projects are undertaken. In most cases, a PMO is not the place to grow junior project managers—junior project managers have a role in the organization of leading projects and growing their capacity to lead larger projects. Unless the PMO is spending a significant amount of time formally leading project efforts, this experience is best gained in the organization's functional units, where the majority of project work is being undertaken.

Additional resources. In addition to a competent staff of project management practitioners, the PMO must have an ability to reach beyond the PMO itself to provide guidance. Believing that a PMO staff will have a definitive answer to every project management question raised by members of the organization is unreasonable. Either within the organization or externally, the PMO staff must have access to additional resources to effectively serve as a consulting organization. From within the organization, this may include access to other project managers or a directory of key project managers within the organization's business units and their particular areas of expertise. Growing the network of project management resources beyond the PMO resources themselves ensures that the PMO staff has support in the event that a request for assistance is made that represents an area in which the PMO staff members do not possess the necessary expertise. The PMO must also have access to expert advice beyond the organization. This may involve expending funds to allow PMO staff members to join PMO-specific interest groups or professional organizations, encouraging staff to attend conferences on PMO-related topics and build a network of PMO practitioners outside of the organization, or subscribing to project- and PMO-relevant newsletters, journals, or trade publications that allow PMO members to stay abreast of trends in the project management and PMO disciplines.

Support activities. As a consulting organization, the PMO may also assist with certain project activities in which project managers themselves may not have sufficient time or expertise. Typically, these activities include assisting with functions such as conducting project kick-off meetings, providing team-building exercises to help build effective project teams, or assisting business units with categorizing and ranking potential projects to maximize return on investment. These are only a sample of the potential areas of involvement, but the general goal is to build a PMO consulting structure that supports project managers and teams directly (as well as other stakeholders) in a way that meets the needs of these constituencies without adding unnecessary overhead. To require that the PMO be involved in the process of kicking off every project that the organization undertakes would, in general, seem to be an excessive effort, but providing the ability for the PMO to assist with a project kick-off when a project manager determines that a more formalized kick-off is required might add value by ensuring a quality experience that starts the project team moving down a path toward success.

Engagement. Not all consulting that the PMO participates in will necessarily occur on an as-needed basis. In some cases, organizational standards or PMO-created standards may dictate involvement by the PMO at certain key stages of the project life cycle. For example, the PMO may review project cost or time estimates created by individual project managers for large projects to ensure accuracy and compliance with organizational standards, or it may be involved in reviews of project progress at defined milestones to help ensure success and to mitigate risk by providing insight and advice to the project manager and project stakeholders. In a less favorable case, the PMO may be involved in reviews of projects that appear to be heading off-track despite corrective action by the project manager to assist in determining root causes of issues or to define action plans for resolving project difficulties. The roles and rules of engagement for these types of activities are often defined as part of the organization's project management standards and practices. As such the extent to which the PMO is involved in any particular project effort that it does not manage directly should be well understood by project managers.

Regardless of whether consulting occurs on an ad hoc basis or at certain predefined points in the project life cycle, the goal remains the same—to provide competent, expert advice to project managers, project teams, and stakeholders. The consulting role can build significant organizational value by having a central center of expertise at the disposal of project managers.

Although project managers certainly will have their own network of colleagues to rely on for day-to-day questions and issues, having a centralized body that can be utilized to assist in resolving larger questions or problems or to request advice on best practices gives project managers in the organization an additional tool to ensure project success. Although the PMO will likely not be a 24-hour-a-day helpdesk for all project management questions, knowing that expert assistance is available can lead to faster resolution of significant project issues. If managed through periodic involvement of the PMO in project review at key project milestones, the consulting role may actually lead to proactive identification and troubleshooting of potential project issues before they become significant events. This can result in saving the organization significant amounts of time and money and increasing overall customer satisfaction.

The PMO as a Knowledge Organization

The knowledge role of a PMO includes the activities associated with acquiring, organizing, maintaining, and disseminating organizational knowledge as well as activities related to project management training and professional development. As organizations undertake and complete projects, typically a significant amount of documentation regarding the project efforts is produced. Many of these items are relevant project assets that have potential for reuse within the organization either for the direct benefit of another project effort or as learning tools for the organization overall. Unfortunately, a significant number of organizations lack the ability to centrally organize and make these key assets available to the project management community.

Knowledge Management

The PMO can play a significant role as the source for knowledge management within the organization as it relates to project activities. Knowledge can range from internal project assets to organizational know-how and lessons learned to external knowledge sources such as books, externally provided training courses, and industry standards. Over time the amount of potentially available knowledge can become large. Without some practical means of cataloging and maintaining this knowledge, it becomes extremely difficult for an organization to provide access to it in a way that provides knowledge users with the ability to find the specific type of information they are seeking in a timely manner.

Knowledge repository. The processes of capturing, cataloging, and maintaining knowledge can be time consuming, especially in large organizations in which numerous projects are undertaken and a significant number of project assets exist. Without a central knowledge repository, project assets tend to either remain within the division or department in which particular projects were undertaken or over time become lost within the organization. The PMO may improve this situation by positioning itself as a central repository for items such as project status reports, project closeout reports, lessons-learned documentation, and key project deliverables. By publishing a set of knowledge management standards, the project community gains awareness of the types of knowledge that are of interest to the PMO and can include forwarding these knowledge assets to the PMO as part of their project processes. The PMO then assumes the role of reviewing the knowledge assets received and cataloging relevant items within the knowledge repository and discarding duplicate or irrelevant items. Over time a significant database of organizational project management knowledge will emerge. When a new project is chartered, the project manager can look to the organizational project management knowledgebase as a source for documentation on past, similar projects or for organizational best practices relevant to the type of project being undertaken. This provides significant value to the organization in terms of eliminating rework as well as in encouraging the use of project best practices to increase the likelihood of project success.

Capture and dissemination. From the standpoint of knowledge management, it is important to consider the practical mechanisms by which knowledge capture, management, and dissemination occur. Typically, the process of knowledge capture works best when a set of standards for the type of knowledge desired is provided to the organization. The PMO will likely set these standards and communicate them to the organization. In addition to the types of knowledge to be captured, the method of transmission to the PMO must be considered. The role of technology will be critical from both an acquisition and dissemination standpoint. Ideally, electronic archives of key knowledge assets would be maintained, with project resources submitting electronic documents, spreadsheets, presentations, deliverables, and other relevant knowledge assets to the PMO. The PMO would then take overall responsibility for building a master knowledgebase that is accessible to the organization via some internal electronic delivery mechanism such as a website. The PMO holds responsibility for maintaining the website and users within the organization take responsibility for using the site's resources as they undertake projects. In smaller organizations, a technology solution may not be practical. These organizations may instead rely on project archives that are physically stored in a knowledge library or that are maintained in a more simplistic electronic format such as a shared file area within the organization's computer network.

The process. Regardless of the method of submission, management, and dissemination chosen, knowledge management is an *evolutionary* process. Typically, an organizational project management knowledgebase will begin with a small subset of all of the potentially available knowledge assets and focus on those areas in which creating a centralized knowledgebase will yield the most benefit. If the organization struggles because of making many of the same types of project mistakes repeatedly, it may be appropriate to begin the process of building a knowledgebase with lessons-learned documents from past projects. If the organization struggles with estimating project costs, it may instead be appropriate to begin by cataloging the methods of estimating used within the organization that have a track record of success and making those methodologies available to the organization. Unless the organization is relatively small, an attempt to capture every potential project asset for every current project in the organization initially will likely result in a loss of focus and an inability to manage the knowledge. Similarly, developing a process for attempting to retroactively capture knowledge for projects already complete may prove to be a challenging exercise because it is likely that no standards were in place relative to knowledge management at the time these projects were undertaken. As a result, the level of available detail and the form and structure of the knowledge assets may vary widely.

Knowledgebase evolution. Over time, the types of knowledge captured will likely increase. As the organization becomes more proficient in capturing and submitting knowledge to the PMO, the level of detailed knowledge available to the organization will increase as well. At this stage in the PMO development process, the specific types of knowledge and the method of capture and dissemination should be considered at a high level so that appropriate resources can be factored into the detailed business case. However, it is not necessary at this stage to develop detailed implementation plans. The knowledge management role is just one potential role for the PMO and, as discussed previously, is likely a role that will evolve over time. It is perfectly acceptable to start with small, limited domains of knowledge that, when captured and disseminated, will assist in addressing one or more of the challenges facing the organization. As the PMO role grows in the organization, the types of knowledge captured will likely grow and the organization's project management knowledgebase will begin to provide value for a broader range of individuals and project situations.

Training and Professional Development

In addition to a knowledge management role, the PMO may play a significant role in training and development as well. As the center of expertise for project management in the organization, the PMO is a logical place to house central responsibility for project management training. This does not necessarily imply that the PMO will have sole responsibility for the execution of training activities, but project-relevant training should minimally be coordinated through the PMO to assure consistency with organizational standards and practices and to ensure that quality training is being provided to the organization.

Materials. Developing quality training materials requires a significant investment of time and resources, which is often best accomplished through the involvement of professional training developers who understand the methodologies and training constructs that are most appropriate for adult learners. The role of the PMO in training development may be limited to providing content to training developers. Alternatively, the PMO itself may take the lead in directly developing training materials by relying on members of the PMO staff. Another choice is for the PMO to outsource training to external providers with expertise in providing project management training.

Trainers. The extent to which the PMO involves itself in training will likely be limited in the early stages of PMO operation. In many organizations, project management training is conducted either internally or externally via qualified providers. The initial focus of the PMO will likely be on understanding the types of project management training in place in the organization already, the effectiveness of these programs, and the gaps in the project management training curriculum that should be addressed. Often it is not practical for the PMO to initially assume responsibility for all project management training in the organization. However, it may be appropriate for the PMO to be involved in developing or sourcing all new project management training activities, relying on the divisions or business units within the organization to assist in identifying gaps in the training curriculum and then developing plans to bridge those gaps via new training offerings. It is also important to realize that the pure concepts of project management are typically not the only types of knowledge that members of the project management community within the organization must acquire. Additional skills in areas such as negotiating, time management, interpersonal communication, and other related topics are very relevant for project practitioners. Planning by the PMO for training should consider these and other relevant general business topics as well.

Training opportunities. Although the range of topics to be offered and the frequency of training do not require a detailed level of consideration at this point, the intended role for the PMO in managing and providing training is very relevant. In organizations with dedicated training departments or divisions, it may be appropriate for the PMO to provide input on the types of training activities that are provided or sourced by the training organization rather than to assume responsibility for these experiences directly. In organizations without a central training organization, or with a central training organization that does not provide support for project management training, the PMO may take the lead in developing a centralized, standard set of project management training opportunities, potentially partnering with other groups within the organization, as appropriate, on topics of broad business interest beyond pure project management. Regardless of whether the PMO plays an active or an advisory role, it is critical that the PMO ensures that any project management training being delivered within the organization is aligned with the organization's project management standards and best practices. This advisory role is critical to ensure consistency across the organization and alignment with the intended benefits of standardized project processes.

Professional development opportunities. In many organizations, training is linked to the broader topic of professional development. Professional development focuses on the entire range of activities that are available to employees to help encourage career growth and personal development. Training is one key aspect of professional development. In addition, access to external industry resources, participation in symposia and conferences on relevant project management topics, and exposure to Best in Class and new project management techniques are among other areas of professional development. The PMO should play a role in finding suitable professional development activities beyond pure training and then making those activities available to project managers and project team members on a regular basis. These activities do not necessarily need to involve significant investments of time and money. Learning experiences such as quarterly lessons-learned reviews or monthly lunch sessions to review new trends in project management can provide significant value to the organization without extensive investment. The PMO may choose to provide more structured offerings such as access to conferences or seminars on project management topics, but these activities typically involve more significant commitments of both time and money and are often limited to only a small portion of the project management community within the organization. Smaller, more accessible professional development activities can yield significant benefits.

As planning for the PMO progresses, the role of the PMO from the training and professional development standpoint should be considered at a high level. It is not necessary to develop concrete plans in the detailed business case, but it is important to recognize that the PMO should be providing benefits to the project practitioners and other relevant stakeholders within the organization from a training and professional development standpoint. The specific benefits to the organization are often intangible, but nonetheless they are significant—quality training and professional development opportunities build stronger project management practitioners and often increase employee job satisfaction. The extent to which the PMO can build strong opportunities will also help to foster a stronger link between the PMO and project practitioners and strengthen the project management culture within the organization.

The PMO as a Standards Organization

The third core role of a PMO is that of a standards organization. One of the benefits often mentioned in discussions regarding the concept of the PMO in general is its role is establishing and maintaining organizational project management standards. The importance of having standardized project processes cannot be overlooked. Without standardized processes and methodologies, project managers and project team members are left to develop their own tools to manage projects. For some project managers, this may be a workable model, but from the standpoint of having organizational consistency and enabling cross-project functions, e.g., consolidated resource management and project portfolio reporting, this inconsistency makes it nearly impossible to effectively execute these initiatives. Therefore, it is in the best interests of organizations to align on standardized processes for core project activities. It is not necessary to dictate a standard process for every aspect of project management. Yet, especially in areas in which the organization faces challenges, defining and aligning standardized processes may be one way to help bridge the gap between the current challenges and the desired state for these processes.

Some of the common areas in which standardization is often used include the processes of selecting projects, chartering projects, delivering detailed plans and statements of work, reporting project progress, assessing and managing risk, and managing contractual relationships. There are certainly many other potential areas of impact in which standardization can provide benefits as well.

The Portfolio Management Role

Of particular note is the role of the PMO as maintainer of the enterprise project "portfolio," a high-level view of all of the projects that the organization is undertaking or considering undertaking along with the status of each effort. The enterprise project portfolio represents the complete view of project efforts within the organization. It is best maintained by a central body that is responsible for the portfolio contents and for reporting on the status of the portfolio to management, along with specific recommendations for action in cases in which one or more projects in the portfolio are not meeting their intended objectives. The portfolio process is enhanced when a single set of standard methods for reporting project progress, adding or removing projects from the portfolio, and providing status to management is maintained. The PMO can play an active role in ensuring that these processes exist and are consistently followed. Absent these processes, portfolio data is often inconsistent, and thus the benefits to the organization of maintaining a project portfolio are limited. The specific details regarding managing a project portfolio will be discussed in Chapter 6, but as part of the detailed business plan development process, understanding this key potential role for the PMO from a standards and management standpoint is an important consideration.

Establishing and Maintaining Standards

Depending on the current state of standardization, the process of establishing and maintaining standards may either begin with a review of the current practices within the groups or divisions that currently undertake projects (if no core standards exist) or by reviewing the individual standards used by the different divisions. The purpose of this process is to determine how to best align existing standards with a single set of standards that will meet the needs of the organization overall. The process of determining the existing level of standardization in place in the organization and defining a single set of standards can be time consuming. It requires input from a broad cross section of the organization. Standardization will not occur overnight. Therefore, the initial focus of PMO efforts in the standards area should be to understand what is currently in place and to develop a plan to standardize existing processes in a common model that can be used broadly within the organization.

The ability of the PMO to enforce standards within the organization is also a topic of interest as the standards role for the PMO in the organization is considered. In models such as the strong PMO model, the PMO may be able set standards directly by establishing standardized processes, documenting those processes, and deploying them to the organization. When the PMO has significant influence over the project organization, this process may be achieved with limited risk of nonacceptance (although no guarantee exists that the new standards will be accepted with great joy). In PMO structures in which the PMO serves in a more advisory role and projects are primarily left to the business units or divisions themselves to manage, deploying standards can be challenging because some groups may believe that the standards do not adequately consider their unique business scenarios and are more advisory guidelines rather than pure standards that must be followed. Certainly, standards can be viewed as guidelines, but if conformance is optional, there is little hope that significant benefits from establishing the standards will be achieved. Rather, the standards will merely become part of a toolset available to project managers to use as they wish as they undertake project efforts. For some organizations, this may be acceptable. The impact of this approach should be considered versus the need for the organization to improve processes in a meaningful and lasting way.

Standards Development and Implementation

The process of standards development and implementation is significant. For many PMOs that are chartered to initially address specific current project management challenges, the standards role may be the area that gets the most initial attention. Undertaking the process of developing standards requires examining the current processes in the organization, documenting the areas of concern, and designing standards that will address these concerns, while also implementing best practices. Developing standards by starting with a clean page and having no organizational context may sound appealing because it facilitates deriving standards from best practices only (assuming the organization has visibility to external best practices in the area being standardized), but the end result may create significant initial internal upheaval if the revised standard processes vary significantly from the way the organization typically operates. Although this situation may be an acceptable risk for some organizations, a more-tempered approach may be appropriate for the majority of organizations. Regardless of the approach taken, it is critical that a standards exercise initially focus on a subset of all of the organization's processes and then develop and implement meaningful and lasting change in these processes before addressing other areas. This method ensures that well-thought-out standards are developed and implemented rather than merely developing a broad set of interim, quick-fix standards that will likely need to be modified and evolved later.

Standards Setting and the Detailed Business Case

Because of the critical role of standards setting, several key considerations must be addressed as part of the process of considering how standards setting will be addressed in the detailed business case.

Scope. The level of control over standards setting and compliance with established standards must be considered. If the intent is for the PMO to serve as the primary standards organization responsible for establishing and maintaining organizational standards, this role must be clearly documented in the detailed business case and receive agreement from management. If the PMO will primarily serve in an advisory role, establishing and documenting best practices for use by the organization on a voluntary basis, this must similarly be documented and aligned with management. The resources required to maintain a standards library can be significant depending on the scope of standards to be created and maintained. Limiting the scope of applicable standards initially is often a good idea to ensure that the PMO can adequately focus its efforts on the key areas identified. In a similar sense, the PMO may be involved in establishing and maintaining certain key standards that require compliance by the organization, yet the PMO may operate in an advisory role for other areas of standardization. This model ensures that for the key processes identified by the organization, a single, uniform set of standards is in place and used. For other less critical areas, the PMO may provide guidance on suggested best practices, but leave specific implementations to individual divisions or project managers. This flexibility facilitates allowing for scenarios such as regional differences in operation and unique situations that may create significant variance in how processes are undertaken within different areas of the organization. As long as permitting these variances is acceptable from a process improvement standpoint, this level of flexibility is largely permissible. At the detailed business case development phase, it is not critical to define each potential area of standardization in detail, but it is important to determine whether the PMO will play a true standards setting role, whether it will serve primarily in a consulting and advising role, or if it will be a combination of the two.

Balanced focus. Although developing a detailed list of all potential areas of influence from a standards point of view is not necessary, it is important to consider the key areas within the organization where the PMO will first concentrate. These areas will likely be drawn from the key challenge areas defined as part of the assessment process. Although standards cannot solve every project management challenge, there is clearly a link between process standardization, the related idea of process maturity, and project results. However, developing standards is not enough. The standards must be developed in a way that creates meaningful benefits without excessive organizational overhead. Striking a balance between meaningful standards and the level of effort required to operate within the standards is critical. There is no hard science that facilitates striking this balance. Focusing on a few critical areas of improvement, developing and piloting standards that create meaningful improvement in the processes, and deploying those processes in a way that encourages understanding the goals and methods of the standards will go a long way toward ensuring that the intended benefits are achieved. To this end, the detailed business case should include a few areas of focus with the understanding that the standards role will evolve over time as the PMO focuses on fixing the immediate challenges facing the organization, measuring success, and then expanding its role into new areas of focus.

Management support. Another important consideration, which has been discussed previously but bears repeating here, is the role of management in the standards process. For initial areas of focus and standards processes that are defined as part of the initial start-up of the PMO, the members of management chartering the PMO must be committed to allowing the PMO to do its job. When the PMO is to set mandatory standards for use in the organization, management should provide the necessary support to allow the PMO to enforce these standards and address noncompliance. It will certainly be necessary to keep management abreast of any standards work being undertaken and to obtain concurrence on standards prior to dissemination to the organization, but once this process is complete, management must communicate their commitment to the goals of standardization to the organization and clearly articulate expectations regarding compliance with the standards. Even when the standards will be primarily advisory in nature, a management commitment to the goals of standardization should be communicated and voluntary compliance with the advisory standards should be encouraged.

Finding the Right Mix

In most cases, attempting to foster the consulting, knowledge, and standards PMO roles equally in the early existence of the PMO is not practical. Doing so tends to dilute the attention paid to each and results in building acceptable, but often not ideal, practices for each of the process areas. A better approach is to determine an appropriate mix of focus on the various roles that accounts for the immediate needs of the organization (thus helping to allow the PMO to provide value to the organization quickly) while still planning for long-term development of each of the roles as the PMO matures. The detailed business case should include planning for the roles that the PMO will play in the organization. This planning should be linked to the needs of the organization as discovered in the assessment process. Developing these links will be the topic of the next section.

DETERMINING PMO SCOPE

The first step in the development of the PMO detailed business case is to determine and document the intended scope of the PMO in a single scope statement. The scope statement will have several dimensions. It will articulate the intended scope of the PMO in terms of organizational reach, roles and responsibilities, and intended outcomes from operations. The scope statement will be the single guiding document for development of the detailed business case, and as business case development progresses, it will be critical to ensure that the detail provided in the business case is aligned with the intended scope of the PMO. The scope statement should also be validated with management, ideally before work begins in earnest on the detailed business case, to ensure that management is aligned with the general direction that is being proposed for the PMO via the scope statement.

It is also essential that the PMO scope statement is aligned to the organizational challenges and opportunities addressed in the assessment process and validated with management as part of the base business case review. The initial focus of the PMO should be on addressing the challenges articulated in the base business case as well as any other organizational challenges brought forth by management for consideration as part of the PMO planning process. Documenting both the short-term scope of the PMO (in terms of addressing organizational challenges) and the long-term scope of the PMO (in terms of intended final mode of operations and broader challenges facing the organization that cannot be solved within the first few months of operation) is certainly appropriate. Doing so will clearly show that the PMO development team has considered the ability of the PMO to affect business results in the near term and has also developed a vision for establishing long-term benefits. Yet, it is critical to make a very clear distinction between what the PMO will deliver in the short-term and what it will deliver in the long-run so that management understands in unambiguous terms what to expect during the first few critical months of operation—the time frame when management will be looking at the PMO operation most closely and assessing the PMO's value to the organization the most.

Scope Dimensions

Several key dimensions of PMO scope must be addressed in a PMO scope statement.

Organizational reach. The first important dimension of the scope statement is the intended organizational reach. Organizational reach reflects the intended audience for the PMO. If the proposed PMO is to serve as a single point of contact for the organization for project matters, its status as the primary organizational unit responsible for project management processes and practices should be reflected. If a decentralized structure is being proposed, and there is an intent to have multiple PMO entities within business units, divisions, or geographies providing localized support while still maintaining a link to a central governing PMO that retains responsibility for certain PMO functions, that structure should be articulated and should include the intended roles of both the central PMO and the associated divisional or geography-based PMOs as well. The organizational reach of the PMO may be an area that is intended to be evolutionary. Especially if management intends to pilot the PMO concept before broadly deploying it to the organization, the scope statement may initially reflect only the intended scope for this first phase, but also have a statement indicating what the intended final structure will be after the full rollout is complete.

Roles and responsibilities. In addition to the intended organizational reach, a clear statement of the intended roles and responsibilities that will be undertaken by the PMO should be included. In some cases, it may be necessary to focus only on the initial intended scope, but in general it is more appropriate to describe both the initial areas of focus in terms of roles and responsibilities and the long-term roles and responsibilities of the PMO, noting a distinction between initial focus areas and the final end set of general responsibilities for the PMO as part of the document. These roles and responsibilities should be segmented along the domains of consulting, knowledge, and standards. At minimum, for the initial phase of PMO deployment, roles and responsibilities will likely align with many of the organizational challenges that establishing the PMO is intended to address. There may be additional intended roles and responsibilities that do not directly link to any challenge facing the organization, but that reflect opportunities for continuous improvement, additional revenue, or some other organizational benefit. These may be documented as well to provide a complete picture of the intended end scope of operations for the PMO. Establishing these roles and responsibilities reflects a starting point. The actual roles and responsibilities of the PMO will likely evolve over time, with the PMO initially focusing on the key challenges facing the organization and then expanding its role into new areas. Some of these areas will be documented in the scope statement and others will be established over time as management determines the right fit for the PMO within the organization. It is not necessary to document every potential area of responsibility in the scope statement. Rather, focus on the few key areas that will be addressed immediately upon start-up of the PMO as well as several additional areas where the PMO could most likely provide value over time.

In general, the majority of the roles and responsibilities will fall into either the consulting, knowledge, or standards areas, but there may be additional responsibilities that are envisioned that do not align well to one of these distinctions. It would be extremely difficult to list all of the possible roles and responsibilities that the PMO could play in an organization. To guide creation of the intended roles and responsibilities, a few of the major areas of responsibility that typically fall within the domains of consulting, knowledge, and standards are provided for reference:

- Consulting
  - Mentoring project managers
  - Providing consulting for troubled projects
  - Assisting with implementation of organizational best practices for particular project efforts
  - Leading lessons-learned sessions and conducting project audits
  - Assisting business units with project selection, vendor analysis, and other project processes
  - Leading project efforts

- Knowledge
  - Assembling project assets from across the organization
  - Identifying and documenting organizational best practices
  - Creating knowledge repositories and providing access to these repositories to the organization
  - Creating project management training materials
  - Conducting introductory project management training for new project managers and advanced project management training for experienced project managers
  - Providing access to white papers, journals, conference proceedings, and other external resources of interest

- Standards
  - Defining organizational standards for key project processes
  - Creating standard tools for use by project managers for project tracking, estimating, or other common project functions

- Leading the implementation of standards and tracking compliance with organizational standards
- Managing centralized project functions such as portfolio management and enterprise project status reporting

The process of determining roles and responsibilities for the PMO should begin with a review of the current challenges and PMO opportunities, include a broad view of the potential long-term roles for the PMO, and should be aligned with management in advance of creating the detailed business case.

The Scope Statement

The structure of a PMO scope statement is fairly straightforward. It may follow a general format such as the following:

GOTPMO CORPORATION—PMO SCOPE STATEMENT

The GOTPMO Corporation seeks to establish a Program Management Office (PMO) to provide a single point of management, control, and accountability for the establishment, development, implementation, and maintenance of a single set of project management standards, practices, and procedures, to serve as the single enterprise point of contact for project management consulting and education and to lead the implementation of major enterprise projects for the organization. The PMO shall engage with the business units within the organization and collaborate to leverage existing practices and to develop useful tools for deployment to the organization.

The PMO shall initially undertake the following responsibilities:

- Establish itself as an organizational entity, recruit sufficient staff to support start-up operations, develop a plan to present the PMO concept to the organization, and have an ongoing communications plan to keep the organization abreast of PMO activities
- Design a standard project status reporting process, document the status of all current project efforts, and create a single summarized report for management on a monthly basis that reflects project efforts in the organization

- Design and implement a single project chartering process to be used by all divisions within the GOTPMO Corporation for establishing and authorizing project efforts
- Build a set of standard templates for use by project managers for documenting project assumptions and managing project risks
- Establish a PMO steering committee to guide further development of the PMO based on business needs

In addition to the initial PMO activities mentioned above, the PMO shall also pursue the following long-term objectives:

- Develop a standardized project management training curriculum to provide new project managers with the essential skills required to competently execute projects
- Conduct a complete review of existing project control processes and create a standardized process library and project methodology for use by project managers that leverages organizational and external best practices
- Review major project management software solutions and recommend to management a suite of solutions to address current limitations in project governance, management, and reporting
- Maintain a master catalog of project assets including charters, schedules, budgets, progress reports, issues logs, lessons-learned documents, and related project documents and establish a process to allow project managers to search these assets and extract relevant knowledge for use in current and future projects
- Lead the delivery of major enterprise project efforts by attracting and retaining a core group of talented PMO project managers with primary focus on the successful delivery of enterprise projects

The scope statement begins with wording that clearly articulates the role of the PMO in terms of serving as a single point of accountability and management for project management processes and as a contributor to project delivery via undertaking major project initiatives. It further recognizes the importance of collaboration with the business units within the organization to leverage existing practices and ensure that developed standards and practices are aligned with business needs. These statements define the intent for how the PMO will operate within the organization and provides the general framework for its responsibilities. The scope statement alone will not provide the PMO with any formal authority, but it should be reviewed with management to ensure alignment with management's needs because these general principals will guide development of the detailed business case and subsequent presentation to management to seek approval to begin work to formally commence operations. Approval of the detailed business case and subsequent communication from management to the organization regarding the role of the PMO in the organization will provide formal chartering and authority to the PMO and ensure that this authority is communicated to the organization.

The remainder of the scope statement is divided into two sections. The first focuses on the initial focus areas for the PMO (likely those activities that will be undertaken within the first 90 days of PMO operation) and includes the processes of establishing the PMO as well as several initial areas of focus for the PMO (which, ideally, should be drawn from the current project management challenges facing the organization). The second section focuses on long-term objectives that the PMO will eventually undertake once the initial phase of PMO implementation is complete and the PMO has demonstrated value by delivering results in the few initial areas of focus.

It is also important to note that the scope statement is provided at a fairly high level and focuses on *what* is to be accomplished rather than *how* the work is going to be accomplished. The scope statement is not designed to be a detailed implementation plan, but rather a guiding document that can be referenced as the detailed business case is built. The detailed business case will include a start-up roadmap that documents the specific details on how the initial focus areas will be delivered, the required resources, and the time line for completing work in the initial focus areas. It is not necessary to provide this level of detail within the scope statement itself.

SUMMARY

In Chapter 2, several important PMO models have been presented to allow the reader to understand the relative benefits of several different PMO models.

Although no one model is effective for everyone, certain models lend themselves more readily to certain types of organizations. It is critical to consider the intended role of the PMO, the size and structure of the organization, and other similar factors when considering how a PMO will be positioned within the organization. In addition to an appropriate model, a clear and compelling business case must be made for the creation a PMO. The first step in this process, establishing a clear PMO scope, ensures that there is clarity regarding the intended roles and functions of the PMO. The PMO scope statement serves as a basis for constructing a detailed business case, which will be discussed in Chapter 3.

THE DETAILED BUSINESS CASE

BUILDING THE DETAILED BUSINESS CASE

With a base understanding of the intended scope of the PMO now documented in the PMO scope statement, the process of developing a detailed business case can begin. A detailed business case should accomplish the following objectives:

- Present the key project management challenges facing the organization and define how the PMO will address these challenges
- Document the intended PMO objectives, roles, responsibilities, and structure
- Provide an implementation plan for the PMO including required resources, time line, and costs for start-up and initial operations
- Request authorization to proceed with implementation of the PMO

A detailed business case should contain sufficient data to allow management to make an informed decision regarding the benefits of the PMO as well as the ability of the PMO to return value to the organization. It should also demonstrate that a cogent plan exists to implement the PMO. A strong detailed business case also acts as a detailed charter for the PMO team, outlining what is to be delivered and the resources, time line, and the constraints that will govern establishing the PMO. With an approved detailed business case in hand, the work to formally establish the PMO and commence operations can begin.

Inputs to the Detailed Business Case

Before beginning work on the detailed business case document, assemble documentation regarding the key PMO planning work that has been completed to date for use as input to the detailed business case, including:

- The base business case document and feedback from management regarding the base business case
- Output from the assessment process including current organizational challenges and opportunities
- The PMO scope statement
- Summaries of discussions with management regarding the scope, roles, responsibilities, and expectations regarding the function of the PMO

Input from this documentation provides a number of important data points that are essential for development of a detailed business case. The base business case document provides the groundwork upon which further investigation of the PMO concept has been built. As an approved document, it represents management's commitment to further investigation of the PMO concept as well as management's intent regarding how further PMO development work should proceed. As the detailed business case is developed, it should be validated against the major findings in the base business case to ensure alignment with management direction. Output from the assessment process will provide important detail regarding potential areas of focus for the PMO. The assessment findings have also been used as a vital part of developing the PMO scope statement (see *Determining PMO Scope* in Chapter 2). Therefore the major challenges and opportunities that have been identified in the assessment process have already been included as part of the scope statement. Revalidating the detailed business case with the assessment findings ensures that the intended areas of focus are completely represented in the detailed business case and also notes any findings from the assessment to be excluded from the scope of the PMO.

Other essential input to the detailed business case includes summaries of discussions that have been conducted with management. These discussions include formal reviews such as the review of the base business case and assessment findings as well as informal updates, reviews of draft documents such as the PMO scope statement, and others. As the process of developing the detailed business case begins, review past input from management regarding PMO development to ensure that management feedback regarding roles, responsibilities, intended tasks and benefits, and other areas is appropriately incorporated into the detailed business case. Reviewing key validation points with management such as a review of the PMO scope statement and revalidation of the base business case prior to beginning development of the detailed business case will help ensure that the detailed business case aligns with management's expectations. This increases the probability that the detailed business case will be accepted by management when completed and formally presented. Although reviewing every detail with every potentially affected manager in the organization is not practical, validating key high-level plans with the appropriate levels of management to ensure alignment is essential. Assuming that management has been kept informed of the PMO work on a regular basis, only reviewing input and ensuring that this input has been included in the detailed business case should be necessary.

Structure of the Detailed Business Case

A detailed business case should be structured into several logical sections. The format may be adapted to any relevant organizational standards or management requests, but in general the format should include these sections:

- Section 1: Introduction
- Section 2: Summary of Current Challenges and Opportunities
- Section 3: PMO Roles, Responsibilities, and Organization
- Section 4: Initial PMO Goals and Measures
- Section 5: Anticipated Costs and Expected Returns
- Section 6: PMO Start-Up Roadmap
- Section 7: Authorization to Proceed

Each of these sections will now be introduced along with suggestions for how to best format and communicate the details intended for each section. In addition to specific detail for each section, several general guidelines should be considered as the detailed business case is developed.

Remember that a detailed business case is designed to be a management report. The concept of a detailed business case implies some level of detail beyond the base business case, but the detailed business case document itself should not provide so much detail that it becomes cumbersome. For example, if a detailed cost/benefit analysis is conducted to help quantify the value of the PMO to the organization, it would be appropriate to include the general findings from this analysis within the detailed business case document itself, but to include the detailed inputs and analysis in an appendix. Placing detailed inputs and analysis in a separate appendix following the document allows management to review the detailed data if needed while still preserving space within the document itself.

Another consideration is to provide a certain level of customization of the document that addresses the needs of the intended audience. If the intended audience consists primarily of senior members of the project management staff, providing more detail regarding the specific project management challenges facing the organization may be appropriate. However, if the primary audience will be business unit managers or corporate staff members who do not regularly participate in project activities, but who do request that projects be undertaken, focusing on the details of how the PMO can help make the processes of project selection, initiation, and status reporting easier might be more appropriate. Detail regarding the current project management challenges and PMO opportunities would still be included as part of the report to a general management audience, but the scope of coverage and level of detail may vary. The key principle to be followed is to tailor the document to the needs of the audience.

Ensuring that the document represents a fair and honest assessment of the state of the organization, the challenges faced, the opportunities provided by the PMO, the expected costs and benefits, and any relevant assumptions or potential negative aspects of PMO implementation on the organization is critical. There may be a tendency by the authors of the detailed business case (who are often charged with leading the PMO efforts and who genuinely want the PMO effort to succeed) to focus primarily on the positive aspects of implementing the PMO and, to some extent, to minimize the discussion of potential challenges and drawbacks to the PMO. Yet, creating a biased or overly optimistic view in the detailed business case may set up the PMO for failure before the implementation even starts if what is promised in the detailed business case cannot be delivered. Therefore, the PMO concept, intended benefits, potential costs, and potential drawbacks must be represented fairly so that management will have a complete understanding of the required effort and potential costs and savings. Because the detailed business case will provide a plan for implementation, the document must also fairly represent the anticipated cost and time line to complete the PMO implementation effort as per the detailed business case. Because management could choose to adjust the cost, scope, or time line based on organizational priorities and available resources, this situation should be addressed as part of the detailed business case review process.

Preparation of the detailed business case document must also estimate as accurately as possible the resource and cost requirements and provide a viable time line that reflects the work required to implement the PMO and commence operations. The following sections will address in detail each of the major components of a detailed business case.

Section 1: Introduction

Section 1 of the detailed business case provides *an overview* of the document as well as relevant background information that aids a reader, who may not be familiar with past discussions regarding the concept of the PMO and the intended implementation in the organization, to gain an understanding of the base concepts that will be discussed in the document. It is appropriate to include a brief review of the PMO concept, several of the reasons why a PMO is being considered, and a discussion of the content included in the detailed business case. This section may be renamed as an "Executive Summary" if that term is used within the organization. Having a long introductory section within a detailed business case is unnecessary. As long as a reader can gain an understanding of the basic concepts of the PMO and what will be presented in the detailed business case, a compact, precise introduction should be sufficient.

Section 2: Summary of Current Challenges and Opportunities

Section 2 consists of two parts: an *overview* of current management challenges and a *focus* on PMO opportunities.

Project management challenges. The first part should concentrate on an overview of the current project management challenges facing the organization. This data may be drawn from the base business case document or from additional research conducted as part of the process of preparing to develop the detailed business case. Identifying every challenge facing the organization is unnecessary, but identifying challenges that currently have significant visibility to the organization and completely reviewing the challenges that are likely to be addressed by the PMO are critical. Additional impacts, either beyond the scope of the PMO or challenges that can likely only be addressed by the PMO in the long term, may be mentioned as well if doing so will provide a more complete view of the challenges facing the organization. For each challenge presented, include the following key elements:

- An overview of the challenge
- The impact on the organization in terms of rework, lost revenue, wasted time, or other relevant factors
- A known root cause(s)

The overview should briefly summarize each challenge and help a reader understand a specific existing problem. The impact on the organization should focus on specific, quantifiable impacts if possible, but it may also focus on "soft" impacts that are a direct or indirect result of the challenge that the organization is facing. If one or more root causes have been identified, including that detail as well is appropriate to help a reader understand any underlying issues that may exist.

As part of the assessment process, a list of PMO challenges was created and used as an input to the base business case (see Chapter 1). A modification of Table 1.3 that was used to present the challenges and PMO opportunities in the base business case can similarly be used in the detailed business case. Table 3.1 provides an example of a possible format.

Table 3.1 Organizational Project Challenges

Current Challenge	Impact(s)	Root Cause(s)
Lack of consistent methodology for authorizing/chartering projects	• Of projects undertaken annually, 15% are canceled due to lack of management support or a clear business need.	• Business units lack training on project chartering.
Inability for management to have a consolidated view of project statuses across the organization	• Extensive additional effort required to gather data leads to lost productivity. • Lack of clear visibility of project statuses by management often leads to late identification of potential project problems.	• No concise, single report format exists for documenting project status. • Methods of determining cost and schedule variance vary widely within the organization.

If a more-detailed discussion of the current challenges is required, a paragraph format may be more appropriate. Regardless of the format used, it is important to ensure that each challenge is presented with sufficient detail to allow the reader to understand not only the nature of the challenge being faced, but also the impacts on the organization. Providing information on the impacts to the organization is critical. The information provided should fairly represent the true impact in terms of relevant factors such as lost time, wasted money, reduced quality, or some other factor of importance to the organization.

PMO opportunities. The second part focuses on PMO opportunities. This is a critical section of the document that deserves significant attention. The purpose of describing the PMO opportunities is twofold: discussing opportunities early in the document helps provide an understanding of what the PMO can achieve and, perhaps more important, it provides the first opportunity to *sell* the PMO concept. Therefore, focus this section on two key sets of opportunities. The first set is the key opportunities in which the PMO can provide value to the organization in the near term (ideally within the first 90 to 180 days of operation). The second set is the areas in which the PMO will be able to build and sustain value over time. These opportunities can be thought of as "short-term" and "long-term" opportunities. They can be separated within the document.

When presenting the PMO opportunities, several factors must be considered. First, ensure that the PMO opportunities are linked to the organizational challenges which have been presented in the first part of this section. Additional opportunities beyond those that directly address these challenges may also exist. Therefore, it is also appropriate to list these challenges in a separate list of potential focus areas that are beyond the immediate challenges. Yet, it is critical to primarily describe the key opportunities that address challenges that the organization is currently facing. They must be described in sufficient detail to allow management to understand how implementing the PMO will effect positive change in relation to the challenges being faced. Any additional opportunities mentioned should not dilute the focus on how implementation of the PMO will address the current challenges that the organization faces. If a table has been developed as part of the assessment process (see Table 1.3 in Chapter 1), this data may be used as a reference along with the challenges and opportunities presented to management in the base business case review. Additionally, the discussion of current challenges created for the detailed business case document should be referenced to ensure that each of the challenges presented is addressed.

Another factor that must be considered is the information that will be presented for each of the identified opportunities. For each opportunity presented, provide several key elements:

- An overview of the opportunity
- A review of how the opportunity addresses one or more of the current challenges facing the organization
- The expected benefits to be achieved in terms of reduced rework, cost savings, increased customer satisfaction, or some other relevant factor
- An expected time frame in which benefits will be achieved (short term or long term)

The overview of an opportunity should focus on *what* will be done. The overview does not need to be extensive if the essence of what will be delivered is clearly communicated. The second key element focuses on a review of *how* the opportunity addresses one or more of the challenges in the organization. It is important to clearly describe how implementing the opportunity will improve the current situation facing the organization. If the opportunity does not directly align with one of the challenges facing the organization, an overview of the intended additional benefit to the organization provided by the opportunity should be included. The third key area of focus describes *the expected benefits* to be provided to the organization. If specific benefit targets can be forecasted, these benefit targets should be provided as a statement such as "decrease process rework by 30% on average," which is a stronger statement than "decrease process rework." If providing a forecasted benefit is not possible, a detailed description of the specific benefits is sufficient as long as the expected benefits are clear to the reader. The fourth key area of focus is *the expected time frame* in which the benefit will be achieved. A statement containing "short term" or "long term" is acceptable as long as the definitions of "short term" and "long term" are articulated. Ideally, short-term objectives should represent those objectives that can be achieved quickly, ideally within at most 90 days of start-up, but in no case longer than 6 months after start-up. Long-term objectives may represent objectives that will require significantly longer than 90 to 180 days to implement. Distinguishing short-term and long-term benefits is critical so that the reader has an understanding of which benefits will impact the organization soon after the PMO is established.

Another consideration is the format to be used for presentation of the opportunities. Creating a table to identify the opportunities, benefits, and time frames that is similar to the table that was used earlier in this section to describe the PMO challenges may be tempting (see Table 3.1). If only a few opportunities will be presented, using a table might be appropriate, but given the importance of presenting the opportunities and *selling* the opportunities to management, briefly describing each of the opportunities in paragraph format is preferable. The discussion of each opportunity does not need to be excessively verbose, but describing each opportunity in sufficient detail to allow a reader to understand what will be achieved is important. When formatting the opportunities discussion, logically separate the opportunities into short-term opportunities and long-term opportunities to clearly distinguish what is envisioned to be delivered in each time frame. The following example provides a possible format for a potential PMO opportunity:

Develop and implement a standardized project chartering and approval process for the organization. A standardized process for chartering and approving projects will address the issue of project cancellation or delay due to lack of clear management support for a particular project by creating a framework for validating business needs; documenting project goals, benefits, and costs; and providing a mechanism to formally authorize work. A standardized process will ensure accountability for projects by requiring explicit management authorization to undertake project work, creating savings for the organization by ensuring alignment with organizational goals and strategies before projects are undertaken. Furthermore, a standard process used throughout the organization will eliminate several nonuniform management processes in place today and create a uniform basis for the first key step in the project process—reviewing and authorizing projects. The PMO will develop, in consultation with the business units, a standard template for documenting project efforts (the "project charter") as well as a standardized management review and authorization process for use by the business units. The PMO will also obtain data on authorized projects for input into enterprise project status reports (when developed). This process will be implemented as a short-term PMO objective.

Section 3: PMO Roles, Responsibilities, and Organization

Section 3 also has two areas of focus: the *specific roles and responsibilities* that the PMO will undertake within the organization and the *organization of the PMO* itself. *Section 3* will be based on data from the PMO scope statement as well as data from discussions with management and the review of the specific opportunities discussed in *Section 2*.

Roles and responsibilities. The roles and responsibilities presented should represent the specific work that will be undertaken by the PMO. Also included should be statements that define the level of management and control that the PMO will exert in each of the areas presented. It is critical to distinguish between roles and responsibilities that will be vested with the

PMO for direct and exclusive management versus those roles and responsibilities in which the PMO will either share responsibility with another group or serve in a consulting capacity. *Section 3* will define the base set of undertakings that will be the responsibility of the PMO. This base set of undertakings should include those relevant opportunities in which the PMO will have direct responsibility or influence and any additional areas in which the PMO will provide insight or guidance.

Because the role of the PMO will likely expand over time, listing every possible role and responsibility that could be conceived for the PMO is unnecessary. Instead, the focus should be on those areas of responsibility in which the PMO will initially focus as well as additional areas in which the PMO will likely focus within the first 12 to 18 months after start-up. Limiting the time frame will ensure that the list maintains a reasonable length. Additionally, because management will expect to see action in the areas described as the key roles and responsibilities to the PMO, it is important to focus the list on those items that can be reasonably delivered. The following is an example of a sample statement of roles and responsibilities:

GOTPMO CORPORATION—PMO ROLES AND RESPONSIBILITIES

- Development and implementation of a standardized project chartering and approval process
    - Define and maintain a standard project charter template for validating business needs and documenting project goals, benefits, and costs.
    - Define and manage a single, organization-wide process for project review and approval.
    - Monitor and report compliance to ensure uniform use of the developed standards.

- Coordination of project management training and development
    - Define a standard set of project management training opportunities for new project managers.
    - Develop or source training materials and identify qualified instructors.
    - Manage scheduling and continuous improvement processes for provided training opportunities.

- Collaborate with business units to determine advanced project management training needs for existing project managers and facilitate implementation of advanced training opportunities as business needs require.

- Development, implementation, and management of the enterprise-wide project portfolio management process
  - Collaborate with corporate management and business unit heads to identify consolidated project reporting requirements to support management information needs.
  - Develop standard reporting templates and processes to track project progress that facilitates summarizing data at the enterprise level.
  - Deploy the developed templates and processes to the organization and facilitate monthly reporting to management for the complete project portfolio.

This example provides a view of only a few potential roles and responsibilities. It is intended to demonstrate a basic format for presenting the roles and responsibilities within the detailed business case. The structure is designed to allow the reader to understand the core areas of responsibility (first-level bullet points) as well as the areas of focus that the PMO will undertake within each core area of responsibility being discussed (second-level bullet points). In some cases, providing second-level detail within the detailed business case document itself may make the roles and responsibilities section unreasonably long (especially if a number of roles and responsibilities are to be presented). To keep the list presented in the document manageable in these cases, only first-level bullet points should be presented. Complete multilevel definition may be provided as an appendix.

As noted earlier, the roles and responsibilities themselves should be presented in the context of areas that the PMO will *manage directly* and areas that the PMO will *influence*. In the example provided, words such as "define," "develop," and "manage" are used to distinguish items that the PMO will deliver directly. The same goal may be achieved by distinguishing the areas in which the PMO will have *direct responsibility* for communicating standards, processes, templates, or other items to the organization and the areas in which the PMO will have *influence* in managing process compliance by separating the roles and responsibilities list into two sections. The first section will focus on "management activities" and the second section will focus on "consulting activities." The specific terms used may differ, but the intent is simple—to clearly distinguish between the areas in which the PMO has *authority* and the areas in which the PMO has *input*.

Organization. The second area of focus relates to the organization of the PMO. The PMO organization must be considered in two dimensions: the structure of the PMO organization itself in relation to the *specific roles* that will be defined and staffed within the PMO and where the PMO will be *positioned* within the organization's overall organizational structure. In a centralized PMO, the fit will be in relation to a central PMO only. In a decentralized PMO, the structure of each business unit or divisional PMO and the relation of these groups to a centralized, enterprise PMO must be considered as well.

From a structural standpoint, the PMO will, at minimum, require a PMO manager to lead the PMO efforts. This individual may already be identified. If so, the PMO manager is likely already part of the PMO planning efforts. If the PMO manager has not been identified, the process for selecting a PMO manager will be included as part of the PMO start-up activities. For the purposes of a detailed business case, specific names are not required, but a general design for how the PMO will be structured is needed. Beyond the PMO manager, additional roles supporting the operation of the PMO may be defined based on the intended scope of PMO operations. These resources may include PMO project managers to manage central projects, PMO support personnel to manage administrative functions, and other relevant roles. A number of these positions may be full-time positions within the PMO; however, based on available resources, it may be necessary to staff some positions using resources who additionally serve as project resources within the broader organization. Some PMO roles may also be facilitated through use of committees of part-time resources that meet periodically to address specific areas of interest to the organization from a project standpoint.

As a general guideline, it is practical to present the PMO organizational structure in terms of the intended structure at start-up. If complete staffing of the PMO is not to be completed as part of the initial start-up efforts, note that

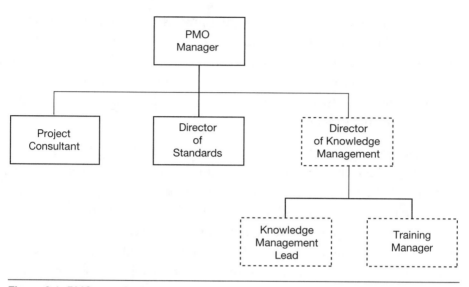

Figure 3.1 PMO organizational structure.

additional roles may be added over time as the PMO rollout continues and as additional areas of responsibility are undertaken. Figure 3.1 shows one possible representation of this structure.

In Figure 3.1, roles that will be staffed as part of start-up activities are indicated with solid-lined boxes, and roles to be added to the PMO as the PMO evolves are noted with dashed lines. The fact that a particular role will not be staffed as part of the start-up effort does not imply that the work that would normally be associated with that role will not be undertaken at start-up. Rather, the available resources at start-up may initiate work in these areas and manage the efforts themselves until such time as the PMO grows to the point that a dedicated resource is required. For example, as part of the PMO start-up effort, it may be envisioned that the PMO will develop a training and development curriculum for project resources, with implementation of the curriculum to occur at some point after the plan is developed, reviewed, and agreed to by management. The initial development of this plan may be undertaken by a committee of resources from different areas of the organization. Alternatively, the initial plan may be drafted by a member of the PMO staff as a part of his or her general PMO responsibilities, with no need for a dedicated resource to focus exclusively on developing the curriculum. Because deployment and management of the curriculum would likely occur at some point in the future, a full-time training manager may be required. Therefore, this future role should be represented on the proposed PMO organizational structure, but with the understanding that the role does not need to be filled in order for the PMO to begin operations.

Defining the structure of the PMO is a critical exercise that must be thoughtfully considered. The level of required staffing will be a key input to the determination of start-up and ongoing PMO costs. It will also assist in providing management with an understanding of the impact of the PMO on utilization of current resources as well as where new resources may potentially need to be recruited and hired. In addition to the structure of the PMO itself, the structural placement of the PMO within the organization must be considered. For some organizations, an appropriate fit may place the PMO within the part of the organization that most closely aligns with the area in which the majority of the projects that the PMO will influence are undertaken. For example, if the PMO is scoped to influence all of the information technology projects in the organization, the PMO may be most logically placed within the information technology division, with the PMO manager reporting to a high-level manager within the information technology organization or perhaps to the chief information officer or chief technology officer.

In a decentralized PMO structure, a governing enterprise PMO would most logically reside within some central area of the organization. The decentralized divisional or regional PMOs would then be placed within the divisions or regions that they serve, with the manager of each divisional or regional PMO reporting to the manager of the enterprise PMO and potentially additionally to a member of the management team for the division or region served by the PMO. Although dual-reporting relationships are often not preferable and may not be appropriate for every organization, maintaining a link to the enterprise PMO is essential to ensure some level of control over the operations of a decentralized PMO (e.g., to ensure compliance with standards, consistent operation, etc.). Also essential is that the management of a division or region that is served by the PMO has a direct relationship with the enterprise PMO and the local PMO leadership, either formally or via local

PMO leadership that serves in a liaison capacity to ensure that the needs of local management are met.

Another essential consideration is determining an appropriate "fit" for the PMO within the organization. The PMO must be placed within the broad structure of the organization at a level that ensures that the mission of the PMO and its roles and responsibilities can be carried out efficiently. Additionally, an appropriate level of management support must be directly available to address issues that affect the ability of the PMO to deliver its intended benefits. Placing the PMO at a conspicuous place in the organization's hierarchy demonstrates management's commitment to the PMO. This structure also ensures that the PMO has a voice in broad organizational decisions that affect the project management function and key projects that are undertaken by the organization.

Section 4: Initial PMO Goals and Measures

Section 4 extends the general discussion of roles and responsibilities in *Section 3* to concretely define a *specific set of initial goals* for the PMO as well as the *measures* that will be used to determine performance versus these goals. The purpose of *Section 4* is to define the specific efforts that will be undertaken early in the life of the PMO and to specifically define how success relative to these efforts will be measured. Defining the initial goals and measures as part of the detailed business case helps to demonstrate that a firm set of goals is in place for the early life of the PMO and that a means of determining and reporting progress and accountability for delivering these goals has been defined. When the PMO implementation activities are complete, the PMO will begin to work to deliver these goals. Management will be kept apprised of progress by the PMO manager. Agreeing to the goals and measures well in advance helps to ensure management alignment with the plans and also provides clear guidance for the PMO team regarding the areas of focus for the initial few months of PMO operation.

Initial goals. The goals that are presented in *Section 4* should be aligned with the general roles and responsibilities that have been discussed in *Section 3*. They should focus on the subset of the overall PMO roles and responsibilities that will be implemented within the first few months of PMO operation.

Constraining the time frame to the first 90 days following implementation is ideal, but if necessary the goals and measures may be extended to focus on items to be completed within the first 6 months of operation. Having a time frame beyond 6 months is problematic because one of the general ideas underlying the process of setting short-term goals is to demonstrate that the PMO is providing value early in its life.

As a starting point for developing *Section 4*, review the complete list of roles and responsibilities presented in *Section 3*. Identify the specific areas of responsibility that the PMO will undertake and implement within, ideally, the first 3 months of operation. If some other time frame will be used, validate the specific time frame before continuing. Identifying the specific areas of focus and initial goals for the PMO first and then attempting to fit those goals into a specific time frame is not a recommended practice. Instead, an initial or a "phase one" time frame for PMO operations should be set, and a reasonable set of attainable goals should be agreed upon that represent a challenge to achieve, but a challenge that is attainable. The desire to make an immediate impact in a number of areas from the start may sound tempting, but diluting effort over too many areas of focus or attempting to solve too many problems at the onset of operations can lead to a situation in which many things get done, but only in a marginal way. It is much better to focus on a few key areas and achieve quality results than to focus on many areas and achieve quality results in some areas and marginal results in others.

For the purposes of this section, the activities associated with PMO start-up (e.g., identifying a PMO manager, obtaining office space, etc.) should not be included. These activities will become part of the start-up roadmap and will be measured as part of the implementation of the PMO. If a bulleted-list approach for documenting the roles and responsibilities is used (such as the method proposed in *Section 3*), the top level of bullet points will likely contain the major roles and responsibilities for the PMO, and the next level of bullet points under each of these roles and responsibilities will define the specific goals or deliverables for each role or responsibility. If a paragraph format or some other type of format for presenting the roles and responsibilities is used, it will be necessary to identify the key deliverables or goals for each area discussed. Regardless of the method used to describe the roles and responsibilities, the goal for this section will be the same—to identify the specific goals that are targeted to be achieved within the first months of operation.

The initial goals list will likely be fairly short if the proposed time frame is 6 months or less. An extensive list of goals to be attained early in the life of the PMO may indicate a plan that is too aggressive to be attainable in a quality way. Ideally, at most, five to seven discreet goals spanning at most two or three general areas of responsibility should be considered. Having fewer than five to seven goals identified is acceptable if the goals identified represent fairly large areas of scope. Each of the initial goals should be documented in terms of what will be achieved. Documenting how each goal will be achieved at this stage is unnecessary because the PMO implementation planning process will include determining how each goal will be addressed.

Validation. With an initial list of goals in hand, the next step is to validate the goals in terms of several key characteristics. For each goal identified, the following factors should be considered:

- Specificity
- Measurability
- Attainability

The first and most critical factor is *specificity*. Identified goals must document specific, discrete areas of undertaking and provide enough detail to allow the reader to understand what will be delivered. For example, making an early PMO goal to "develop and deliver project management training" is too broad to allow the reader to understand what specific outcome will be achieved. A better goal might be to "develop an introductory 2-day project management training course and conduct a pilot course offering." The revised goal clearly articulates the type of training to be developed (an introductory 2-day course) as well as a specific delivery (one pilot course).

Measurability refers to the ability to provide specific measures that will determine whether or not a specified goal was achieved. If a particular goal cannot have any specific measures defined for it, the goal is likely too general. Defining specific measures will be discussed later in this section.

Table 3.2 Initial PMO Goals Matrix

PMO Initial Goals and Measures Ninety-Day Plan	
Goal	**Measure(s)**
Create and align with business units a standard template for reviewing project proposals and chartering projects.	
Define a standard project training roadmap for training and developing new project managers during their first 12 months in a project management role.	

Attainability refers to validating whether or not the specific goal can be reasonably attained within the time period allotted for achievement of the initial PMO goals. Goals that are too broad or far reaching will likely fail the test of attainability and should be scaled to a level that provides a reasonable probability of success within the allotted timeframe. Attainability must be considered both at the individual goal level and in sum. Once each individual goal has been validated as being attainable within the initial start-up time frame, the entire set of goals should be evaluated against the previously discussed criteria of ensuring that a set of initial goals that represents a reasonable challenge and reasonable probability of success is developed.

Documentation. Once the set of goals has been established and validated, the goals should be formally documented. A simple table format may be used to document the initial PMO goals and measures. An example format is provided in Table 3.2.

A table format such as Table 3.2 is not the only possible format, but it does provide the three critical elements that must be included in the goals and measures documentation—the specific goals, the time frame in which the goals are envisioned to be achieved, and the specific measures that will be used to determine whether or not each goal has been achieved.

Measurement. Once each of the initial goals is identified and documented, the next area of focus is the measures that will determine whether or not a goal has been achieved. The measures will be used to gauge progress versus the goals and provide management with a view of progress. For each goal presented, one or more measures should be defined. These measures may be in terms of specific deliverables, quantifiable data, or some other factor that can be reliably captured and presented to show progress versus each specific goal. General measures such as, "increased employee satisfaction" or "improved project delivery" should be avoided because these statements are too broad to provide any meaningful information for management. A better set of measures might include such measures as "customer satisfaction increased by 10% as defined by corporate customer satisfaction survey" or "project estimating accuracy increased by 20% for pilot projects using revised project estimating practices." These examples provide concrete targets (10% increase in customer satisfaction and 20% increase in project estimating accuracy) and also provide a basis (customer satisfaction survey) or scope of measurement (only pilot projects using revised project estimating practices) to clearly articulate the population of measurement or specific tool or gauge that will provide the basis for validating the measure. Not all measures need specific quantifiable targets. For a goal of "creating and aligning a standard template for project chartering" that was proposed as one of the goals in Table 3.2, a reasonable set of measures might simply include validating that a final document format was produced and that the affected divisions within the organization that will use the chartering document have agreed to its format (or "signed-off" on the document itself). Table 3.3 is an extension of Table 3.2 and includes some possible measures for the initial goals defined.

The measures listed in Table 3.3 represent concrete deliverables that can be validated to determine if the components required to meet the listed goal have been achieved, but these measures do not include a time line for delivery of each goal at this stage. An appropriate time line will be developed later.

Section 5: Anticipated Costs and Expected Returns

Section 5 addresses the cost and benefit aspects of implementing the PMO. The first element of the cost section will define the *start-up* costs required to implement and start-up the PMO. The second element of the section will address the *ongoing* costs associated with PMO operations.

Numerous potential start-up and maintenance cost categories may be relevant. These costs depend on the specific scope of responsibilities that the

Table 3.3 Initial PMO Goals Matrix with Measures

PMO Initial Goals and Measures Ninety-Day Plan	
Goal	**Measure(s)**
Create and align with business units a standard template for reviewing project proposals and chartering projects.	• Standard project charter template created • Alignment and sign-off from Information Technology, Sales, and Business Development units obtained
Define a standard project training roadmap for training and developing new project managers during their first 12 months in a project management role.	• Project management training roadmap developed and delivered to Corporate Training division

PMO will undertake. General cost categories applicable to most PMOs and thus applicable to most PMO cost discussions include:

- Personnel
- Office space (including office furniture, phone, computer networking, etc.)
- Equipment (computers, copiers, software, etc.)
- Office supplies (including base supplies, mailing costs, etc.)
- Training and development (for PMO staff)
- Marketing (to the organization)
- Travel and expense
- Reward and recognition

Minimally, a cost analysis should be segmented into a section for specific start-up costs required to facilitate PMO implementation and a section outlining ongoing costs to facilitate operations and grow the PMO over time. The start-up costs will include fixed costs such as procuring equipment and variable costs such as personnel salary costs which will change depending on the length of time required to complete the start-up activities. (*Note:* Other relevant costs may require inclusion or following standard corporate accounting policies may be mandated as part of the process of developing a cost analysis for the PMO.)

Because the development of the specific start-up time line is discussed later as part of the start-up roadmap and because time lines may need to be adjusted later based on management requirements or other factors, merely expressing variable costs such as salaries in terms of cost per some reasonable unit of time (e.g., per month) and making a best guess as to the duration required to start-up the PMO based on the roles, responsibilities, and initial goals for the PMO is appropriate at this stage of development. A specific duration can later be used to adjust the estimates. Alternatively, this section may be temporarily skipped and returned to after the completion of the start-up roadmap.

Personnel. From a personnel standpoint, costs to recruit, interview, and hire new personnel should be included if an external search will be required to fill one or more of the initial PMO roles has been defined in *Section 3.* If internal candidates are already identified or if an internal search for initial staffing of the PMO is envisioned, the costs associated with replacing individuals moved into PMO roles or reassigning their responsibilities to other members of the organization should be considered. Additionally, once the staff is identified and in place, the cost of the staff (including salary and benefits) should be included in the start-up budget for the period of time required to implement the PMO. Ongoing, the cost of the PMO staff will be included in the operations budget for the PMO and will likely be budgeted as part of the organization's ongoing budget processes. Because start-up activities are a one-time occurrence, budgeting staff costs for this duration as a separate cost within the start-up budget is appropriate.

Facilities and equipment. In addition to staffing and training costs, the start-up costs associated with the physical facilities and equipment required to support the PMO must be included. If the PMO will rely on existing office space, the likely office location for the PMO staff should be identified and the existing reusable equipment should be inventoried. The start-up budget should include the costs to convert the existing office space for PMO use, to purchase or reconfigure furniture, to activate phone and network connections, etc. Additionally, funding for office supplies, computers, printers, and other necessary office automation equipment should be considered, especially if external staff that does not already have computer equipment, phone numbers, etc. assigned to them will be hired. The PMO should be a self-sufficient, autonomous unit to the greatest extent possible. As such, the core PMO staff should be situated in the same general office area if all members are local to a particular office location, should have access to meeting space and other similar facilities, and should have access to standard office equipment such as copiers and printers in addition to core office supplies. If members of the PMO are widely dispersed across several buildings or in multiple office locations in different cities or countries, costs for establishing audio conferencing and/or video conferencing capabilities for PMO members, communication and collaboration software, and other similar equipment should be included in the start-up costs.

Initial staff training. An additional and often overlooked personnel cost associated with start-up of a PMO is the cost of training for the PMO staff. As part of the PMO start-up, providing the PMO staff with internal training or potentially using externally provided training on PMO operations, advanced project management techniques, software, or other business-relevant areas will likely be necessary. Even if internally provided training is primarily envisioned, the cost of meeting space, refreshments, training materials, and other associated items must be included as part of the start-up budget. Additionally, costs for purchasing PMO and project management-related books, magazine subscriptions, and memberships in professional associations should be considered.

Marketing materials. Marketing expense represents the cost of developing educational materials, presentations, or other communications to help educate the organization on the goals of the PMO and the expected role of the PMO within the organization. For a PMO that operates on a smaller scale such as a single group or division within the organization, marketing may only entail a single presentation to the members of the affected group on the PMO concept and implementation plans. For a PMO with a larger scope, a number of presentations may be necessary. More formal communications may be required for the PMO implementation plans. If the PMO is expected to interact with external customers or serve in a customer relationship role, additional communication to these external customers may be necessary. This communication could include on-site visits to customer sites to explain how the PMO will affect the interaction between the customer and the organization. Other types of communication to assure customers that the PMO will provide an enhanced customer relationship rather than an additional layer of complexity in the interactions between the customer and the organization may be required. Marketing the PMO to the organization and its customers (if appropriate) is critical for a successful start-up. Sufficient resources should be available to support a reasonable marketing effort that educates and informs PMO stakeholders.

Travel and incidentals. A separate and important component of the PMO start-up budget should include travel and miscellaneous expense allocations for PMO start-up activities. Travel costs may include costs to attend industry conferences, to participate in training activities, or to meet with key business stakeholders who will be affected by PMO activities. If members of the PMO are widely dispersed, travel costs should be included to facilitate bringing all PMO members and key stakeholders together for a PMO kick-off and one or more in-person working sessions during the implementation of the PMO. Also include an additional start-up budget for expense items that are not covered in other budget categories and incidental expenses such as catering occasional working lunches, purchasing small ancillary office equipment, and so forth.

Team recognition. The final component of the PMO start-up budget should include funds to support recognizing the PMO implementation team at the completion of the implementation effort. Chapter 4 will address this category in more detail, but from a budget planning standpoint, reserving funds to provide some form of recognition of the team that will make the PMO a reality in the organization is important. This recognition could be monetary recognition in terms of a bonus or perhaps a lunch or dinner to celebrate a successful implementation. Plaques or other similar forms of tangible recognition may also be considered. Ensure that some form of recognition is planned for and built into the budget and that the level of recognition is commensurate with the level of effort required to perform the PMO implementation activities.

Cost estimate. The start-up costs should represent a "best estimate" for the cost of implementing the PMO in the organization and should provide management with an understanding of the level of financial commitment associated with PMO start-up. This should not be a rough order of magnitude estimate, but rather a reasonably definitive cost estimate. Sufficient funds should be included to cover the full cost of PMO implementation. Assuming authorization to proceed with PMO implementation is obtained, the PMO should be able to be established with the funding requirements described in this section. Establishing base budget numbers for implementation plus an appropriate reserve to cover unknowns or assumptions used in establishing the start-up budget is appropriate and should be disclosed along with any budget figures presented in this section. The start-up activities related to the PMO are essentially project activities—one-time undertakings that meet a business objective. As such, standard budgeting techniques such as reserve analysis are appropriate when developing the start-up budget.

If the organization has a standard budget template that is used for projects, using this template in the detailed business case is appropriate. If no standard exists, a simple list of the major cost categories, associated cost items, and budget amounts may be used. If the budget requires many detailed line items in order to comply with organizational budget policies or if a number of expense categories have been defined, a budget summary may be included in the detailed business case. Supporting detail such as the complete budget with all line items may be included as an appendix. The start-up budget should clearly show the total required funding commitment that will be needed to ensure a successful start-up of the PMO as well as any assumptions or other relevant factors that have been considered as part of establishing the budget.

Operational expense. The second element of the PMO cost section is ongoing costs associated with PMO operations. This cost category represents the "day-to-day" costs of operations and the associated budget to facilitate managing and growing the PMO. As appropriate, these costs should include the following general cost categories:

- Ongoing personnel expense (salary, benefits, bonuses, etc.)
- Ongoing facilities expense

- Recurring utility expense (phone service, teleconferencing services, network access services, etc.)
- General and administrative expenses (including office supplies, etc.)
- Travel and entertainment expenses

These and other relevant ongoing costs will create the PMO operating budget, which likely will be included as part of the organization's budget planning process and updated annually as part of annual budget planning processes. Accordingly, an extensive discussion of annual budget planning processes will not be included because it is important to consult standard organizational budget planning documentation or the organization's finance or accounting department to determine the appropriate structure for presenting an annual operating budget.

Because the scope of the PMO will likely expand as it takes on more responsibility, the budgetary requirements to support the PMO will likely grow over time. It is important to consider the scope of the operating budget that is presented. Two basic approaches may be used:

- Consider the operating expenses required to support the start-up scope and any anticipated additional responsibilities that will be added during the first operational year (or until the next budget-planning cycle).
- Determine the required operational costs for the first year (or until the next budget-planning cycle) and forecast expenditures in subsequent years based on an analysis of required implementation resources for areas of PMO responsibility that are envisioned to be implemented beyond the first year.

The first approach considers the operating expenses required to support the PMO within its start-up scope and any anticipated additional areas of responsibility that will be added within the first year of operations (or, if appropriate, until the organization's next regular budget planning cycle). Adding these operating expenses to the required start-up budget would yield the complete expenditure for start-up and 1 year of operations (or start-up until the next budget planning cycle) and would provide management with a complete picture of the monetary commitment required to fully deliver the initial goals established for the PMO.

The second approach is an alternate method that determines the costs required to operate the PMO in its first year of operation (or until the next regular budget planning cycle) and then forecasts expenditures in the subsequent years based on an analysis of the resources required to implement the additional areas of PMO responsibility that are envisioned to be implemented beyond the first year. This method provides management with a more complete view of potential ongoing costs, but requires considerable additional analysis because a time frame for implementing the complete set of PMO objectives must be developed and required resource commitments must be forecasted. If this method is chosen, the applicable assumptions used in deriving the forecast for subsequent years should be included as part of the analysis. At this stage, avoid trying to completely map the potential areas of focus for the PMO in the long-term. Considering long-term plans is a significant exercise in its own right and is best achieved as part of a long-term PMO planning process rather than a PMO budgeting process. (The process for developing a long-term PMO roadmap will be discussed in Chapter 5.)

Assumptions. The concluding section of a cost analysis should include a statement of any major assumptions that were used in developing the cost model that is presented. This statement could include assumed resource rates, assumptions relative to the availability of resources within the organization that limit the need to expend funds in certain areas, or other relevant items that either contribute to the costs presented or represent items that are not included as cost line items because some other form of sourcing makes these items available for use by the PMO without cost. The assumptions should be discussed and, ideally, validated prior to or as part of the review of the cost portion of the detailed business case with management.

Return on investment. Once the costs for PMO start-up and ongoing operation have been established and documented, a set of anticipated returns must be developed. The purpose of identifying the key returns (or benefits) is to provide management with a basis for determining if the value to be provided by the PMO justifies the anticipated expenses required to implement and sustain the operation of the PMO. This discussion extends the discussions of PMO opportunities (*Section 2*) and the initial PMO goals (*Section 4*) by bringing together the short-term goals (*Section 4*) and a complete view of opportunities that may be provided by the PMO (*Section 2*). However, in this section, the difference will be that justification primarily focuses on a financial benefit basis rather than an organizational benefit basis as described in the previous sections. When possible, the returns discussed here should include analysis of the potential savings in terms of funds expended, reduced resource requirements in other areas of the organization, or some other factor (or factors) that allows management to see that the investment in the PMO will pay back benefits to the organization over time. Essentially, this section focuses on a return on investment discussion.

If this section cannot show that the PMO will provide the organization with a return on the investment required to implement the PMO and maintain operations over time, the likelihood of approval of the PMO by management is small. Therefore, undertaking a thoughtful and detailed analysis of potential returns and documenting these returns with associated data, hard savings calculations, or other measures when applicable is important.

The first step in the process is to document expected returns based on the initial PMO goals and long-term PMO opportunity areas, roles, and responsibilities. Each of the initial PMO goals should be included, as well as additional areas beyond the initial goals in which the PMO will have responsibility. Because not all of the expected returns will be achieved immediately, the items identified in this section should be segmented into categories representing a time frame for achieving the expected return. Often identifying expected returns in terms of the expected return in the fist year of operation, second year of operation, and so forth is preferable. Thus, the return on investment can be considered in similar terms to the expected costs identified previously. For each of the goals identified, consider the following:

- Is there an opportunity to reduce duplicate work and free resources to perform other activities?
- Is there an opportunity to realize economies of scale and thus reduce costs to the organization?

- Is there an opportunity to reduce errors or increase control, thus reducing cost overruns, excess expense, or wasted organizational resources?
- Are there other real savings that can be quantified by undertaking the activity?
- What are the "soft" benefits which, although not quantifiable, provide a benefit to the organization?

The purpose of this exercise is to review the list of goals and opportunities and begin to identify how realization of each goal or opportunity provides benefit to the organization and, additionally, to attempt to accurately quantify that benefit. If the goals and opportunities are documented in sufficient detail, framing the potential areas of return fairly easily should be possible. The difficulty often comes in determining an accurate quantifiable value for the return. Ideally each item identified would be quantified in terms of hard monetary savings and thus the return on investment for the PMO would be easily determined by summing the total required investments over time and comparing those investments to the total expected returns over time, similar to how return on investment is calculated in pure financial terms. Unfortunately, a number of the benefits that are identified as part of this exercise may be difficult to quantify. For example, the cost of reduced work effort due to implementing a standardized project chartering process and the potential for increased project success due to uniform review of project benefits and costs prior to chartering certainly contribute benefit to the organization. However, it is difficult to quantify the number of potentially unsuitable projects that might be avoided due to a standardized review process unless historical data exists or can be obtained to identify past projects that were undertaken that should have been avoided but were not due to lack of consistent review and chartering processes. If no such data exists, the best alternative is either to approximate the likely benefit and document the associated assumptions used in approximating the benefits or to provide a list of returns in "soft" terms, such as "improved reliability in the project approval and chartering process," rather than in terms of actual projected monetary savings.

Documenting the anticipated returns is most easily accomplished in a table that lists the opportunities, time frame for implementing each, and the expected return(s) that will be achieved once the opportunity is implemented. Table 3.4 provides an example of this structure.

The objectives in Table 3.4 align to either the initial PMO goals or one of the long-term PMO opportunities identified. Time frames are indicated in terms of elapsed time after implementation of the PMO so that a clear understanding of when the objective will start to provide returns is available to management. The expected returns are indicated in terms of true cost or productivity savings when possible and in terms of "soft" benefits in cases when actual forecasted cost savings cannot be easily produced or when an understanding of the additional savings beyond quantifiable amounts provides additional perspective that may be of interest to management. By looking at the table in total, management should be able to understand how achievement of the intended PMO goals will result in benefits to the organization. The complete list should be validated to ensure that the returns listed are accurately captured and that any estimates are realistic. For this process, guidance from the organization's accounting or finance department may be advisable because these functional experts may have organizational standards or best practices already in use that can be leveraged to ensure that the final data presented to management is realistic.

This exercise also serves as a good internal check to validate the expected returns before presenting the detailed business case to management. Documenting the expected returns as part of developing this section may clearly show that the value provided by the PMO exceeds the expected investment. Alternatively, the analysis may show that in the near term the expected investment will not be offset by the expected returns, but that in the long-run the expected benefits will outpace the ongoing costs and eventually will also recover the initial investment in one-time PMO implementation activities. If, however, the analysis shows that the expected returns will not exceed the expected costs over time, then additional analysis of the business case will likely be required before making a detailed presentation to management. Restating the potential returns alone to make the business case look more appealing to management is not advisable—if the data suggests that the benefits realized will not exceed the costs to implement and maintain the PMO, adjusting the PMO scope to focus only on areas of higher likely return or to

Table 3.4 Anticipated PMO Returns

Implementation Opportunity	Expected Time Frame	Benefits/Returns
Create and align with business units a standard template for reviewing project proposals and chartering projects.	90 days after PMO implementation	• Increased scrutiny of potential projects reduces risk of undertaking projects with low return potential. • Analysis suggests 60% of projects canceled in the organization are canceled due to lack of identification of clear business benefit at project onset (at a cost of 230,000 USD to the organization in 2005).
Define a standard project training roadmap for training and developing new project managers during their first 12 months in a project management role.	90 days after PMO implementation	• Standardized curriculum reduces division-specific training formats and facilitates implementing standardized project methodologies, decreasing rework and facilitating standardized management reporting. • Knowledgeable project management staff increases likelihood of project success.
Implement enterprise project management software for tracking resource utilization.	Within 2 years after PMO implementation	• Eliminate one project scheduler position (60,000 USD savings per year).

reduce the funding requirements to bring the cost to benefit ratio into line may be necessary. If this is required, additional discussions with management may be necessary prior to the presentation of the detailed business case so that management input and alignment to the revised plans is obtained in advance of finalizing the business case and PMO implementation plans.

Section 6: PMO Start-Up Roadmap

Section 6 will focus on the PMO start-up roadmap, which defines the major required activities and time line for the implementation of the PMO. The definition of start-up may vary depending on the intent of PMO implementation. For some organizations, start-up will represent the first day that the PMO is staffed, functionally situated within the organization, and ready to begin work. For other organizations, start-up may include having some base deliverables already in place that the PMO will begin to implement in the organization when operations commence. If the intent of PMO implementation is to develop a first set of processes, procedures, or other deliverables and to deploy these to the organization immediately, the start-up time line will likely be longer than if the intent is to get the base PMO structure in place and create a plan for how the PMO will deliver its initial plans within the first few months of operation. If possible, start-up should be viewed from the latter perspective.

Time frame. The initial PMO goals and time frames were presented in the first part of *Section 4*. These goals and time frames were based on an intended implementation time frame that began on the date when the PMO implementation activities were complete. From this viewpoint, adequate *planning* should be part of the PMO start-up roadmap, but *execution* of the activities required to achieve the intended goals should not commence until after the PMO officially begins operations. This viewpoint is preferable not only because it shortens the required start-up time frame, but also because it facilitates focusing implementation activities on building a solid foundation from the perspective of the base items needed to establish a functional PMO rather than focusing on beginning to create detailed processes and deliverables to deploy to the organization (rightfully be the job of a functioning PMO). This approach also creates a clear delineation between the implementation of the PMO (the project aspect) and the activities of the PMO (the operations aspect).

Required detail. The start-up roadmap is similar to a project plan in many ways. It will identify the major activities that are required in order to implement the PMO and will specify a reasonable time line for completing these activities. For the purposes of the detailed business case, a project plan is best presented at a high level rather than at a detailed task level. A detailed project plan may be prepared and used as a project management tool to guide the PMO implementation team in implementing the PMO, but this level of detail is not necessary for a management report. Thus, the start-up roadmap may either be prepared as a high-level plan for the purposes of the detailed business case and expanded to the task level later in order to facilitate detailed management of the implementation effort or, preferably it may be prepared as a detailed implementation plan initially with a summarized rollup of major phases or deliverables within the plan presented in the detailed business case. The method chosen may differ among individuals based on their preferences, but the start and end points will remain the same. Approval of the detailed business case and receiving authorization to proceed with implementation should be prerequisites for executing the work associated with a start-up roadmap. The roadmap should conclude with commencing operation of the PMO.

Considerations. Numerous factors will affect the structure of a start-up roadmap and the time required to implement the PMO. The intended initial scope of the PMO, required time to recruit PMO staff, availability of office space, and reliance on internal resources that have primary commitments to other projects are just a few of the potential factors that must be considered when developing a start-up roadmap. From a management perspective, implementing the PMO in a timely fashion is likely a priority. Yet from a PMO perspective, implementing with quality should be the primary objective. Finding the balance between these two objectives is critical to ensuring the early success of the PMO. If implementation is rushed, the likelihood of a substandard implementation increases. If implementation is expected to take a significant amount of time, management may prefer to implement stopgap measures for the most significant issues facing the organization, which will later have to be retooled or removed and new processes implemented to align with the long-term project management vision that the PMO will create and implement. Although all PMO implementations differ, a general guideline that may be useful is to plan the scope and timing for implementation to be no longer than the suggested time frame for implementing the first few key PMO goals—ideally within 90 days of approval of the implementation plan.

Activities such as external staff recruiting and hiring, locating available office space for the PMO, or other long-lead-time activities can significantly affect this general guideline and should be considered if applicable. If no long-lead-time activities are expected, setting an initial goal of implementation within 90 days is reasonable in most cases.

Implementation activities. Because the variety of activities that will be included in any particular start-up roadmap may be significantly different depending on the nature, structure, and goals of each PMO, creating a single, uniform roadmap that will be widely applicable is not possible. Each PMO implementation will rely on the expert judgment of the PMO staff members (who ideally are experienced project managers) to define the appropriate tasks required for implementation. However, a brief discussion of the major categories of activities that should be considered as part of developing the start-up roadmap as well as some general guidance on structuring the start-up roadmap is appropriate. The major categories of activities that are relevant for a start-up roadmap include:

- Personnel
  - Identifying resource needs
  - Recruiting PMO personnel
  - Hiring personnel
  - Initial training and development for the PMO staff

- Facilities
  - Identifying appropriate facilities including office and conference space as needed
  - Preparing or renovating facilities to meet the needs of the PMO
  - Securing services such as phone connections, network access, etc.
  - Moving and unpacking

- Equipment
  - Securing access to printers, FAX, and related technology

- Marketing and communication
  - Developing a PMO marketing and communication plan

- Executing the plan to inform stakeholders of PMO goals and activities
- Processes
  - Identifying initial areas of focus
  - Detailed planning to support achieving initial PMO goals

Specific details for each of these areas will be provided in Chapter 4, which focuses on PMO implementation. For the purposes of the detailed business case, an overview of each of these areas is provided here so that the type of work to be undertaken can be considered as part of the process of developing the start-up roadmap.

Personnel requirements. Personnel requirements for the PMO will likely be the first critical area of focus in implementation planning. With the initial goals and broader roles and responsibilities for the PMO already established as part of the detailed business case development process, required resources to facilitate implementation of the PMO and initial operations can easily be identified. The required time to facilitate recruiting and hiring resources, if applicable, may vary considerably depending on the need for an external search, the availability of internal resources to join the PMO team, existing corporate human resources policies and procedures, and many other factors. Completion of the initial staffing activities will be a predecessor to many of the tasks in the start-up roadmap—staffing activities should not be rushed. If resources are not already identified, sufficient time should be allocated for identifying qualified resources and conducting a comprehensive interview process. If an external search is required, the process could take several months. For an internal search, the length of time required may be less, but it will likely span at least several weeks.

Staff training. Ensure that time is included in the plan for initial training and development activities for PMO staff members. At the conclusion of implementation activities, the PMO staff should be in a position to commence operations and begin working toward achievement of the initial goals established for the PMO. In order to ensure that the staff resources have the skills and knowledge needed to be effective, some level of training and development will be required. This may include training in areas such as PMO objectives, corporate policies, advanced project and program management skills, consulting skills, or other important areas as determined by the intended scope of PMO activities. Factoring training time into the implementation plan will ensure that time is set aside for these activities. Often scheduling training on a best-effort basis results in training being set aside in favor of "getting the work done," thus robbing staff resources of the opportunity to build their skills and become more effective contributors to PMO efforts.

Office space. From a facilities perspective, it is important to ensure that the PMO has a defined physical "home" within the organization. This includes ensuring that all full-time PMO resources are located together in the same general office area (assuming all resources are local to one particular office location) and that adequate space is provided for team meetings and meetings with management and customers. If office space is readily available, the task of identifying available facilities may be completed fairly quickly. If office space must be located or reconfigured to accommodate the PMO, the time required to locate the space, plan for its use, and make any necessary adjustments to the space configuration should be included in the implementation plans. On a temporary basis, the implementation plan may be executed without permanent physical office space for the PMO staff, but locating the PMO resources together should be a priority for completion prior to start-up of the PMO.

Office equipment. The time required for securing the resources required for the facilities, such as phone service, access to corporate networks, and other related activities, should be considered and included as part of facilities planning. These activities will likely be closely aligned with identifying and procuring the necessary office equipment to ensure that the PMO has the resources needed for day-to-day operations. Include procurement of items such as phones, FAX machines, office supplies, and other related resources as part of the planning activities. If the organization has a central purchasing organization, this organization should be consulted to identify appropriate suppliers and to determine required lead times for ordering items that are not readily available within the organization. Implementation of the PMO can certainly progress without some of these items in place, but it is important that planning for them occur and that the majority of technology and equipment requirements are solidified as part of the implementation planning process and that plans are in place to ensure that required items are available prior to start-up.

Marketing. The marketing and communication component addresses the tasks required to inform the organization and its customers (for an externally facing PMO) of the PMO's goals, plans, and roles and responsibilities. Sufficient time should be allocated in the schedule to facilitate development of the marketing and communication plan as well as execution of the plan. Although detailed marketing literature and related collateral materials may not be necessary, some base level of marketing materials that explains the PMO's goals and plans will likely be required. Additionally, formal presentations to the organization and/or its customers may be helpful for defining the role of the PMO within the affected groups and for addressing questions or concerns and gathering feedback.

Functional readiness. A last, but not least, area of focus to consider in a start-up roadmap will be the planning required to ensure that on the start-up date the PMO is prepared to begin developing and implementing the items identified as initial PMO goals. Having each of these initial goals fully developed and ready to implement when the PMO commences operations is not necessary, but ensure that all required preplanning is complete and that a plan exists to define how the PMO will achieve its initial goals within the time frame specified in *Section 4*. This area of preplanning may include tasks such as further defining each of the initial goals in terms of a detailed work plan, consulting with management and other stakeholders to determine specific scope and requirements for each of the goals, researching root causes of current issues in the organization related to the initial areas of focus, interviewing members of the organization to understand their needs, and other relevant areas that will provide the PMO team with the data needed to develop and execute a plan to meet the initial PMO goals. Time should be allocated, at minimum, to define what will be in place at start-up and what key activities will be undertaken as of the start-up date.

Risks. In addition to identifying the specific categories of work that will be included as part of the implementation effort, the start-up roadmap should also clearly identify any major assumptions or risks that could materially impact the ability of the PMO team to execute the plan. Proactively identifying these items is in itself a risk-mitigation effort, but it also allows management to understand some of the potential roadblocks that could limit the ability of the PMO team to implement the PMO in a timely manner. When appropriate, management assistance should be solicited to help validate major assumptions or to develop plans that address one or more of the major risk areas identified. Discussion of the relevant assumptions and risks associated with the proposed plan will be an important part of the presentation of the detailed business case to management. Document these areas as well so that a formal record exists.

Section 7: Authorization to Proceed

Section 7 of a detailed business case should summarize the content of the business case and request authorization to proceed with the implementation plans as described in the document. This authorization should include authorization to spend any required funds and assign or recruit resources as needed. It also serves as a formal statement of management's commitment to making the PMO a reality in the organization. The detailed business case thus becomes the base charter within which the PMO implementation team will operate. As the implementation progresses, detailed planning and execution of the PMO start-up should align with the intended goals and plans detailed in the business case. If significant deviation is required as the implementation project progresses, it may be necessary to return to management to restate the business case and request concurrence on a revised plan.

Approvers of the detailed business case should be the key stakeholders who have authorization to expend funds and who will be responsible for guiding the PMO implementation efforts from a management perspective. For an enterprise PMO, these individuals will likely be the key corporate officers or directors who will have responsibility for the PMO. For a regional or divisional PMO, a region or division head (or his/her designee) will likely provide the approval for the effort. The approvers will likely continue to monitor the PMO implementation efforts once approval is granted, either as a formalized PMO steering committee or as a group of representative stakeholders. Whether or not a formal group is established, the key managers who are authorizing the PMO should be regularly updated on the progress of the implementation effort and involved as needed to resolve issues or provide guidance to the PMO implementation team.

PRESENTING THE DETAILED BUSINESS CASE TO MANAGEMENT

When the detailed business case document is complete, the next step is to present the detailed business case to management and secure approval to move forward with the PMO implementation. Ideally, this process will include distributing the detailed business case for review as well as making a formal presentation to management. Although the detailed business case document contains the essential details required to allow management to understand the goals of the PMO, implementation plans, and the required investment to support the PMO, the management presentation offers the opportunity to directly address questions or concerns regarding the detailed business case. The presentation also provides an opportunity for the PMO team to *sell* the PMO concept and implementation to management. If a review of the base business case has been conducted with management as part of the approval to move forward with development of the detailed business case, management is likely already aware of the basics of the PMO concept and some of the potential benefits to the organization. However, the base business case did not include a level of specificity that would allow management to completely understand the goals, impacts on the organization, costs, and benefits associated with the implementation of the PMO in their specific organization. The management presentation provides an important opportunity to present a strong case for the benefits of the PMO to the organization.

Attendees. The key manager or managers who will be asked to approve the detailed business case, any additional stakeholders that management or the PMO team may identify, and the team that created the detailed business case document should attend the management presentation. For PMO proposals that span a relatively small area of scope such as a division or region, attendees may include only a few key individuals from the divisional or regional management team. For a PMO that will span an entire organization (even if the organization is relatively small), ideally key members of the organization's central management team as well as leaders from affected divisions within the organization should attend. When considering attendees, keeping the group of attendees relatively small and limiting attendees to the key "influencers" who will determine if the PMO implementation will proceed is important. A broad education session regarding the PMO concept and goals is not a necessary goal of the management presentation. The goal of the presentation is to present the detailed business case, to address questions and concerns regarding the detailed business case, and to secure approval to implement the PMO as per the plans included in the detailed business case document. (*Note:* Chapter 4 will address broad communication for the organization's general management regarding the PMO, education about the benefits and goals of the PMO for the organization's staff, and related PMO marketing efforts that will be part of a broad communications plan. This broad communications plan is a defined part of the PMO implementation process.)

The presentation. A detailed business case presentation should be structured to focus on the relevant factors that management will need to understand in order to make an informed decision regarding approving the PMO. A possible agenda may include the following:

1. Introductions
2. Agenda
3. Review of PMO Opportunities
4. Proposed PMO Structure, Roles, and Responsibilities
5. Initial PMO Goals and Measures
6. Anticipated PMO Costs
7. PMO Start-Up Roadmap
8. Discussion/Questions

The format of the management presentation closely aligns with the format of the detailed business case document; however, the presentation does not serve the purpose of merely restating the detailed business case itself. Instead, the presentation provides an opportunity for the PMO team to provide background, perspective, and additional detail that contextualizes the PMO concept for management in terms of the specific implementation being planned. When needed, the detailed business case document can be referenced within the presentation itself.

Introduction. The presentation begins with introductions and a review of the agenda to ensure that participants understand the roles of everyone involved in the presentation, including members of the audience, and are familiar with the planned format for the presentation. The next section of the presentation focuses on a review of PMO opportunities. These opportunities have already been presented as part of the base business case presentation, but providing a brief discussion prior to addressing the detailed business case directly helps to frame the context of the discussion for management by briefly reviewing what can potentially be achieved through establishing the PMO. Ideally, the opportunities presented in this section of the presentation will be further developed and included as goals for the PMO, so it is important to focus this portion of the discussion on the specific opportunities in which the PMO will have direct influence. It may also be beneficial to initially focus briefly on reviewing the fundamental concept of the PMO in terms of the specific opportunities that the PMO can provide for creating value in the organization if many of the attendees are not familiar with the PMO concept already. This section of the presentation does not need to be long or in depth, but it should be included as a segue to a discussion of the detailed business case.

The remaining sections of the presentation focus on the detailed business case itself. With a review of the PMO opportunities complete, the focus of the discussion should center on the specific intended structure and roles of the PMO in the organization.

PMO structure. An overview of how the PMO will be structured (both from the standpoint of organization of the PMO itself and placement in the organization) as well as a review of the intended roles and responsibilities of the PMO should be included. When discussing the PMO roles and responsibilities, it is important to concentrate on the types of roles and responsibilities that the PMO will undertake immediately as well as the vision for the role of the PMO in the organization in the long term. This approach allows management to understand what changes in the organization will occur in the near term as well as how the PMO will grow over time. Additionally, it is important to focus the discussion on not only the roles and responsibilities themselves, but also the linkage between the roles and responsibilities and one or more of the opportunities presented in the previous section of the presentation. Thus, the presentation will flow from *what is possible* (the opportunities), to *what will be undertaken* (the roles and responsibilities in the near term and long term), to *what will be done* (the initial PMO goals and measures).

Initial PMO goals. The next topic of the presentation describes the initial PMO goals and measures and focuses on demonstrating to management that a set of initial goals and measures are indeed in place to guide the initial development and implementation of the PMO. Describing the initial goals in some reasonable level of detail provides perspective on the specific areas of influence in which management can expect to see results soon after implementation of the PMO. Defining and presenting a set of initial measures for determining performance when measured against these goals helps provide assurance to management that progress will be tracked, measured, and reported and that a firm set of criteria are in place to allow management to determine the level of achievement relative to the goals established. This section can be one of the strongest selling points in the presentation. By establishing a clear set of focus areas and a sound means of determining success in these focus areas, the PMO team is demonstrating that a detailed and thoughtful analysis and plan has been developed for how the PMO will provide benefit to the organization in the near term. When considering a PMO, two common areas of management concern are unclear objectives and a lack of understanding of how the PMO will benefit the organization as opposed to merely consuming resources in hopes of attaining some broad, long-term gains (which are often not clearly defined or quantifiable). It is acceptable to include some discussion of long-term goals and measures here if these long-term goals and measures have been elaborated in the detailed business case document, particularly if management has questions regarding how the PMO will be able to sustain and build value over time. However, it is critical to demonstrate that the creation of the PMO will benefit the organization in terms of solving immediate challenges and building a strong foundation in the near term for continued success in the long term.

Required resources. The next section of the presentation focuses the resources that will be required for support of the PMO implementation and its ongoing operations as well as the development of an implementation plan itself. Because a detailed cost analysis for the PMO has been included as a part of the detailed business case itself, only a summary of the anticipated costs is required for this presentation. It is important to provide the cost data in terms of anticipated start-up costs as well as anticipated ongoing operating costs. If these costs have been forecast for 1 or more years into the future, demonstrating how costs will change over time as the PMO evolves its role and scope is appropriate. If quantitative analysis of the potential returns from PMO operations has been conducted, the results of this analysis may be included as well to demonstrate the potential savings that will offset the required initial investment and PMO operating expenses. If the majority of the potential benefits are soft benefits, these may also be mentioned briefly in the presentation. Make some statement, quantitative or qualitative, that demonstrates to management what value will be returned for the investment made. Discussion on PMO opportunities and initial goals has helped to set the stage for what will be achieved. Providing some detail on anticipated returns will help to reinforce the message that the PMO will return real value to the organization, thus helping to justify the investment.

Milestones. Focus discussion of the start-up roadmap on the key milestones that must be achieved in order to ensure a successful start-up rather than giving detailed information on each activity that is relevant for PMO start-up. The presentation attendees are primarily interested in what major activities will be undertaken as part of the start-up and when start-up activities will be complete. If specific resources are already assigned to assist with implementing the PMO (or are contemplated to be assigned), mention these key resources and their roles. This section of the presentation should tie together many of the details already presented in a way that will provide a clear path to complete implementation of the PMO. It also provides assurance that a firm plan is in place and details the specific time line from approval of the PMO implementation to PMO start-up. Therefore, management will better be able to understand when the PMO will start to influence and enhance the project management function within the organization.

Value statement. Conclude the presentation with a strong statement regarding the value of a PMO to the organization. By relying on the opportunities identified and the intended goals of the PMO, this statement should be simple to prepare, particularly if the PMO team has done a good job of investigating and documenting the PMO opportunities. End the presentation with a positive statement about what is possible, what will be achieved, and how the PMO will benefit the organization.

Discussion. The final *sell* should be followed by an opportunity for participants to ask questions and to discuss the content of the presentation and the detailed business case document. Ideally the presentation and the accompanying documentation will have set the stage for a positive discussion. Even so, the possibility still exists that some dissention will be included in the discussion as well. To the extent possible, the PMO team should steer this type of discussion in a positive direction while still fully addressing any concerns raised by the attendees.

Authorization to proceed. Assuming no major issues have been raised that would require additional investigation and follow-up with the management team, the final presentation activity should be a request for authorization to proceed with PMO implementation as per the detailed business case. This authorization should include an authorization to spend funds, commit resources, and execute the required start-up planning. Required planning will include developing plans to keep management informed of implementation progress and ensuring that a quality implementation is completed within the time and cost constraints in the detailed business case. Authorization should also include the work required to fully implement the PMO and to commence operations. When authorization is in hand, the last major step in planning for the PMO has been completed. Now, the start-up work required to make the PMO a reality can begin.

SUMMARY

Chapter 3 has described the process of developing a detailed business case, which is a critical component of establishing a PMO within an organization.

Without a clearly articulated set of benefits and returns, the value of a PMO to an organization may not be well understood and therefore limit the likelihood of obtaining management support for a PMO. A detailed business case establishes a base set of goals for a PMO team. It provides guidance and helps ensure that a PMO will remain focused on a few key areas that are of immediate concern to management. The PMO must address these immediate management concerns as part of its initial work. A detailed business case documents the required effort and time line to implement the PMO. It also requests approval to proceed with implementation, which is a critical juncture in the PMO process.

The activities associated with the development of a detailed implementation plan will be discussed in Chapter 4. Also discussed will be the process of developing a PMO marketing and communication plan. This plan will be used to guide the PMO team to effectively communicate the PMO concept, goals, benefits, and detailed implementation plans to management and the organization.

4

IMPLEMENTATION PLANNING

INTRODUCTION

Now the work begins! Chapter 4 will address the subject of PMO implementation planning. Assuming that the review of the detailed business case was successful and permission to proceed with the PMO implementation has been obtained, it is now time to make the PMO a reality in the organization. Numerous details must be addressed in order to start-up a PMO. Some of these are very practical, straightforward matters such as securing phone lines for the desks that the PMO staff will utilize or obtaining access to trade publications or associations that address topics relevant to project management and PMOs so that the PMO staff can stay up-to-date on trends in project and PMO management. Other areas, however, address more tactical and strategic aspects of implementation and start-up and seek to ensure that a solid foundation for long-term PMO success will be built. For the purposes of Chapter 4, attention to the base administrative matters that must be considered when starting up the PMO will be kept to a minimum. Topics of a more strategic and tactical nature, such as developing a PMO communications plan or identifying key stakeholder groups and stakeholder needs, will be discussed in greater detail to provide a perspective on some of the key areas that are important to fully address as part of implementation and start-up planning.

THE PMO IMPLEMENTATION PLAN

A successful PMO implementation begins with good planning. The goal of a PMO implementation plan is to develop a workable plan that will ensure that the necessary tasks that must be completed prior to commencing operation of the PMO are delivered within the time and cost constraints set forth in the detailed business plan. The essential areas of focus in PMO implementation plan include:

- Assembling the PMO implementation team
- Developing a detailed implementation plan
- Developing a management communication plan
- Introducing and training the PMO implementation team
- Developing a PMO marketing and communication plan
- Transforming PMO goals into strategies
- Executing the plan

Each of these major areas will be discussed in detail in Chapter 4. Once the work associated with each of these planning areas is complete, the implementation plan can be executed, and the initial PMO operations can commence. Details related to the actual implementation and the early life of a "live" PMO will be the subject of Chapter 5.

Assembling the PMO Implementation Team

Implementation of the PMO will be addressed much like a project. With the detailed business case and the PMO start-up roadmap in hand and agreed to by management, many of the major constraints that will affect the implementation of the PMO (such as the available budget and a high-level schedule) are known. The first step in developing the PMO implementation plan is to assemble a team to perform the detailed planning and execution within the budget and time frame approved by management. Parties interested in the information in Chapter 4 are likely to either be serving on such a team, to be planning for a PMO implementation that will utilize such a team, to represent organizational decision makers within the management structure of the organization that are considering implementing a PMO, or are project management practitioners with an interest in the PMO concept. Each of these groups, as well as others, will have a role in the implementation of a PMO. The PMO implementation team will be made up of more than just the PMO manager alone or the PMO manager plus the PMO staff. In order to effectively implement the PMO in a way that brings value to the organization early in its life, a number of constituencies within the organization will likely be involved at some level. The primary constituencies that will have a role in the PMO implementation include:

- PMO manager and staff
- Project management subject matter experts
- Project managers and project team managers
- Members of management
- Project stakeholders and internal customers

Although each of these groups will have a role in the implementation and start-up of the PMO, the role may not necessarily be at the same level of involvement. The bulk of the implementation work will fall to the PMO manager and PMO staff, as would be expected. Other members of the project management community within the organization, including senior project managers or other project subject matter experts, should be involved (as is appropriate) so that as the implementation planning and execution occur, valuable input from these experts is obtained and considered as needed. Performing detailed planning for and implementation of the PMO's intended roles and responsibilities "in a box," without input from the project management community, is a sure way to ensure PMO failure. The PMO should exist, in one sense, to serve the project management community within the organization. In order to serve the project management community effectively, there must be consultation with and input from the community so the needs of the members are met. Although there may be broad management goals for the PMO that seek to transform the project management community, that transformation will take place over time and will be more readily accepted if there is input obtained from the project managers and project team members who are working on projects daily. A heavy-handed PMO that sets its goal and priorities, and then forces its will on the project managers and team members who are delivering projects, will face resentment and, possibly, outright rebellion. If members of the project management community think that they have a voice in the PMO's plans, this resistance is more easily overcome. Furthermore, the community likely has insight that will be of great value to the PMO as the PMO staff starts to take the goals set for the PMO and transform them into actionable plans and deliverables.

Members of the organization's management team working in the areas that will be influenced by the PMO (or the entire organization itself in the case of a centralized enterprise PMO) will also have an important role. These managers will want to be kept apprised of the implementation progress and will be important resources for clarifying intended roles, resolving issues, and providing guidance to the PMO team as the implementation progresses. Many of these key managers were likely part of the group that reviewed and approved the detailed business case, but there may be other members of management that would also be appropriate to consult on certain PMO-related issues. Depending on the size of the PMO, the size of the organization, and the level of involvement that management wishes to have in the PMO implementation effort, a PMO steering committee or PMO sponsor may be identified to serve as the key point of contact for management involvement in the PMO effort. For relatively small PMOs or for PMOs that have a limited focus (such as a single group or division PMO), a single management point of contact may be sufficient. For PMOs of larger scope, a steering committee comprised of several members of the management community may be useful in order to ensure adequate representation from a broad cross section of the management community. Regardless of makeup, the goal of continued management involvement in the PMO process is important and must be adequately considered and agreed to with management before detailed planning and implementation commences.

The last two key constituencies that must be considered as part of planning for the PMO implementation team are project stakeholders and internal customers. These constituencies represent the community within the organization that requests projects and receives deliverables from projects. If the PMO primarily serves internal customers, these individuals will be relatively easy to identify. If the PMO is intended to serve as a link between the organization itself and the organization's external customers, key customer relationship managers such as account managers or engagement managers may be appropriate points of contact. The purpose of identifying and involving key project stakeholders and internal customers is to ensure that the implementation and specific deliverables from the PMO align with the needs of these stakeholder groups. Although the PMO may most broadly influence the project organization directly in terms of standards setting, education and training, and other areas of influence, the end deliverables from most projects address some business need supplied by individuals not directly involved in project management. Instead, accountants, sales representatives, customer service personnel, client account teams, and other such groups are the key stakeholders of projects. Their satisfaction is a critical measure of the effectiveness of project management and project delivery. Although the role of these individuals in the PMO implementation process will be relatively small, primarily providing guidance and input on perceptions of project management and delivery from a customer perspective, not having this perspective robs the PMO implementation team of valuable insight that can help guide how the PMO addresses the key goals established for the PMO.

Of course, not all of these groups will be engaged to the same extent in the PMO implementation activities. The core PMO implementation team will have the responsibility for making the PMO a reality and should be composed primarily of dedicated resources. For a smaller PMO, the core team may be comprised of the PMO manager only. For a medium or larger PMO, more than one resource will likely be required in order for the PMO to function effectively and as such all members of the PMO staff will serve as members of the implementation team. In some cases, these members may already be identified. In other cases, they may have to be recruited internally or externally. Even the PMO manager may not yet be in place if the PMO planning was conducted by a team within the organization itself with the expectation that upon approval of the PMO concept, a full-time PMO manager would be identified. If this is the case, recruiting and hiring a PMO manager must be the first priority. Assembling the PMO implementation team may still take place if time is of the essence and if appropriate individuals can be identified, but the implementation team should be led by the individual who will assume responsibility for the PMO once it is in place and functioning. Ideally, this individual should have input into the selection of the PMO staff. A complete discussion of acquiring core PMO staff is provided in the next section, *Staffing the PMO*.

Beyond the PMO team itself, part-time participation from members of the other key constituencies that have been identified in this section should be considered as well. The representatives of these constituencies should be identified and asked to participate in the PMO implementation effort. If appropriate or required by the organization, short job descriptions may be created to help these individuals understand their role in the PMO implementation process. As an alternative, a brief bulleted list of these roles may be created such as the example shown below:

- Project subject matter experts
  - Provide insight into current project management challenges facing the organization
  - Review draft standards, procedures, training, and other deliverables that will be deployed as part of the initial PMO implementation or early post start-up activities
  - Represent the project management function in key discussions regarding PMO roles, responsibilities, and influence

- Management
  - Serve as project sponsors or steering team members, reviewing implementation progress and providing guidance to ensure that the PMO implementation meets management expectations
  - Serve as the escalation point for issues that cannot be resolved by the PMO implementation team
  - Champion the PMO implementation by demonstrating commitment to the PMO concept and implementation

- Project stakeholders and internal customers
  - Provide insight into project delivery issues that result in decreased revenue, customer satisfaction, or other key performance measures

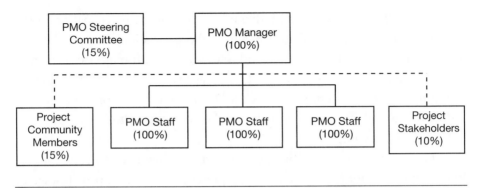

Figure 4.1 Implementation organization chart.

- Provide insight into additional areas of need in which value could be created or enhanced from a customer perspective

Because these individuals will not serve on the PMO implementation team full time, an estimate of the required level of their participation should be included so that the time commitment is clear. In many cases, some level of internal recruiting and negotiations with these key individuals' managers will need to take place in order to ensure the availability of appropriate resources to fill these key consulting and influencing roles. A short job description or, at minimum, an estimated time commitment will make it easier to fairly represent the required effort and commitment to the individuals themselves and their management.

It is also helpful to create an organization chart that depicts the implementation roles. This chart may also include the expected required time commitment for each role in order to set expectations regarding participation in the implementation effort. A sample PMO implementation organization chart is provided in Figure 4.1.

Figure 4.1 depicts the organization chart in terms of the key roles that are required as part of the PMO implementation team. Also included is an estimation of the required effort per role (indicated as a percentage of each individual's time) as well as a distinction between the core PMO implementation team and the influencing and consulting roles that will be included (indicated by the dashed lines). Because the purpose of the organization chart is to help facilitate an understanding of the required roles, specific names are not required on the chart. Once all individuals who will be participating in the implementation effort are identified, a formal organization chart can be produced and distributed with names and roles identified. It may also be helpful to identify the implementation roles (i.e., roles that will exist for the duration of the *implementation* effort) versus PMO staff roles (i.e., roles that will be staffed by individuals who will make up the *permanent* PMO staff once the PMO start-up is complete).

The importance of identifying appropriate individuals to serve on the PMO implementation team (ensuring representation from a broad range of affected groups) and gaining commitment from team members early in the implementation process cannot be underestimated. Without an understanding of the resources available, the PMO implementation manager will not be able to effectively develop a detailed implementation plan. Additionally, forming the team early in the process provides time for team-building activities and ramp-up prior to extensive implementation work commencing. Even for those resources who will commit only a fraction of their time to supporting the PMO implementation effort, a base level of understanding of the PMO's intended roles and responsibilities, initial goals, and other relevant background knowledge must be provided. These individuals must be welcomed to the PMO implementation team and acquainted with the other members of the organization who will be supporting the PMO effort before the implementation formally commences. Recruiting a solid implementation team is the first critical step in ensuring a successful start-up.

Staffing the PMO

Staffing the PMO includes the processes of identifying and acquiring the resources that will serve as the permanent PMO operational staff once the PMO implementation is complete. These resources should also serve on the PMO implementation team to allow them to be fully engaged in PMO efforts prior to formal start-up of the PMO. The process of staffing a PMO may be as simple as finding one internal project manager to serve as the PMO manager (in the case of a PMO with a small initial scope). This project manager must have the desire to lead an effort to better the project management culture in the organization. Alternatively, to support broader implementation or a wider range of roles and responsibilities, the process may be more time consuming and include internal or external recruiting of a full complement of PMO staff. (In this section, the PMO manager role will be discussed separately from the PMO staff roles because the skills and experience required for a PMO manager differ from those of the PMO staff.) In addition to the roles themselves, some general process discussion is included to help guide the process of recruitment and selection. Initially, the following base questions should be addressed:

- Who is needed to staff the PMO?
- Where will they be found?
- What skills should they bring?
- What will they do?

An understanding of who is required (i.e., what PMO roles will be staffed as part of the implementation) should already be complete. The PMO implementation organization chart includes the structure of the PMO core implementation team and should identify those roles on the implementation team that will remain as PMO staff roles once the implementation is complete. If resources are intended to serve on the PMO staff "part-time" in addition to their other job functions (not ideal, but acceptable if human resource or budget constraints are significant), these part-time roles should be noted because they will likely come from resources within the organization. The staffing practices for obtaining part-time assistance from existing resources will vary significantly from staffing for full-time, dedicated roles.

One key to effective PMO start-up is to clearly identify the required PMO staff positions that will be needed to support the initial operation of the PMO and to recruit individuals with appropriate skills and experience to fill these roles. Depending on the required number of resources needed, available budget, management intent, and organizational policies regarding staff acquisition, the process of finding candidates for PMO staff roles may be as simple as identifying internal resources with appropriate skills or as complex as undertaking a complete external search and recruiting process. In some cases, appropriate internal resources may already be identified for some (or potentially all) of these roles. If so, the availability of these resources should be confirmed and appropriate plans to transition them to PMO roles should be established. Once these internally staffed roles have been confirmed, any remaining roles that do not already have candidates identified should be considered.

Search scope. The first step in the process of locating appropriate resources is to make a decision regarding whether an internal or external search (or both) will be conducted. Utilizing internal resources to staff the PMO typically results in a lower up-front cost because recruiting and hiring costs are greatly reduced, but finding internal resources with appropriate skills that are not already devoted to key project efforts may be difficult. Additionally, unless a clear career path is established that provides some assurance that a PMO role will be valuable from a career perspective, it may be difficult to entice exceptional individuals to leave their current roles to join the PMO. Conversely, conducting an external search for candidates for PMO roles may lead to a broader array of qualified candidates (especially for the key PMO manager role); however, the costs associated with conducting an external search and interviewing qualified candidates can be significant (especially if a national or international search is conducted). External candidates bring the potential advantage of a broader range of industry and project management experience. Although this may be highly desirable from the standpoint of acquiring staff that is not ingrained in the organization's culture and processes, costs such as relocation, signing bonuses, and potentially higher salary and bonus requirements may create a financially restrictive proposition. Discussions with management regarding the scope of the search, available budget to support hiring candidates, and other factors are critical. Additionally, relevant human resource policies and procedures must be reviewed and strictly adhered to regardless of the scope of the search conducted.

If a decision is made to advertise one or more of the available PMO roles externally, the organization's corporate recruiting or human resource department should be immediately engaged to assist with the process of creating appropriate job descriptions, advertising the positions, accepting and screening résumés, and identifying candidates for interviews. If an internal search will be conducted, communication regarding the available positions via corporate job boards or other means of communication should be initiated as soon as approval to advertise the positions is obtained. A complete job description for each position will still be required, but the interview and hiring guidelines will likely be different for candidates within the organization. Because the time and effort to recruit and hire PMO staff may vary significantly depending on whether an internal or external search is conducted, it is critical that the staffing processes begin as soon as practically possible.

Skills and experience. In order to ensure that qualified individuals are in place to support the PMO, considering the skills and experience desired in the PMO staff is important. These skills and experience may vary significantly depending on the specific role, and it is not possible to list every possible skill requirement that may be necessary. However, there are a few general qualities that are fairly universal across roles. First and foremost, members of the PMO staff should have significant experience in managing projects. The PMO will ideally be viewed by the organization as a center of expertise in project management knowledge and practice, and the staff will be viewed as being able to provide expert guidance and advice to the organization. Additionally, the PMO staff may be called on to lead key project efforts if one of the PMO's roles is to perform some level of active project management. It is critical that if this role is being considered, that one or more members of the PMO staff are senior project managers capable of leading large project efforts. Even if the PMO will serve primarily in a standards management or consulting capacity only, it is important to ensure that the staff can effectively contribute expert knowledge and advice. There is no formula that can be used to determine how much project management experience is appropriate. A track record of successfully leading significant project efforts over a number of years may be used as a general guideline. It is certainly not necessary to staff the PMO with only the most experienced internal project managers or external candidates with multiple decades of project management experience. However, it is also not advisable to staff the PMO entirely with junior project managers and use the PMO as a means to grow these individuals' project management skills. Project management experience may also be demonstrated through exposure to recognized project management standards or achievement of relevant project management certifications. These items alone do not make a project manager successful, but experience with standards and achievement of certification does demonstrate a level of understanding and commitment to the practice of project management.

Level of experience. Beyond project management experience, significant experience in one or more of the key domains that will be addressed by the PMO—consulting, knowledge, and/or standards—should be required. Because the role of the PMO in these areas will evolve over time, it is important to consider not only the immediate needs in terms of implementation and achievement of the initial PMO goals, but also how these skills will benefit the PMO and the organization over time. Experience developing project management standards, providing project consulting to internal teams or external customers, developing best practices, documenting lessons learned, or developing and delivering project management training are just a few of the areas within the consulting, knowledge, and standards domains that may be beneficial. There are certainly many others. As staffing the PMO roles and determining the appropriate skills and experiences for the PMO staff are discussed, the short-term needs for PMO implementation and start-up, as well as the long-term direction that the PMO will take, will guide the specific combination of skills in these domains that will be desirable. It is important to also consider whether *deep* experience in one of the domains or specific areas of interest to the organization is preferable over *broad* experience in a variety of areas within these domains. Staffing the PMO with individuals possessing deep expertise in a few key areas can be beneficial if these key areas are critical areas of need that the PMO will address; however, this approach may rob the PMO of the flexibility to be influential in other key areas. Conversely, staffing the PMO with individuals with broad experience in a variety of relevant areas, but who lack deep expertise, can create more opportunities to influence the organization. This approach will likely require more effort on the part of these members of the staff in terms of conducting research and determining best practices in certain areas in which the PMO is expected to provide influence, but in which staff resources do not have a level of expertise that allows them to develop optimal solutions through relying on their own experience and expertise alone. This tradeoff must be considered in terms of the intended roles and responsibilities of the PMO as well as the intended long-term PMO staffing model. If the PMO staff will be grown over time as the role of the PMO expands, it may be possible to utilize experts in a few areas of influence initially and obtain additional resources later to fill gaps in knowledge as the PMO expands. If the initial PMO staff will be in place for some time without significant expansion, having resources in place that can serve in a broad range of capacities may be desirable.

Industry or geographical experience. Broad industry or geographical experience should also be considered. If the PMO will influence a large or geographically diverse portion of the organization, experience working in multiple industries and/or geographies (or in the case of an external candidate, within the industry or closely related industries that align to one or more of the industries in which the organization serves) may be highly desirable. Hiring an individual from outside the key business areas in which the organization currently operates can provide fresh perspective to the organization as long as the individual being considered has the capacity to learn the business that the PMO serves; however, the time required to gain this experience may be significant. Of course, individuals with extensive experience within the same or closely aligned industries can still provide perspective based on their past experience. It is critical to ensure that any candidates who have gained experience in the same industry via having worked for one of the organization's competitors are not bound by any employment agreement that forbids them from working for a competitor for a period of time and that relevant intellectual property considerations related to the individual sharing practices that were developed to benefit a competitor are given appropriate thought.

Communication skills. In addition to project management expertise and experience in one or more relevant PMO domains, skills in interpersonal communication, conducting presentations, and customer relationship management are critical. The PMO staff will be the resources that will be responsible for establishing policies and procedures, consulting with individuals and teams on project management topics, representing project management and the PMO to the organization's management, and potentially interacting with external customers on project matters. These resources will be the "ambassadors" of project management to the internal project organization as well as to customers (as required). They should possess a high level of interpersonal communication skills as well as an ability to communicate and to build influence at different levels of the organization. Clearly, the PMO manager must be able to communicate effectively and build relationships with the mangers who will oversee PMO operations as well as with other organizational leaders whose groups will be affected by PMO operations. Beyond the PMO manager, the PMO staff should also be able to effectively communicate with management and members of the project management community, build consensus, and influence the organization. If the PMO staff will be conducting training, presenting standards or procedures to the organization or regularly communicating in a forum or group setting, advanced presentation skills and experience will be required.

This discussion certainly does not encompass all of the potentially desirable skills and experiences that members of the PMO staff might possess. A specific combination of the skills discussed and others that are required will be determined by the specific role that is being staffed. Additionally, organizational human resource policies may dictate certain "standard" skills or required levels of experience based on the level of the position within the organization or how closely the position aligns to a standard job description or skills map that the organization may use to baseline salaries, define job descriptions, or for other purposes.

With an understanding of the specific roles that will be filled, the type of search that will be conducted, and the general set of desirable qualities that will be important, beginning to develop job descriptions for the available positions is possible. The format and content of the job description must be developed in consultation with appropriate recruiting or human resource contacts to ensure compliance with organizational policies. A general format for the job description may include the following items, but specific formats will be determined by local laws and regulations and organizational human resources practices:

- Position title
- Department
- Work hours
- Salary range
- Position description and job responsibilities
- Education and experience requirements
- Application procedures

An example of a possible sample job description for a PMO training manager is provided below:

GOTPMO CORPORATION—JOB POSTING

Position: Program Management Office (PMO) Training Manager

Department: Corporate Information Technology

Work Hours: Full-Time

Salary Range: Salary commensurate with experience and qualifications

Position Description: Under the direction of the PMO Manager, the PMO Training Manager will lead the development and implementation of a consolidated, standardized training curriculum for project management resources within the GOTPMO Corporation Corporate Information Technology division. Responsibilities include:

- Determining the project management training needs for new and existing project managers within the division
- Identifying existing training opportunities, gauging training effectiveness, and reusing existing training content when possible
- Working closely with the PMO Standards Manager to align the Corporate Information Technology Division's project management training curriculum with PMO project management standards and industry best practices
- Developing new training courses based on identified training needs
- Identifying, selecting, training, mentoring, and evaluating qualified instructors
- Working with the Corporate Training Division to ensure compliance with corporate training standards and to leverage standard training tools and technologies when possible
- Other duties as assigned by the PMO Manager

Required Skills and Experience:

- Bachelor's degree in business, computer science, information systems, or other relevant field; Master's degree preferred
- 3+ years working in a training and development capacity as a trainer or curriculum developer

- 7+ years experience with project management tools, techniques, and best practices, including leading significant project efforts
- Strong interpersonal skills and ability to influence decision makers
- Strong training delivery skills and ability to lead and mentor training staff
- Excellent written communication skills

Application Procedure: Submit a current résumé, salary requirements, and two professional references to the address indicated on the cover of this job posting.

In the example job description, the position description is used to provide the specific duties associated with the position being advertised in terms of a specific set of expectations for the position as well as an understanding that additional duties beyond those outlined in the position description itself may be assigned. Additionally, the required skills and experience expected are outlined. Providing specific requirements such as a certain number of years of experience managing projects or a specific level of educational experience helps to set clear expectations with potential candidates and also ensures that appropriately qualified individuals are considered. In addition to project management skills and experience, general business skills such as a high degree of skill in oral and written communication should be included as appropriate.

Once the job descriptions are complete, the processes of posting the job descriptions, reviewing applications, conducting interviews, and making hiring decisions can begin. Because these processes will vary significantly from organization to organization and country to country, in accordance with corporate policies and government regulations, a discussion of these phases of the staff acquisition process is not included here. At the conclusion of the process, the initial PMO staff should be in place and ready to begin the process of developing the PMO and commencing operations.

Developing a Detailed Implementation Plan

With team requirements identified, the next step is to review the start-up roadmap and to develop a detailed implementation plan based on the core focus areas and time frames in the start-up roadmap. The implementation plan will be the primary document that the team will use to understand and manage the work required to implement the PMO. The document should reflect all of the work required to complete a successful implementation and should reflect this work at a detailed level. As with most project plans, work should be detailed to the work package or task level and scheduled according to standard project scheduling practices. For the purposes of this section, a detailed review of the process of developing a project plan will not be provided. Instead, some general guidance regarding the form and content of the implementation plan for the PMO specifically will be provided.

Because the start-up roadmap already contains the high-level work that will be completed for each of the major areas that must be addressed as part of the PMO implementation and start-up, developing the implementation plan should primarily be an exercise in further decomposing the major tasks provided in the start-up roadmap as needed, validating that no major tasks have been missed and ensuring that sufficient resources are available to complete the required work in a time frame that is acceptable to management. If a detailed project plan was created as part of developing the detailed business case as a result of management request or for some other reason, the decomposition step may not be required. However, even with an understanding of the full set of resources available to assist with the PMO implementation effort available, it is still important to perform a validation that the work to be undertaken can be completed in a timely fashion utilizing the resources available as well as to review the start-up roadmap to validate that there have been no omissions.

An important component of this exercise will be validating that the time frame initially proposed for PMO implementation in the start-up roadmap is still accurate. If the start-up roadmap was completed using sound estimating techniques, the detailed implementation plan should approximately reflect the time frames proposed in the start-up roadmap. If, however, some important areas of scope were missed in the start-up roadmap or if other factors now exist that were not considered as part of development of the start-up roadmap, it may be necessary to make minor adjustments to the implementation scope to ensure completion within the time line committed in the detailed business case, or it may be appropriate to determine if additional resources are available to assist with portions of the implementation effort or to develop a revised implementation time line that reflects current business conditions. At this stage, it is appropriate to consider these options if it appears that the original scheduling assumptions are no longer valid, but it is not necessary to develop a final plan of action. The implementation plan will be reviewed with the PMO implementation team and input from the team may lead to other options to address any potential scheduling issues. The first exercise is to draft a plan that is representative of the work that must be completed and to make a first attempt at developing a detailed project schedule that can be used to manage the implementation effort.

As each section of the start-up roadmap is elaborated, the resources required for completion of the work associated with each of the major tasks or deliverables should be identified and documented. In cases in which one (or more) of the required resources is not part of the PMO implementation team, the resources should be noted as additional required resources. Their availability should be secured once the implementation plan is finalized. For example, a telecommunications technician may be required to set-up phone service for the PMO staff. Availability of telephone service may be needed by some particular date to ensure that the PMO has everything needed to begin operations in its designated facilities. The technician would not need to be involved in the PMO implementation team; however, the technician (or the telecommunications group if a specific technician cannot be named) would need to be informed of the requirement for telephone service and the required delivery date. Follow-up would also likely need to occur to ensure that resources are available to complete the work without delay.

This may represent the simplest case because the resource required has minimal potential for contention within the PMO implementation project itself. A more difficult scenario arises when many of the same PMO implementation team resources are assigned to multiple implementation tasks. This scenario is analogous to many of the challenges faced by project managers in general—more work to complete than the available capacity to complete the work. The simplest answer, of course, is to ensure that appropriate planning and schedule development practices are followed. However, although this is certainly a preferable option and well in line with project management best practices, it is occasionally not practical when, for better or worse, expectations have been set either by or with management regarding implementation and start-up time frames. As mentioned previously, options should be considered that utilize the available resources as efficiently as possible, but that still allow for learning and professional development as part of the implementation process. It is critical that resources are not assigned to so many areas of responsibility within the plan that there is no flexibility left to allow the PMO team to "settle in" to their new roles, conduct internal training and development, and develop a workable model for how the PMO staff itself will operate once the PMO is in operation. Consideration of these internal process issues must be included in the detailed planning process so that the internal mechanisms of operation are appropriately developed in addition to the deliverables that will impact the organization and lead to the achievement of the initial PMO goals.

As part of developing the detailed business case, the initial focus of the PMO implementation in terms of deliverables that support the base roles and responsibilities of the PMO has already been considered. One of the key questions addressed was whether the PMO implementation would result in having a set of initial deliverables ready to implement in the organization at the start-up date or whether the implementation would focus primarily on developing internal PMO operational policies, securing facilities and staff, and training the PMO staff, thus making the start-up date the first date that the PMO staff would begin working toward achievement of the initial PMO goals. If the intent of the PMO implementation is to prepare the PMO for operation at the start-up date and then to begin development of PMO deliverables to support achievement to the initial PMO goals, the detailed implementation plan should include any necessary preparations to ensure that the initial areas of focus for the PMO are identified and plans are in place for beginning to address these areas as of the start-up date. If the intent is for the PMO implementation to include developing deliverables to support achievement of the initial PMO goals as part of the implementation process, detailed planning for these deliverables should be included in the implementation plan. As the detailed implementation plan is developed, the required resources necessary to work on these initial focus areas should be considered in the context of the other PMO implementation work that must be completed. It may become apparent that focusing on both the core implementation tasks as well as delivery of certain PMO deliverables will result in a diluted effort in both areas. If this is the case, management should be consulted. This situation should be explained to management in detail. To commence PMO operation with less than full attention having been paid to the base tasks required for a successful PMO start-up may have long-term consequences in terms of rework in the future or reduced effectiveness in the near term. A focus on the base tasks is seldom worth sacrificing in order to focus less-than-full attention on another key area—developing and delivering PMO services.

When complete, the plan that has been developed should be reviewed in detail with the PMO team to ensure that team members understand the plan completely and to provide the team with an opportunity to provide feedback before the final plan is reviewed with management. As a result of this review, further refinement of the plan may be required. Once finalized, the implementation plan should be reviewed with the PMO sponsor or PMO steering committee to ensure that these PMO stakeholders understand how the implementation team intends to proceed. Validating the plan with management also provides an opportunity to review any major risks or areas of concern and to highlight important implementation milestones that may be of interest.

Developing a Management Communication Plan

As PMO implementation efforts progress, keeping members of management informed regarding implementation progress is important. These members may include members of the PMO steering committee, the PMO sponsor, and other managers that need to be kept apprised of the status of the implementation effort and any issues that may affect the timely start-up of the PMO. The management communication plan establishes a formal process that defines the types of communications management can expect to receive, the frequency of communication, and the means of communication. The types and frequency of communications to management differ significantly from the frequent, detailed communication that will occur between members of the PMO implementation team. It is important to ensure that a plan is in place to communicate key messages regarding progress, issues, and other items of interest to management on a regular basis. By creating a communication plan and aligning it with the members of management who will be the recipients of the communications in advance, expectations can be set and managed. Additionally, formalizing a communication plan ensures that management is kept up-to-date at a frequency that is based on their needs and thus minimizes the risk of over- or undercommunicating status, issues, and other relevant items.

The first step in developing a management communication plan is to identify the members of management who will be the recipients of management communications. Many of the members of the management team that reviewed the detailed business case as well as the key individuals who authorized the PMO implementation will clearly be included among those that will be targeted in the management communication plan. These individuals should also be consulted to determine if other members of the organization's management should be included as well. For a smaller PMO implementation that impacts only a particular area of the organization, the list of members of management who will receive management communications may be relatively small. For larger implementations, potentially dozens of managers (or more) may be included in some or all of the management communications. For larger groups, defining the managers who are the key decisions makers and who will be involved in resolving PMO issues and authorizing changes to the implementation plan (if required) is advisable. This group may be made up of the PMO sponsor or the PMO steering committee only (or a subset of the steering committee) or it may include other individuals beyond the steering committee itself. Regular, routine updates and communications should be addressed to all identified managers, but certain communications that require management action may be directed to only those individuals who have been identified as decision makers in order to maximize the timeliness of response to issues.

Once the members of management who will receive communications as part of the management communication plan have been identified, the next step is to identify what, when, and how various types of communications will be disseminated. Two important types of communications should be considered. The first type includes routine communications such as status reports. These reports typically represent the "state of the project" and are provided to keep management informed of progress on a regular basis. The second type

Table 4.1 Management Communication Plan

GOTPMO Corporation
PMO Implementation—Management Communication Plan

Communication	Frequency	Audience	Format
Status report	Weekly	All	Electronic mail
Project plan updates	Monthly	All	Electronic mail with attachment
Implementation review	Monthly	All	In person
Issue log	Weekly	Steering Committee	Electronic mail
Issue escalation	As needed	Sponsor with copy to Steering Committee	Electronic mail with in-person follow-up

includes exception reports such as issues summaries, project variance reports, or other communications that require management attention or action. Although many potential types of reports can be included, keeping the number of reports to a minimum is desirable. The goal is to ensure that sufficient reporting is available to meet management's communications needs, but without unnecessary communication, and to ensure that the reports provided are timely and accurate. In order to document the management communication plan, a table such as Table 4.1 should be developed to define the specific communication requirements that will need to be addressed.

Table 4.1 includes some of the common types of management communications that may be included as part of a management communication plan. Each organization may have their own requirements concerning management communication, and the communication plan that is developed should be reviewed and aligned with management to ensure that management needs are being met. In addition to the specific types of communications that will be included, the frequency of communication, intended audience, and format of communication are provided so that a clear understanding of what will be delivered, to whom, and when is included in the plan. Responsibility for aligning the plan with management and executing the plan as the PMO implementation effort progresses rests with the PMO manager or his or her designee. It is important that management communication needs are given appropriate attention and that the plan developed is consistently executed throughout the implementation effort. Once the PMO implementation is complete, revision of the document to reflect ongoing communication regarding PMO operations should be undertaken. A revised operational communications plan should then be put in place to ensure continued consistent communication throughout the life of the PMO.

The most common form of communication in the management communication plan will be the status report. The status report provides regular updates to management regarding accomplishments, progress versus the implementation plan, and issues that the project team is facing as it completes its work. In many organizations, a standard status report template may exist. If available, this report should be utilized. If no standard report is available, a simple report format such as the format below may be used.

GOTPMO CORPORATION–PMO IMPLEMENTATION STATUS REPORT

Reporting Period: June 10–17, 2006

Prepared By: Joe Smith, PMO Manager

Project Percent Complete: 25% (on track)

Project Percent Spent: 21% (under budget)

Accomplishments this Reporting Period:

- PMO staff completed Earned Value Management training
- Office facilities agreement completed with corporate facilities department
- Project management tools subteam met with two potential enterprise project reporting vendors

Work to Be Completed during the Next Reporting Period:

- Complete office space set-up documentation and finalize move-in date
- Develop questionnaire for project contract management effectiveness survey
- Identify key project management training requirements for Information Technology organization

Summary of Key Project Issues:

- Delay in hiring Training Manager requires modifying training deliverables schedule in project plan

The goal of a status report is to create a concise summary of the key items that will be of interest to management and to communicate these items in a way that facilitates quick review. If any recipients of the report have questions regarding the report content, the PMO manager or his or her designee should be available to address these issues. In addition, key supporting documents such as the detailed project plan, budget updates, or issue documentation may be included for reference if appropriate.

Other standard forms of communication such as issue logs, issue summaries, budget update documents, and any other items identified as necessary components of the management communication plan may be developed as needed to support management's information needs. Most likely, the status report will serve as the primary vehicle for informing management of progress. An issue log or issues summary will provide a vehicle for keeping management apprised of issues and seeking management intervention when required. If the management communication plan is executed consistently and any relevant issues are communicated swiftly using the processes established in the communication plan, there should be few surprises that catch management off guard.

Introducing and Training the PMO Implementation Team

With the PMO implementation team organizational structure in place, PMO staff identified and hired, and a detailed implementation plan ready, the process of planning the initial introduction and training session for the PMO implementation team can now begin. A "kickoff" session serves several purposes:

- It allows the members of the implementation team to meet and conduct initial socialization and team building.
- It facilitates a uniform understanding of the PMO goals and objectives by providing an opportunity for the team to hear from key members of the PMO planning team and to understand the importance of the PMO to the organization.
- It provides an opportunity to review the PMO implementation plan and seek comments from the team regarding the plan's structure, time line, and intended goals. This feedback is invaluable and

serves as a validation that the plan is accurate and reasonable and that the resources that will be involved in executing the plan are aligned to the plan's goals and time line.

From a practical standpoint, several important considerations must be addressed as part of planning for the PMO implementation team kickoff meeting. The first key consideration is attendance. An attendance list should be developed by the session leader (who will be the PMO manager in most cases) as soon as is practically possible. All members of the PMO implementation team, including core PMO staff members as well as members from outside of the PMO staff that will be participating in the implementation, should be required session attendees. Even if the roles of some of these individuals are not full-time PMO implementation team roles, the information being presented is of sufficient criticality that it is important that everyone involved attend. In addition, the PMO sponsor or members of the PMO steering committee should be invited to attend. The kickoff provides an opportunity for the key managers who are overseeing the PMO implementation to provide management perspective on the PMO. Management attendance at the kickoff also demonstrates commitment from management to the success of the PMO. Because this session is designed to inform the project team and serve as a forum for finalizing implementation plans, it is not appropriate to include other managers or members of the project management community at large. The PMO marketing and communication plan will include activities that will allow the broader organization to be exposed to the PMO prior to start-up.

With an attendance list confirmed, the next consideration is the timing of the meeting. In order to set a firm date for the meeting, the expected duration must be estimated and an appropriate date set with sufficient lead time to allow attendees to make calendar adjustments as needed to ensure that they are available to attend. Ideally, a 1-day session should be planned. Planning for less than 1 day typically does not leave sufficient time in the schedule to encourage socialization among the participants and it may lead to a rush at the end of the agenda if one particular area requires significant attention. Conversely, planning for more than 1 day may lead to an agenda that is too broad and that dilutes focus on the primary goals of the kickoff. An exception to this general rule may be cases in which the kickoff meeting is intended to

include one or more working sessions on topics of interest to the PMO implementation team or if other training opportunities beyond the core areas of
focus for the agenda will be conducted. In this case, the core agenda for the
kickoff should still be constrained to 1 day if possible, with additional time
planned following the completion of the kickoff agenda to facilitate training,
breakout meetings, or other working sessions.

Finding a suitable date that exactly aligns with the schedules of a significant number of individuals is a nearly impossible task. The importance of
attendance at the kickoff meeting should be communicated by the PMO manager or designated session leader along with the selected date with appropriate follow-up from management to ensure attendance on the part of all
required parties. It is critical that a date be set early and communicated
broadly. Providing only 1 or 2 weeks of notice may create situations in which
calendars are already well booked and difficult to adjust. Setting a date should
be one of the key session planning priorities that the PMO manager addresses.
Alternatively, if possible, the date for the kickoff meeting can be included as
part of the start-up roadmap so that a placeholder is available even if all of the
details and required participants are not yet known. This is especially important in cases in which individuals may need to travel to a central location to
attend the session. Attendance in person by everyone involved in the effort
should be strongly encouraged. Although remote participation via video conference or audio conference may be possible as a last resort, remote participants will not have the opportunity to meet their fellow team members in
person and begin to develop working relationships. This is especially important for members of the PMO staff who will remain key contributors after the
implementation is complete. If one or more of the part-time resources from
constituencies beyond the core PMO staff must attend remotely, this is a much
lower risk than if a core member of the full-time PMO team is unable to
attend in person.

Finding a suitable date should be conducted in concert with finding a
suitable location. For most groups, a large conference room at one of the organization's facilities should be sufficient. If working sessions or other small
group activities are included in the agenda, one or two smaller "breakout"
rooms should be considered as well to accommodate these sessions. Access to

standard resources such as whiteboards, data projectors, and other similar meeting essentials must be ensured for any location under consideration. Clearly, the most preferable location is one that minimizes disruption of the normal routines of team members. An office location where a number of the team members already work or a nearby offsite location is ideal. Because the meeting will span an entire day and includes opportunities for informal conversation and discussion, access to catering facilities that can provide breakfast, lunch, and periodic refreshments during the day should be considered. As needed, access to corporate networks, phone service, and similar services should be verified as well. These practical logistics may seem trivial in nature, but comfort and convenience will go a long way toward ensuring that meeting participants remain active and positive participants in the session.

Once the location and date have been set, a formal agenda should be developed and provided to all meeting participants. The agenda should be tailored to the specific objectives of the session. All kickoff meetings will likely be somewhat different, but in general the following agenda provides a practical starting point for structuring the session:

GOTPMO CORPORATION—PMO IMPLEMENTATION KICKOFF MEETING AGENDA

1. Introductions
2. Agenda Review
3. Executive Perspective (optional)
4. PMO Overview
   a. Opportunities
   b. Roles and Responsibilities
   c. Initial Goals
5. Implementation Planning
   a. Expectations
   b. Time Line
6. PMO Marketing
7. Next Steps
8. Questions and Answers
9. Wrap-Up

Other agenda items beyond the areas presented here may be added as needed. The agenda may seem a bit sparse at first glance, but the intent of the agenda is not to attempt to fill an entire day. Rather, the agenda is designed to provide meaningful content for the participants while still allowing sufficient opportunity for discussion, extension to other relevant areas, etc.

The day should begin with an informal gathering, light breakfast, and sufficient time to allow for informal introductions and networking. The formal agenda begins with a call to order by the PMO manager (or other session leader if appropriate) and an opportunity for attendees to briefly introduce themselves and explain their roles in the PMO implementation effort. Other pertinent information such as the formal role within the organization for resources that are not assigned to the PMO staff, past project experience, any expectations or initial questions, and so forth may be included as appropriate. Once the introductions are complete, the session leader should review the agenda for the day to ensure that the agenda aligns with the expectations of the participants. If any major additional areas of discussion are requested by the attendees, they should be noted and worked into the agenda as time permits. If not determined in advance, a timekeeper and/or secretary should be appointed to create minutes of the meeting for distribution and archiving purposes and to ensure that the group uses the available time allotment efficiently so that the entire agenda can be adequately covered within the timeframe allotted.

An optional section (Executive Perspective) in the base agenda is provided to allow time for one or more members of the organization's management team to address the group and to provide perspective on the PMO effort. These individuals could include one or more members of the PMO steering committee (or the PMO sponsor) or some other organizational leader that was involved in planning for the PMO and approval of the PMO implementation effort. To the extent possible, an effort should be made to ensure that an appropriate resource is available to provide this perspective. Starting the meeting with a message from management regarding the importance of the PMO to the organization and demonstrating support for the PMO implementation team sets a positive tone for the meeting and can be used as a motivator to encourage a successful kickoff session. This portion of the agenda may also be used to allow the participants to address any initial questions to management if appropriate, but should be kept relatively brief (ideally to 30 minutes or less).

The next section of the agenda provides an opportunity to educate the participants on the PMO concept and intended role of the PMO. The participants will likely have some base understanding of the concept of the PMO by virtue of having been recruited to participate on the PMO implementation team. However, providing a baseline understanding of the intended role of the PMO in the organization and the goals of the PMO implementation helps to ensure alignment among the team and provides an opportunity for questions or concerns regarding the intended goals, roles and responsibilities, and opportunities to be addressed. The content for this overview section of the agenda can be drawn directly from the detailed business case (and summarized as appropriate for presentation) or portions of the management presentation of the detailed business case can be adapted for this purpose. The first portion of the presentation should focus on the opportunities that the PMO has to influence the organization. These opportunities may be framed in the context of current challenges facing the organization from a project management perspective or they may be presented as opportunities to evolve the practices that are in place currently without explicitly detailing the exact challenges that will be addressed. The discussion of the opportunities should be followed by a review of the PMO roles and responsibilities, with an understanding that the roles and responsibilities represent, to some extent, a desired end state at some point in the future rather than a broad group of areas in which the PMO will immediately attempt to focus. The subsequent review of the initial PMO goals will help to link the broad list of roles and responsibilities to the precise areas of focus in which the PMO will initially begin to operate and to create value for the organization.

Because the PMO roles and responsibilities and initial goals have already been reviewed and agreed to with management, the primary goal of this section of the agenda is educational in nature. Although feedback may certainly be solicited from the group, and feedback may help shape certain aspects of how the implementation and operation of the PMO are realized, this section is not designed to be an opportunity to validate these goals and roles and responsibilities with the group or to reshape the core intent of the PMO that was provided in the detailed business case and agreed to by management. Enough detail should be provided to allow members of the implementation team to understand how their specific implementation team roles help to advance the goals that have been set as well as to understand how their efforts help to build a successful foundation upon which the PMO can be built and sustained for long-term achievement of the complete scope of roles and responsibilities that will be undertaken. A complete presentation of the content contained in this portion of the agenda along with sufficient time for discussion and questions may occupy as much as 2 hours of the agenda.

The next, and possibly the most critical, topic on the agenda is PMO implementation planning. This section should include a complete review of the draft PMO implementation plan as well as discussion of the expectations of the team in terms of executing the plan. Unlike the previous section of the agenda, this topic is designed to be a working session in which feedback from the team is incorporated into the draft plan. Ideally, the plan will be provided to the team members in advance of the meeting for review and a copy made available via a data projector so that it can be reviewed and edited in real time. The discussion should start with a high-level overview of the plan in general, including the major deliverables, phases, or task groups and the overall time line for the implementation. Once the overview is complete, a section-by-section review of the major work items and associated tasks should be undertaken. In addition to validating the work requirements for each of these sections, a member of the team should be assigned responsibility (ownership) for the delivery of each major section or deliverable in the plan.

This review is the primary area in which the team will be able to influence and guide development of the final plan. The review also provides an opportunity to validate that no omissions in the plan have been made and that the time line associated with major work items and tasks appears reasonable. If the plan has been developed using sound project management practices and is reviewed in advance, only minor changes should be necessary, and these changes should not impact the overall schedule dramatically. If, however, major areas of work have been missed or if the time frames associated with certain portions of the plan are found to be unreasonable, having the entire implementation team together provides an excellent opportunity to brainstorm possible options for resolving the omissions or constraints and to come to agreement on a resolution that does not cause excessive risk to the overall success of the effort while still striving to meet the implementation time frame objectives.

The PMO marketing section addresses one of the key initial deliverables for the PMO implementation effort—developing a marketing and communication plan to introduce the PMO to the organization. (A detailed discussion of the marketing and communication plan will be provided in the next section.) For the purposes of the kickoff meeting agenda, the goal is brainstorming to gather potential ideas for presenting the PMO concept to the organization and introducing the PMO at start-up. Related to the PMO, different groups within the organization will potentially have different information needs. Identifying the key groups that will be affected by the PMO (directly or indirectly) as well as identifying those additional groups that will need some knowledge of the existence of the PMO, but who will not regularly interact with the PMO directly, is an important part of this exercise. Creating a detailed marketing and communication plan will be one of the objectives of the implementation. Therefore, developing the plan in detail as part of the agenda for the first meeting of the implementation team is not necessary. However, the importance of marketing the PMO to the organization is significant enough to justify devoting a portion of the agenda to some initial discussion regarding potential marketing opportunities and techniques.

The remaining sections of the agenda provide opportunities to review the next steps in the implementation process and to address any questions from the team. Establishing a clear set of next steps and assigning ownership for each will help ensure that every team member understands his or her immediate focus areas. Taking time to address remaining questions ensures that team members do not leave with unanswered questions or ambiguity regarding what will be delivered and what is expected of them. If concerns regarding the plan are raised as part of this review, a discussion of these concerns may be required. Appropriate mitigation efforts may need to be established so that any concerns are addressed by the team. Ideally, communication with the team throughout the process will ensure that any concerns are addressed during the development of the plan as well.

With the kickoff meeting complete, the team should turn its attention to delivering the agreed-to plan. The final plan, along with minutes of the meeting and any other relevant documents presented or created at the meeting, should be forwarded to all team members at the earliest possible time and regular status checks or team meetings should be scheduled so that progress can be monitored, issues addressed, and continuous communication encouraged.

Additional Training Requirements for the PMO Staff

Beyond the kickoff meeting itself and initial training on the PMO concept and implementation, additional training activities should be provided for the PMO staff (and additional members of the implementation team as appropriate) to help ensure that these individuals are well equipped to effectively undertake the PMO's work once the implementation is complete. Topics for these trainings might include advanced project management skills, portfolio management, negotiating, or other relevant areas based on the scope and responsibilities of the PMO. Ideally, an individual training plan should be created for each member of the PMO staff. The plan should addresses topics of common interest to all members of the PMO staff as well as individual additional courses as needed based on each individual's role in the PMO. Including time in the PMO implementation plan for training and development of the PMO staff will be of great benefit in the long run because it will better prepare the staff to be effective team members.

The sources of training for the PMO staff might include seminars or conferences on project management and PMO topics, internal training on PMO operations and specifics related to the PMO conducted by the PMO manager, training on general topics of business interest provided by the organization's training department or Web-based training on relevant project management, PMO, or general business topics that can be completed on-demand. It may be helpful to produce a list of available internal training opportunities that are provided by the organization (and which, conceivably, could have a lower cost than externally provided training) as a starting point for identifying appropriate training opportunities and then to determine the gaps that exist between what is available and the needs of the PMO staff. Most likely, training on topics related to managing a PMO, portfolio management, and related topics that address PMO topics directly will not be generally available and may have to be outsourced to training providers who have expertise in PMO implementation and management. For more general project management topics, extensive resources are available (books, articles, case studies, and training courses). Reasonably priced Web-based delivery is widely available for many advanced project management topics. The PMO training manager or some other designated resource responsible for PMO staff training should evaluate these options as well as live training opportunities and investigate qualified providers to understand how their offerings align with the training needs of the PMO staff.

Another excellent resource for project management training and related topics is the PMO staff itself as well as other internal project managers. Project managers who have had experience in leading large, complex projects may have extensive knowledge and "in the trenches" experience that can be leveraged to create very meaningful training opportunities. Every training opportunity does not have to be a formal, multi-day class complete with a slide deck and formal agenda. Smaller opportunities such as knowledge-sharing sessions, lessons-learned discussions, and reviews of past successful projects can provide excellent opportunities for members of the PMO staff to learn from their peers in the PMO and from other experienced project managers. Also provided are opportunities for the PMO staff to better understand how project work is being done and to gain insight into the factors that lead to success in managing projects.

The appropriate mix of training opportunities that should be planned during the PMO implementation phase will be determined by the existing skills of the PMO staff, the scope and roles and responsibilities that the PMO will undertake, the availability of training offerings, and the time constraints placed on the PMO implementation. Training opportunities will vary from organization to organization. However, general guidance in this area, that is applicable to all organizations, is to ensure that time is allocated in the implementation schedule to facilitate training for the PMO staff; that training plans are developed that consider the needs of each member of the staff; and that a variety of learning opportunities are made available. Even items as simple as creating a small library of project management- and PMO-relevant texts or subscribing to one or more journals of general interest in the field of project management, and making these journals available to the PMO staff, can provide opportunities for learning that do not require major commitments of funds or time. Professional development and growth for the PMO staff will increase the effectiveness of the PMO in the long run and may also lead to increased employee job satisfaction.

A Note about Certification

In addition to training for the PMO staff, the availability today of multiple project management certifications in the project management realm provides additional professional development opportunities for the PMO staff. A staff of certified project managers may provide additional credibility to the PMO in terms of expertise in the skills and practice of project management. Although the investment required to obtain certification can be substantial in terms of effort (often requiring a specific number of hours of formal training as well as experience in managing projects) and cost, the benefits to the organization and the individual can be significant. Part of the development of a training plan for the PMO staff might include discussion of available certification options and individual interest in obtaining certification. Requiring certification within a certain time frame is not preferable. Those who do not have an inherent desire to obtain certification (for professional or personal reasons) may resent a mandated requirement. Yet, the PMO and the organization would be well served to encourage those with an interest to pursue certification and to provide assistance when possible to help individuals achieve project management relevant certification. Assistance might come in the form of monetary assistance to pay for training materials and testing fees or in terms of flexibility in scheduling to allow individuals to study as part of their on-the-job training and development plans.

Among the most widely known of the project management certifications available is the Project Management Professional (PMP®*), developed and delivered by the Project Management Institute. PMP® is widely regarded as a certification of distinction and requires a significant commitment of time and

---

* "PMP" and the PMP logo are certification marks of the Project Management Institute which are registered in the United States and other nations.

energy to study for and to successfully pass the required examination, in addition to additional requirements in terms of education and past project management experience. Certifications such as PMP® provide professional development for the PMO staff as well as recognition of achievement of advanced skill and knowledge in the practice of project management within and beyond the organization itself.

DEVELOPING A PMO MARKETING AND COMMUNICATION PLAN

Because the PMO will likely influence many areas of the organization (either internally or externally depending on scope), it is important to develop a plan to introduce the PMO to the organization so that members of the organization will understand what role the PMO will play and how they will interact with the PMO and to determine how the PMO will sustain marketing and communication to the organization over time. The mission of marketing the PMO is in many respects an undertaking that primarily involves communication. This activity could be considered by developing a communication plan alone. However, although marketing concepts include communication in some form or fashion, they also include the idea of creating specific communications or messages that do more than just present information. Some level of building excitement about the PMO, branding the PMO, and *selling* the PMO to the organization is important in addition to merely providing information.

A marketing and communication plan has several goals. One is to *inform* the organization that the PMO is being implemented. The inform activities will occur during the implementation itself, so it is appropriate that a marketing and communication plan be developed as part of implementation planning. The activities associated with informing the organization primarily seek to raise awareness so that members of the organization understand what work is being undertaken as well as the time line for PMO implementation. A second purpose is to *educate* the organization about the goals, roles and responsibilities, and activities of the PMO. The educate activities will occur as part of PMO start-up. The purpose of these activities is to expand upon the messages that were communicated as part of informing the organization about the

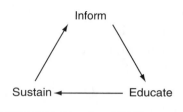

Figure 4.2 PMO marketing cycle.

PMO and to educate members of different areas in the organization about how the PMO will affect them and the expected areas of focus in which the PMO will provide value and/or help them to function more effectively. The educating function is more focused on targeted messages to different groups whereas the informing function is primarily focused on broad messages at a high level that can be distributed to a wide audience. A third purpose of a marketing and communication plan is to *sustain* communication within the organization. The sustain activities will occur and evolve over the life of the PMO. Ongoing marketing of the PMO to the organization and communication from the PMO to the organization should be planned from an operational standpoint. It is also appropriate to include the sustain activity in the marketing and communication plan at the implementation planning phase because planning for ongoing communication is critical for ensuring that the communication occurs.

The activities undertaken as part of the PMO marketing and communication plan are not discrete activities that occur on a one-time basis. PMO marketing should be viewed as an ongoing aspect of PMO operation, and its activities should be viewed as cyclic in nature. Figure 4.2 provides a view of a PMO marketing cycle.

The entry point into the cycle will be the initial activities undertaken to *inform* the organization about the PMO. As these activities are completed, the marketing should transition to the *educate* phase, expanding on the messages provided in the previous phase and targeting these messages to appropriate audiences. The cycle then transitions to the *sustain* phase, which provides ongoing communication regarding the areas that the organization has been informed and educated about already. Finally, the cycle transitions back to the *inform* stage, in which the next set of marketing communications (perhaps as part of a new phase of PMO deployment or completion of a critical area of focus) are prepared and presented to the organization. Over time, the focus and distribution of communications may change as the PMO refines its focus. The intent of a marketing and communication plan is to create a flexible framework that meets the needs of the organization and that can evolve over time as the PMO's constituents change. A number of different versions of the marketing and communication plan will likely be created over the life of the PMO. For the purposes of a PMO implementation, the marketing and communication plan should address the first cycle of informing, educating, and sustaining communication regarding the PMO start-up and its initial set of undertakings.

Developing the PMO marketing and communication plan will involve four primary steps:

- **Step 1:** Identifying the audiences or areas of the organization (and potentially other areas outside of the organization) that will receive communications regarding the PMO
- **Step 2:** Identifying the key communications deliverables that will be created and determining the form and method of delivery for each
- **Step 3:** Developing the PMO marketing and communication plan itself
- **Step 4:** Determining how the effectiveness of the communications will be measured and developing a method of improving communications over time to better meet the needs of those receiving the communications

Step 1: Identifying Audiences

The first step in developing the marketing and communication plan involves identifying the potential audiences that exist in the organization (and outside the organization as well if the PMO will affect external customers or partners) and documenting the information needs of these audiences. Not all groups require the same level of communication. Therefore, it is important to distinguish between areas of the organization that primarily need to be informed about the formation of the PMO and activities related to the PMO over time versus those areas of the organization that will require targeted, educational messages. Because the goal of informational messages is to provide a broad view of the PMO and its activities at a high level, informational messages are appropriate for a broad range of groups within the organization, understanding that some of these groups will not interact with the PMO directly. The PMO's direct customers and other groups in which the PMO will have influence or frequent interaction will require additional educational communications in addition to the informational communications. Additionally, some level of sustained communication will be required for all groups. This sustained communication may be in form of newsletters, website updates, or electronic mail communications that are meant for broad consumption by the organization. Some form of sustaining communication is relevant for all audiences and should be planned.

Identifying intended audiences is most easily accomplished through brainstorming with the project team. Primary audiences such as project managers will be included and will require regular informational and educational communication. However, it is important to look beyond the immediate customers and users of the PMO and to consider other groups that may need to be kept informed regarding PMO activities. For example, the organization's training department may be interested in the activities of the PMO from a training and development standpoint. Therefore, occasional informational communications such as PMO training schedules or updates on PMO professional development opportunities may be appropriate. As potential audiences are identified and their information needs are considered, a document should be created to summarize the audiences and required communications that are identified. A format such as Table 4.2 may be helpful.

Table 4.2 includes a column to identify the intended audience as well as additional columns to specify the communication type (informational or educational) that will be relevant for the audience. A third column is added to document any special considerations in terms of the types of communication that will be provided, the frequency, or the method of communication. Some informational communications will be intended for all audiences, but there may be additional specific communications (such as publication of the PMO

Table 4.2   Intended Audiences and Required Communication

GOTPMO Corporation
PMO Marketing Plan—Intended Audiences

Audience	Communication Type	Special Considerations
Project managers	Inform, educate	Frequent communication required
Division line management	Inform	
Finance Department	Inform, educate	Educate regarding any potential impacts to how project financial data is reported only
Human Resources Department	Inform	
PMO Steering Committee	Inform	Inform via monthly Steering Committee meetings
Training Department	Inform	PMO training calendar

training schedule) that will be of interest to only certain audiences. Determining the specific communications that will be produced as well as their frequency and format will be discussed in *Step 2*.

Step 2: Identifying Marketing Deliverables

Identifying intended audiences for communication in *Step 1* likely caused some amount of thought regarding the specific communications that these audiences should receive. Putting audience identification first was, in part, intended to do just that. With the audiences identified, the next step is to consider the types of communications that will be included in the marketing and communication plan. Likely, it is easiest to consider these communications separately in terms of informational communications, educational communications, and sustaining communications because each have different goals. Even within these categories, it is important to distinguish between specific communications that will be provided during implementation and start-up activities as well as those types of communications that will continue over the life of the PMO. In sum, the entire set of deliverables represents the communications package that the PMO team will build to introduce the PMO to the organization, to market the PMO, and to ensure continued communication to the organization over time. A list of deliverables should be brainstormed and documented by the implementation team. This list will serve as a key input to developing the marketing and communication plan.

As an example of a possible format for documenting marketing deliverables, an overview of possible marketing deliverables for informational communications will now be provided. Initially, these informational communications will serve to introduce the concept of the PMO and raise awareness regarding the PMO implementation. Once the PMO is in place, these communications will provide a vehicle for communicating new PMO undertakings and other items of interest. Some examples of communications in the informational category include:

- Implementation and start-up
  - Introductory communication from management announcing the formation of the PMO and the appointment of a PMO manager
  - Introductory letter from the PMO manager highlighting the major goals of the PMO and an anticipated start-up date
  - Monthly update newsletters or electronic mail communications describing implementation progress and introducing the PMO team
  - Establishment of a PMO website to provide information on-demand to members of the organization regarding the PMO
  - PMO "town hall" meetings to answer questions regarding the PMO and its activities
  - "Giveaway" announcing the start-up of the PMO and directing audiences to the PMO website at start-up

- Ongoing (post start-up)
  - Announcements regarding new PMO areas of focus, completion of deliverables, or revised work processes and standards
  - PMO town hall meetings to answer questions regarding the PMO and its activities

Numerous other activities could be included as well. For the purposes of this exercise, the goal is to examine the audiences that have been identified and to consider the types of informational communications that are relevant to them. At this stage, it is not necessary to define the specific form of communication, frequency, or method of delivery for each because this detail will be included when the marketing and communication plan is assembled. The format presented for informational communications or some other similar format agreed to by the implementation team should be repeated for educational and sustaining activities as well. The following are examples for each of these areas:

For educational communications:

- Implementation and start-up
  - Presentation describing the PMO concept, goals, roles and responsibilities, and specific intended benefits to the organization
  - Sample case studies describing PMO successes in other organizations placed on the PMO website
- Ongoing (post start-up)
  - PMO "users guide" describing how to engage the PMO
  - Publication of and training on processes, tool, templates, or other deliverables that the project management community will be expected to use

For sustaining communications post start-up:

- Implementation and start-up
  - Expectation setting regarding ongoing communication from the PMO
- Ongoing (post start-up)
  - PMO newsletter highlighting PMO activities and upcoming deliverables and events
  - Publication of the PMO training calendar

Many other possible deliverables could be included as well. The implementation team should use its expert judgment to define an appropriate list that meets the needs of the organization. In a smaller organization or in a larger organization in which only one group or division of the organization is impacted by the PMO, more frequent informal communications at team meetings and other similar venues may take the place of more formal communications such as newsletters and town hall meetings. For a PMO of a larger size or scope, formal communications such as newsletters or websites are often more appropriate because they provide an easy means to distribute information broadly. Some form of live communication such as a town hall meeting or PMO start-up event will likely still be necessary from time to time, but for more frequent communications, a method that provides ease of distribution to a large audience is preferable.

Upon first review, distinguishing between the intent of informational communications that are provided post start-up and sustaining communications may be difficult. Essentially, the intent of informational communications is to provide, as needed or on-demand, communication regarding certain items of special interest (such as new tools, templates, etc.). Because these communications are only provided on an as-needed basis, audiences receiving these communications may pay special attention to them because they are not part of regular communications that the audiences expect to receive. The intent of sustaining communications is to provide updates in a standard format that audiences will expect to see on some type of regular basis (such as a monthly newsletter). This helps to ensure consistent communication and keeps the organization informed on a regular basis regarding items of general interest.

Step 3: Developing the Plan

Once all of the potential marketing and communication deliverables have been identified, the next step is to combine the list of intended audiences and their communications needs with the types of marketing and communications deliverables identified in *Step 2* and to add specific formats, frequencies, and distribution mechanisms to form a complete marketing and communication plan. The focus of this exercise should be on those specific items that will be needed as part of the implementation and start-up to inform and educate the organization. It is also appropriate at this stage to develop an ongoing plan so that an understanding of the types of communications that will be required once the PMO is in place is documented and so that plans can be created as part of the implementation to address these ongoing communications needs.

The component that will be developed in *Step 3* that has not yet been considered is the administrative aspect of the plan in terms of how the plan will be executed. Items requiring consideration include:

- Who will be responsible for developing each of the deliverables in the plan?
- What form of communication will be used?
- How frequently will each deliverable be distributed?

In terms of *who* will develop each of the deliverables, the responsibility should be assigned to one or more members of the PMO implementation team for implementation and start-up communications and one or more members of the PMO staff for ongoing communications. Specific roles should be identified to clearly define the team member who has responsibility for each of the deliverables.

The *form* of communication defines the specific type of communication that will be used for each deliverable. The types of communication used might include printed newsletters, live meetings, training sessions, electronic mail, websites, or other appropriate communication vehicles. In some cases, more than one form of communication may be appropriate. Very likely a number of different forms of communication will be required based on the types of deliverables being considered. Documenting the intended format for each type of communication helps to ensure that there is a balance between the various forms of communication when the plan is considered as a whole. For example, always communicating via electronic mail may lead to certain members of the intended audiences eventually ignoring communications if electronic mail messages from the PMO occur too frequently. Conducting numerous live meetings may create an excessive time commitment for some members of the organization. Striking a balance ensures that audience members remain engaged and receptive to PMO communications.

The *frequency* of communication is closely related to the form in terms of ensuring balance. For each communication deliverable that represents a regular, routine communication, a particular frequency should be designated. For

Table 4.3   Marketing and Communication Plan

GOTPMO Corporation
PMO Marketing and Communication Plan

Deliverable	Audience	Form	Frequency	Responsibility
Introduction of PMO staff and PMO Manager	All (inform)	Electronic mail	One time	PMO Sponsor
One-page summary of PMO goals, roles, and responsibilities	Project managers (inform) Division management (inform)	Electronic mail with attachment	One time	PMO Manager
PMO website	All (inform/educate)	Website updates	Monthly	PMO staff
Town hall forum	All (educate)	Live meeting	Monthly	PMO Manager
Giveaway pens with PMO logo and website address	All (inform)	Giveaway at PMO start-up	One time	PMO staff

recurring communications, the frequency of communication must be regular enough to provide information in a timely fashion, but infrequent enough that the potential for audience members ignoring communication from the PMO over time is minimized. For nonroutine communications, indicating "as needed" is entirely appropriate and leaves the decision as to when to communicate with the specific individual responsible for the communication.

Having a base understanding of the three components presented in this step (who, what form, how frequently) and having complete lists of intended audiences and desired deliverables in hand, the marketing and communication plan can now be constructed. A table format such as the example presented in Table 4.3 is preferable, but any other reasonable format may be used. Regardless of format, the key is to link the marketing and communication deliverables to the intended audiences and to indicate the intended frequency and form of communication.

For the purposes of this example table, only the relevant marketing and communication deliverables contemplated as part of the PMO implementation and start-up are provided. An additional section of the table or other indicator within the table itself could be used to document the ongoing marketing and communication deliverables that will be produced as part of ongoing PMO operations. The initial intent of the marketing and communication plan is to provide an internal document that the implementation team can use to ensure consistent communication to the organization regarding the PMO and to ensure that the appropriate messages are reaching the intended audiences.

Once the specific set of marketing and communication deliverables are identified, a time line can be developed to specify when certain one-time deliverables will be produced and distributed and to map the recurring deliverables to a specific schedule that aligns with the implementation plan. This detail will ideally be included as part of the implementation project plan and will include the required due dates for each of the deliverables as well as the associated tasks that are required in order to achieve the deliverable. For example, if the PMO staff wishes to have giveaway items such as pens or notepads available to distribute on the PMO start-up date, these items must be ordered with sufficient lead time to allow them to be available onsite on the start-up date. Additionally, marketing materials such as newsletters, websites, and other communications vehicles may require lead time and potentially vendor involvement, which must be coordinated and managed within the context of the broader implementation project plan. Depending on the number and type of deliverables being contemplated, it may be appropriate to assign one member of the PMO implementation team to the role of marketing and communication coordinator. Although this individual may or may not have responsibility for producing some or all of the marketing and communication deliverables, having a single point of contact to coordinate the efforts can help ensure that appropriate focus is being placed on these critical activities.

Step 4: Execute, Measure, and Improve

With a plan developed and the time line integrated into the PMO implementation plan, the work of executing the marketing and communication plan can begin. The first few communications to the organization will be the most critical because these communications will set the tone for how PMO communications will be received by the organization. If initial communications are well thought out and professionally presented, the likelihood of the intended audience members paying attention to future communications increases dramatically. Deliverables that are rushed, not well prepared, or that do not provide value to their intended recipients will likely lead readers to the conclusion that the PMO is not particularly organized and that communications from the PMO do not provide much value. In some organizations, marketing and communication professionals from either external organizations or internal marketing or communication divisions can be used to assist with the preparation of initial marketing and communication deliverables in order to help ensure quality and effectiveness. However, this is by no means a requirement. Modern word processing, webpage design, and presentation software can create professional-looking deliverables without the need for professional involvement. The content is the key. If the content is well thought out, edited, and prepared with the goals of the material being created in mind, the likelihood of producing an effective deliverable increases significantly.

A critical portion of this final step in the marketing process is determining the effectiveness of the plan and improving the process to better meet the needs of the audiences that the marketing and communication plan serves. Initially, there may be many questions about the PMO, its goals, and how various individuals and groups within the organization will be affected by the PMO. Often it is appropriate to err on the side of overcommunicating initially. In time, the level of communication may decrease as the members of the organization learn more about how they will be affected by the PMO. Gathering feedback on the quality, timeliness, and form of communication is necessary for several reasons. Early feedback helps to ensure that future communications better meet the needs of the intended audiences. Often, gathering feedback also leads to identifying additional unmet communication needs that can be addressed through either additional communication or revisions to the marketing and communication plan. Additionally, gathering feedback will help to gauge initial perceptions of the PMO, allowing the PMO implementation team to tailor future marketing to resolve any potential misconceptions and to ensure that future marketing is appropriately focused.

As a principle, continuous improvement underlies not only marketing and communication, but also the operation of the PMO in general. Striving to improve the value of marketing and communication should be given an appropriate level of attention. As the marketing and communication plan is revised and evolved during the PMO implementation, appropriate adjustments should also be made to the plans for ongoing sustained communication with the organization once the start-up is complete. This is best achieved through gathering regular feedback from members of the organization and incorporating this feedback into revised plans and strategies for communicating with the organization. For initial communication during the implementation, the primary messages relate to what the PMO will accomplish, how the PMO will go about its work, and so forth. Once the PMO is in place, the communications focus will turn to tasks such as distributing useful information to project managers to help them do their jobs better, distributing standards that project managers will be expected to follow, advertising training and development opportunities, and other similar types of operational communications. Understanding the communication expectations of members of the organization by gathering feedback on the quality of communications and developing plans to improve these communications as part of the implementation will help to ensure that future operational communications meet the needs of the organization and that members of the organization continue to pay appropriate attention to communications from the PMO.

TRANSFORMING GOALS INTO STRATEGIES

As implementation planning activities begin to come to a conclusion, the team will start to turn its attention toward execution of the implementation plan and toward work to ensure a timely implementation. This is a good time to consider the first few key areas of focus that the PMO will address once implementation is complete and the PMO commences operations. Although planning for the activities that the PMO will undertake once it is in operation is not an implementation planning activity per se, an important part of the PMO planning process is validating that plans exist to achieve the initial goals set for the PMO. These initial goals are stated in the detailed business case along with a time line for achievement. These goals provide the base expectations as to what will be achieved and the time line specifies the target date for when the goals will be achieved, but the level of elaboration provided in the detailed business case is generally not sufficient to provide a detailed plan for how each goal should be approached. Developing a more detailed plan of action and a work breakdown structure is a prerequisite for beginning to work toward achievement of these goals. Some of this work has been completed as part developing the detailed implementation plan. This work should be referenced as appropriate.

In general, the work to develop a detailed work breakdown structure for each of the initial PMO goals should be assigned to the member or members of the PMO staff who will have primary responsibility for each goal. This work may commence only after start-up if there are already significant amounts of implementation work to be completed that require the attention of the staff members who will be responsible for developing and executing these detailed work plans. However, there is a middle ground between the goal and the detailed work plan that must be achieved. The implementation planning and execution phase is an ideal time to begin this work. Because of the relatively broad nature of the goals, developing one or more detailed strategies for how each particular goal will be achieved is advisable. The primary difference between the goals and strategies is simply that goals define *what* should be achieved and strategies define, at a high level, *how* the achievement of these goals will take place. Strategies play an important role in defining the key overriding themes or guiding methodologies that will lead to the achievement of the stated goals. Strategies also provide a foundation upon which detailed plans can be built, defining high-level methods that can be expanded later to specific work plans.

Taking the time to develop these strategies as part of the implementation process has several advantages. First, it ensures that due consideration is given to the importance of thinking about not only the implementation, but also the role of the PMO in the organization in the first few months of its existence. Developing strategies for achieving the first few critical goals helps the PMO implementation team keep in mind how the implementation activities will support being able to achieve these goals once the PMO is operational. Next, developing these strategies ensures that an additional level of detail beyond the established goals exists so that, as time permits, members of the PMO staff and the extended implementation team can work to develop the more detailed work plans that will guide the work that will achieve these goals. Additionally, utilizing the collective knowledge and experience of the PMO implementation team helps to provide important perspective so that the best possible plan is developed. Although this feedback could be gathered at any time, including it as part of the planning process aligns well with the goal of using the implementation planning process to lay the groundwork for PMO success.

The process of developing the strategies for each of the initial PMO goals is straightforward and is best achieved by using the collective knowledge and experience of the PMO implementation team and any other available relevant project management subject matter experts. A brainstorming session or similar opportunity to propose and discuss potential strategies is a viable forum for performing this work because it encourages thoughtful dialog and debate so that the best possible set of strategies is developed for each of the defined goals. Due to time, resource, or other constraints, it may not be possible to effectively execute all of the strategies proposed. Therefore, a balance must be struck between what is possible and what is achievable when considering the strategies in light of any relevant constraints. The goal is to decide on a reasonable set of strategies that can be implemented to help ensure achievement of each of the goals and, in doing so, to equip the members of the PMO staff who will be responsible for achievement of each goal with some useful approaches that can be used to achieve the goals. They can, in turn, develop a more detailed tactical plan and time line for implementing the strategies.

Each of the initial PMO goals and associated measures that were defined in the detailed business case should be considered individually and discussed in terms of a specific set of actions that can be used to realize the goal. A combination of the goal and its associated measures can be used to perform this exercise by considering what specific strategic undertakings can be used to ensure that the measures specified are achieved. The documentation of these strategies can remain at a high level, and a format similar to the goals and measures table produced in Chapter 3 (see Table 3.3) may be used by simply

Table 4.4   Initial Goals, Strategies, and Measures

GOTPMO Corporation
PMO Initial Goals, Strategies, and Measures—Ninety-Day Plan

Goal	Strategies	Measure(s)
Create and align with business units a standard template for reviewing project proposals and chartering projects.	• Perform analysis of current processes in Information Technology, Sales, and Business Development units to identify data needs. • Leverage the existing project initiation template from Business Development unit as a starting point to minimize rework.	• Standard project charter template created • Alignment and sign-off from Information Technology, Sales, and Business Development units obtained
Define a standard project training roadmap for training and developing new project managers during their first twelve months in a project management role.	• Identify and document key skills required of new project managers to ensure appropriate scope. • Survey major certification providers to determine education requirements that must be met prior to applying for certification to ensure training roadmap provides relevant experiences for project managers seeing certification.	• Project management training roadmap developed and delivered to Corporate Training Division

expanding the table to include a list of the specific strategies agreed to by the team. Table 4.4 provides an example of this format.

If a significant number of relevant strategies are identified or if further documentation of the strategies agreed to with the team is required, a paragraph-form document for each goal may also be used. Once complete, this document should be reviewed with the PMO manager prior to commencing detailed planning. As appropriate, these strategies may be reviewed with the PMO sponsor or steering committee as well to verify alignment with management needs and expectations. The document, once reviewed and finalized, serves as a foundational document to guide further development of the appropriate work plans to deliver the initial PMO goals, but it should not be viewed as a limiting mandate that requires the PMO staff to work within the developed strategies exclusively. As implementation progresses, as more is learned about the needs of the organization, and as the PMO staff gain additional knowledge and experience by working in the PMO environment, new potential strategies may emerge. These new strategies should be discussed among the team, and, as appropriate, the goals, strategies, and measures document should be updated to reflect additional developed strategies that may be helpful in achieving the goals stated in the document.

Once the document is agreed to with management, a good practice is to baseline the current level of performance in the organization in the areas that will be targeted for initial improvement. Depending on the specific goal, it may be possible to gather data that would suggest a current average level of performance in the organization. For example, in a PMO scenario in which one of the initial PMO goals is to develop additional project management controls to help control project costs, cost performance data for a variety of projects undertaken in the organization could be gathered and analyzed to determine the average level of project cost overrun. This data can be used as a baseline for determining improvement as the PMO implements its intended strategies to achieve the goal of increasing cost performance. For areas in which data is not immediately available, surveys or techniques to gather qualitative data may be required in order to capture an appropriate baseline. If, for example, one of the initial PMO goals is to improve the project chartering process, a review of current impressions of how projects are approved or a survey of the percentage of the organization that follows a formal process to charter projects could be conducted to create a general baseline for current performance. As plans to improve the chartering process are implemented, additional data can be obtained on the perceptions of the revised process as a means of measuring improvement. From an initial goal standpoint, some of this data gathering work has already been completed as part of the assessment process. Reviewing the assessment outcomes may provide valuable data that can be used in the development of appropriate baseline data.

The importance of gathering this baseline data may not be apparent from an implementation perspective, but it is critical as part of the planning for measuring the PMO's performance once operation commences. In order to assist in providing a viable value proposition for the PMO, certain improvement expectations have been set with management. Once the PMO is in operation, gathering baseline data on the current level of performance in these key areas will assist with demonstrating to management that the value that was promised is being delivered. Additionally, having baseline data assists the PMO staff with understanding the areas of greatest need as well as with estimating the level of performance improvement that may be possible.

EXECUTING THE PLAN

Now that implementation planning is complete, the implementation work can begin. Before commencing work, it is advisable to validate management alignment with the final plan. This may require a formal presentation to management. Alternatively, a document that provides a summary of the implementation plan, any assumptions, constraints, or risks that were identified as part of the planning and any changes in scope that resulted from detailed planning may be presented to the PMO steering committee or the PMO sponsor. Preparing the documentation to validate management alignment with the final plan provides a good opportunity to review the entire plan to ensure alignment and to confirm that the items contained in the plan meet the needs of management. If a proper level of planning has been undertaken, this review should be fairly straightforward and should result in few questions from management.

From the PMO manager's perspective, commencing work also means commencing measurement of progress versus the agreed-to plan. Tracking project progress, identifying tasks that are off-track, and using other relevant cost and schedule management techniques should be undertaken as needed to ensure conformance with the plan and to ensure a successful start-up. (Chapter 5 will address several considerations related to executing the implementation plan as well as provide guidance on formal PMO start-up and operation of the PMO in its first few months of existence.)

SUMMARY

The PMO implementation planning process lays the foundation for long-term PMO success. Effective PMO implementation begins with assembling a strong team to coordinate the planning and implementation activities and concludes with an effective implementation plan that can be executed within a reasonable time frame and is aligned with management's expectations. By taking adequate time to consider factors such as those addressed in this chapter, additional factors identified by the PMO team, and the guidance provided by management and then developing a detailed plan for the initial PMO deployment, the PMO team will demonstrate its commitment to following project management practices and also demonstrate a high level of professionalism and commitment to making the PMO a success.

5

START-UP AND OPERATIONS

INTRODUCTION

With implementation planning already complete, activities associated with implementation and start-up can commence. The first few months of PMO operation are critical from the standpoint of ensuring that the PMO starts its operation on solid footing as well as from the standpoint of building a foundation for success in the long run. In Chapter 5, several important components of a successful implementation will be discussed, followed by a series of suggestions for ensuring a successful start-up. In addition, a section will be devoted the initial operation of the PMO that provides guidance on ensuring that the first few key months of operation are successful. Also included in this section will be guidance on planning for the next phase of PMO operations once the initial PMO goals are achieved as well as a review of practical techniques for measuring value created by the PMO.

PMO IMPLEMENTATION SUCCESS FACTORS

With a firm plan in hand, resources aligned, and the necessary due diligence performed to help ensure success, implementation of a PMO in many respects should follow standard project methodology. Resources should complete work according to the implementation plan, management should be kept informed regarding progress and issues, and the implementation leader should ensure conformance to the plan and lead and direct the resources performing the work. The factor that differentiates projects in general and the specific task of implementation of a PMO is that most projects do not involve, in and of themselves, planning for the evolution of project management practices. A PMO, on the other hand, is often tasked with leading and directing cultural or process changes in the practice of project management within the organization. As a result, the implementation activities should achieve the base goals of ensuring a successful start-up while also considering the impact of the implementation activities on the broader objective of creating meaningful change and evolution in the practice of project management in the organization.

A few key factors related to PMO implementation will specifically help to ensure a successful start-up and to set the foundation for success over time. For the purposes of this section, the following success factors will be discussed:

- Lead by example
- Know your mission and your market
- Dress to impress

Lead by Example

The first success factor may seem obvious. The idea of leading by example refers to ensuring that the PMO implementation project demonstrates project management best practices and is completed within the scope, time, and cost constraints agreed to with management. Whether explicitly or implicitly, it can be ensured that members of the organization who have heard about the PMO and who will be affected by the PMO (even if not initially) are watching the PMO implementation effort with great interest. Depending on the scope of deliverables within the marketing and communication plan, members of the organization may have already received direct communication regarding the PMO and its goals and intended scope of operations. Conversely, word-of-mouth may have made members of the organization aware that the efforts to implement the PMO are taking place. Word will undoubtedly get around that the PMO is coming so it is important that any questions regarding the PMO and its activities be addressed honestly and that the members of the PMO implementation team represent the PMO positively. It is also critical that the PMO implementation team conduct itself in a manner that is consistent with sound project management practices. A PMO implementation in which members of the implementation team appear disorganized or, perhaps worse, in which the PMO implementation team consistently misses targets or fails to communicate its needs in a timely manner to other parties who are critical to the success of the PMO will cause members within the organization to call into question what value the PMO can hope to provide when the implementation itself does not appear to be proceeding in a manner consistent with good project management.

It is unreasonable to expect that the PMO implementation will proceed without any difficulties. The key to success in leading by example is to proactively identify areas in which potential issues might arise in advance (via sound risk identification and assessment) and to plan, to the extent possible, viable mitigation strategies as well as sound response strategies in the event that one or more of the identified risks are realized. Along the way, as deviations from the plan occur and corrections are made to ensure that the implementation remains on schedule, part of the process of leading by example will be ensuring that the team remains focused on success and that appropriate opportunities are taken to understand why deviations from the plan occurred, to document those deviations and the reasons for their occurrence, and to develop strategies to ensure that future projects do not encounter the same issues (whether further stages of deployment of the PMO or other projects in the organization). This exercise may result in the creation of lessons-learned documents, new or revised project templates and standards, or additional training for project resources.

Know Your Mission and Your Market

Another success factor is to understand the mission of the PMO and know its market. An understanding of the PMO mission by everyone involved in the implementation and regular review of the progress of the implementation, in the context of the PMO mission, help to validate that the end result, the operational PMO, remains aligned with its intended mission. As the PMO implementation progresses, there may be a temptation to address additional areas of need. This is especially true when the implementation is going well. The project team may view success in the implementation process as an opportunity to seek other areas of focus or to accelerate development and implementation of certain additional work beyond the initial PMO scope and goals.

Although these additional areas of focus may in fact be part of the overall PMO strategy for the long term, the mission of the implementation is to successfully start-up the PMO in a manner that ensures that all of the initial PMO goals are met. The desire to provide more immediate value by focusing on additional areas of need in the organization is noble, but this form of scope creep presents its own set of problems and should be avoided. If implementation of the PMO is going sufficiently well and the PMO manager perceives that extra time is available in the schedule, this time is better spent on growing the skills and knowledge of the PMO staff, ensuring that all preparations for PMO start-up are in place, or performing marketing to the organization rather than attempting to plan for and implement additional scope.

Another part of "know your mission and your market" relates to the concept of contextualizing the PMO mission in terms of the market(s) that will be served. As implementation work proceeds, validation of the implementation work in terms of the mission set forth for the PMO must include a focus on the intended markets to be served and on understanding the *current state* of these markets, the *perception* of the PMO in these markets, and the *intended plan* to *sell* these markets on the PMO concept. For this process, "markets" include the specific areas of the organization that will be served by the PMO (e.g., specific divisions, groups, or geographies) as well as other constituent markets such as external partners, customers, or other stakeholders.

The process is fairly straightforward and involves *reviewing* the needs of the markets that will be served (via previous assessment activity or conducting research to determine how project management needs differ by market); *ensuring* that the needs of each market are documented; *keeping* the state of project management in the markets in mind; *guiding* the PMO implementation to ensure that when the PMO start-up is complete that the PMO is equipped to serve these markets; and *using* the marketing and communication plan as appropriate to ensure that the PMO is *selling itself* to the markets that it will serve.

In terms of *selling itself*, the PMO may be able to merely dictate project management policy, assuming that management backing of the PMO in the organization is sufficient to facilitate mandating certain standards, processes, and so forth. In general, however, a process of slowly introducing the organization to the PMO, "socializing" the concept and benefits as part of the implementation, and then gradually implementing changes into the organization leads to greater "buy-in" and reduced implementation time. By first taking steps to understand the needs of the markets and then ensuring that communication is provided about how these markets will be served by the PMO in terms of their needs, the likelihood of success in achieving acceptance of the PMO concept dramatically increases in these markets.

Even if eventual standards deployment requires mandating revised processes that differ from processes currently in place in a market, taking time to first gain a detailed understanding of the specific needs of each individual market and then to ensure that these unique needs are documented and considered as the PMO begins its work (and potentially evolves processes over time) will be extremely beneficial. The PMO itself and the organization will benefit because the PMO has taken steps to ensure that the organization's needs are met.

Dress to Impress

The third factor, in this context at least, does not refer to clothing. Instead, "dress to impress" refers to ensuring that there is an appropriate level of professionalism and "polish" in the presentations of the PMO to the organization. Professionalism and polish will certainly be a critical part of the start-up activities, but they are equally important during the implementation phase. As stated previously, interest in PMO implementation activities will grow as more members of the organization learn about the PMO, its functions, and the potential impacts that it may have on the way members of the organization do their jobs. Part of dressing to impress involves ensuring that the PMO is presented in a positive light. Discussion of its goals and operations should stress the value that will be provided. Ensure that members of the PMO staff and implementation team conduct themselves in a manner that is consistent with a Best-in-Class project organization. Although this factor may seem somewhat obvious, it is important to note because making a positive first impression on the organization is critical. Fixing a negative reputation is difficult. Therefore, the best risk mitigation is ensuring that the PMO does not develop a negative reputation in the first place.

Chapter 4 discussed the implementation planning process in detail, and the first section of this chapter has provided additional detail related to several factors that can help ensure a successful implementation. As implementation project planning reaches its later stages, beginning to turn some amount of attention to transitioning from implementation to operation will become necessary. The bridge between these two phases is start-up.

PMO START-UP

Recognizing that PMO start-up is a unique phase of the PMO life cycle is important. Start-up not only recognizes the success of the implementation, but it also signifies that the PMO is "open for business." Although the initial focus of the PMO may not involve the organization as a whole, it is important to ensure that areas of the organization initially affected by PMO operation are aware that the PMO has commenced operation. Start-up provides an opportunity to recognize the hard work of the implementation team; to formally introduce the PMO to the organization; and to set appropriate expectations within the organization regarding the initial goals of the PMO and the role of the PMO in the organization during the first few months of operation. Conveying this information is most easily facilitated by a well-coordinated start-up event that includes appropriate marketing to the organization and that provides an opportunity for the organization to learn more about the PMO concept and its intended functions in the organization. Necessary areas of focus for a PMO start-up include:

- Recognition of the implementation team
- Review of the PMO marketing and communication plan

- Introduction of the PMO to the organization
- Closeout of the implementation phase

Recognizing the Implementation Team

As implementation work comes to conclusion, members of the PMO implementation team who will not remain with the PMO as PMO staff members will likely be released to other assignments within the organization. Even if some formal recognition for the entire team is planned, intermediate recognition as individuals "roll off" of the implementation project provides an opportunity to thank the individuals who contributed to the success of the PMO implementation effort. Recognizing the implementation team's hard work, collectively and individually, also provides an opportunity to reflect on what has been accomplished. The PMO manager should assume responsibility for this effort and should give consideration to the form of recognition as well as an appropriate time to recognize the team.

Although many members of the implementation team will likely prefer a monetary reward in the form of a bonus or another similar award, the organization's compensation systems and budgets may not support this form of recognition. If so, other options may have to be considered. The PMO implementation budget will provide guidance on funds that are available for team recognition. If a monetary award is not possible, other forms of recognition may be appropriate options (e.g., a dinner to celebrate the implementation of the PMO, a plaque or other similar tangible recognition, or an award of additional flexible time off in addition to each employee's normal time off schedule). Certainly many other options could be considered as well. Although the PMO implementation budget provides guidance about the available funds to support recognition, the PMO manager should also think creatively about additional forms of recognition that do not require significant investments of funds. Writing a positive letter for the personnel file of each team member, securing a note of thanks from a senior member of management, or similar gestures can be used to show the organization's appreciation for the team's hard work.

In addition to considering the type of recognition, considering an appropriate time to provide the recognition is important. Recognition of the members of the implementation team at a formal PMO kickoff with members of management and the organization in attendance provides an opportunity to recognize the team in a broader forum. Inclusion of the names of members of the implementation team in electronic mail or printed communications announcing the start-up of the PMO may be another opportunity. In addition to public forums in which the team can be recognized in the presence of the broader organization, a special team meeting or celebratory lunch or dinner event with the entire implementation team in attendance provides a good opportunity for the team to celebrate its success because it provides an opportunity for some form of recognition and good-natured joking or reflection on some of the challenging parts of the implementation effort with only the implementation team in attendance.

PMO Marketing and Communication Plan Review

A critical area of focus for start-up and ongoing operation of the PMO will be the communication to segments of the organization that will be impacted by PMO activities. A marketing and communication plan has already been created as a part of the implementation planning activities. This plan has provided a framework for ensuring consistent communication as part of the implementation process. It has also laid a foundation for ongoing communication after completion of the implementation phase. Preparation for the formal start-up provides an excellent opportunity to review the marketing and communication plan in the context of start-up and to validate that the needs of the PMO's stakeholders are still accurately reflected in the plan.

This review should begin by considering the effectiveness of the marketing and communication vehicles that have been used during the implementation. Questions to be asked as part of this review should include:

- Was consistent communication maintained with the identified constituencies?
- Were the communicated messages appropriate and understood?
- Were additional groups or constituencies identified that should have been included in communications?
- Was communication to management sufficiently frequent? Was it at a level of detail that met management's needs?

A review of these questions in the context of deliverables that were part of the implementation process will help to guide any required changes or additions to the plan in order to support ongoing marketing and communication to the organization. Determining factors such as the *consistency* of communication and whether the level of communication was *appropriate and understood* will likely require surveying members of the organization who received communications as part of the marketing and communication effort during implementation to determine their perceptions of the effectiveness of communication. Additionally, it may be appropriate to understand from these individuals' perspectives whether or not the communications helped to *sell* them on the PMO concept, thus providing some base level of validation as to whether or not an effective job of marketing was done.

This review also provides an opportunity to determine if *additional groups* within the organization should be reached through marketing and communication. Likely, the major affected groups within the organization have been identified as part of the development of the marketing and communication plan; however, with progression of the implementation, additional individuals or groups may have requested information about the PMO and its activities. In some cases, these inquiries may have been of a general inquiry nature, but in other cases one or more groups or individuals might represent a constituency that has not been considered, but that should be included in ongoing marketing and communication. Identifying these additional constituents and ensuring that their needs are met going forward is an important step that should be addressed as part of the marketing and communication plan review.

Determining whether or not the level of communication to management was appropriate is also important. Once the implementation project is complete, communication to management regarding the PMO may decrease because ongoing operations may not require the same level of management involvement. Therefore, a review of the frequency and content of communication to management that has been a part of implementation can assist in determining the key communications that should be maintained or improved upon to better meet the needs of management once the PMO is in place. From a management reporting perspective, the communication review may identify additional areas of need that the PMO should consider adding to the marketing and communication plan for sustained communication.

Results of the analysis of marketing and communication efforts in the implementation phase should be used as inputs to update the marketing and communication plan. Marketing and communication will be required as part of the start-up effort. Therefore, it is a good practice to align the marketing and communication plan based on any relevant findings from this review. Updates that reflect the needs of the organization are also required so that the plan that is in place to sustain communications over time is aligned with the needs of the stakeholders that the plan is designed to serve. As the PMO evolves and grows over time, the marketing and communication plan should be revisited periodically to validate that the plan aligns with stakeholder needs as well.

Introduction of the PMO to the Organization

The primary event signaling formal completion of the implementation phase and transition to the operations phase ("start-up") should be an introduction of the PMO to the organization. This event formally signifies to the organization that the PMO is "in business" and recognizes completion of the PMO implementation. From the start-up date forward, the PMO will focus on delivering the initial goals established for the first few months of operation and, longer term, on the achievement of broader goals in the areas of focus defined in the detailed business case (and potentially other areas as well as the PMO evolves).

Depending on the size and scope of the PMO, the plans for formally signaling the PMO start-up may vary. For a functional, regional, or divisional PMO, communication to the appropriate groups within the organization that will interact with the PMO may be appropriate. For a large regional PMO or a PMO that exists at the enterprise level, communication to a broader range of parties will be required. Therefore, the specific activities undertaken to formally start-up the PMO may vary. If possible, a live event should be conducted, allowing members of the PMO staff to interact with their key constituents and to address questions and to gather feedback and perceptions from the PMO's constituents. For large or geographically diverse groups, an audio conference or video conference may be required so that a broad range of the organization is reached. If a live event is not practical for the organization, a prerecorded presentation that is available via a website or similar technology may be appropriate. If none of these options are viable, some form of written communication that can be distributed via electronic mail or postal mail may be used; however, a more formal presentation is preferable.

Content planning and communication to the appropriate groups within the organization regarding the event are required. Providing sufficient advance notice of the date and time of the event, distributing an agenda or other marketing materials in advance to encourage attendance, and perhaps offering some sort of giveaway or other incentive to encourage attendance is important. In addition, a short electronic mail communication from a key member of management encouraging attendance and setting expectations regarding what will be accomplished and the benefits of attendance should be considered. This type of communication demonstrates management support for the PMO to the organization and helps to reinforce the importance of attendance.

From a content perspective, several areas of focus are appropriate. Regardless of whether a live event or a set of written materials is being considered, introduction of the PMO to the organization should address five key areas:

- Formally announce start-up of the PMO
- Introduce initial goals and areas of focus to the organization
- Set expectations regarding how the PMO will influence the organization and its work
- Address any questions regarding the PMO and its operations
- Recognize the hard work of the PMO implementation team

The formal announcement. This communication is designed to inform the organization that PMO implementation work is complete and that the PMO will begin to operate as a functional group within the organization. Although prior communication to the organization may have introduced the concept of the PMO at a high level, it may be appropriate to provide an additional overview of the PMO concept along with the general structure of how the PMO is situated within the organizational hierarchy and its intended roles as part of announcing the start-up.

Introducing the members of the PMO staff and the member of management (or members) who will be responsible for guiding the PMO's efforts and ensuring alignment with organizational goals is also appropriate. Include the roles of the PMO manager, other members of the PMO staff, the PMO sponsor or steering committee members, and other organizational leaders who will be involved in ensuring the long-term success of the PMO. These introductions help provide the organization with an understanding of the PMO structure and also demonstrate management commitment to the PMO.

Initial goals and focus areas. Introducing the initial goals and areas of focus is designed to educate the organization on the PMO concept and specific areas of focus that will be initially addressed by the PMO. Many members of the organization will likely already be familiar with the PMO concept as a result of pre-start-up marketing efforts, but others will require a basic introduction to the general operational goals of the PMO and how the PMO adds value to an organization. This component should be kept fairly short, but allow sufficient time to focus on the specific goals that the PMO will seek to achieve and the anticipated benefits to the organization of establishing and maintaining the PMO. It is critical that members of the organization who will be affected by the PMO's operations understand what the PMO will set out to do as well as what benefits are anticipated to be achieved.

A discussion of long-term objectives of the PMO is also appropriate. Include a focus on the general areas of influence that may be explored in the future. Keep this discussion fairly brief. Recognizing the role of the PMO as being a part of the organization that will be a key contributor to the organization's success in the long term is important, but focusing on results that the organization can expect to see in the near term is also important.

Set expectations. With an understanding of the initial goals and areas of focus now complete, begin to set expectations regarding how members of the organization will be impacted by the PMO. If the PMO will be focusing on developing standards that will eventually represent required ways of working in the organization, the manner in which these standards will be defined and implemented (ideally with significant input from the organization) should be discussed. If the PMO will be providing opportunities for professional growth and advancement through training and development opportunities, a summary of the expected areas of focus and plans should be reviewed. If other relevant areas of focus are part of the initial PMO goals, these areas should be mentioned in the context of how members of the organization will be affected as well. The goal of this section is to focus on how members of the organization will be affected in the short term (during the time when the PMO is working toward achievement of the initial PMO goals) while framing the PMO concept in general as a means of achieving evolution in the organization's project management practices in the long term.

Avoid an extensive discussion of how the PMO will evolve and influence the organization over a period of years. The audience will be primarily interested in short-term effects, but it also will likely be curious as to how jobs and current practices will be affected over time. An important part of this discussion is to acknowledge that the PMO is not designed to work in a vacuum. Input from outside of the PMO will be required in order to ensure that work by the PMO best serves the needs of the organization. As such, at this stage include setting the expectation that active participation from outside of the PMO will be encouraged and that its success will depend on engagement from areas of the organization that it will serve.

Be open to questions. Likely, the previous discussion areas have identified some questions or areas of concern. Addressing these questions and concerns in a timely and professional manner is a critical activity that should be taken seriously. If a live event is being used to announce the PMO start-up, a question-and-answer section should be included in the agenda. If a prerecorded or written communication format is being used, provide a series of answers to frequently asked questions or a contact phone number or electronic mail address where questions can be directed. If a live venue is not used and questions are submitted for response, a commitment must be made by the PMO staff to provide timely responses to any questions directed to the PMO.

Regardless of format used, the responses to any questions or areas of concern should be honest and reflect the best knowledge to date regarding the goals and the operation of the PMO. Clearly, the PMO manager and PMO staff will not have answers immediately available for every potential question. Detailed plans may not yet be in place or research may need to be conducted to ensure that full and complete answers are provided. Having a commitment to follow-up on questions that cannot be immediately answered is critical. The PMO staff does not need to have all answers at hand if a commitment is made to provide answers for questions with no available immediate answer. Yet, not having an answer, but committing to provide an answer, and then not following through on that commitment will leave the individual who posed the question with the impression that either the PMO does not take the question seriously or, perhaps worse, that the PMO is disorganized and cannot even properly respond to a simple question (even if the question is not simple in the opinion of the PMO). Follow-through is critical.

Recognize the team. This area of focus is designed to reiterate what has already been presented regarding recognition of the PMO team. The start-up event or communication that signifies the formal launch of the PMO is another excellent opportunity to publicly thank the PMO implementation team for its hard work to make the PMO a reality.

Implementation Phase Closeout

A final important start-up activity is implementation phase closeout. The purpose of implementation phase closeout is similar to the purpose of performing a project closeout, which is to review the recently completed project and identify opportunities for improvement in future projects. In the case of the PMO implementation, this review should focus not only on how the implementation progressed from cost, schedule, and quality perspectives, but also from the standpoint of how the implementation achieved its intended goals in terms of building a foundation for achieving the initial PMO goals that will be undertaken now that the implementation is complete and how the implementation achieved its intended goals in terms of building a foundation for long-term success.

PMO implementation will certainly not be the only project that the PMO undertakes. As the PMO evolves, new areas of responsibility and new phases of design and implementation will undoubtedly be undertaken. Although this new work may not be of the magnitude of the initial implementation, it will share many common features in terms of needing to assess what will be accomplished; to set goals; to inform and educate the organization; and to ensure management alignment. A thorough review of successes, challenges, and opportunities for future improvement is an important component of continuous improvement. These "lessons learned" may also be valuable to the broader organization and may contribute to improving the organization's overall project management practices.

Ideally, a formal session with all members of the PMO implementation team in attendance should be arranged. The agenda for this session should focus on reviewing the plan agreed to at the beginning of the implementation effort; reviewing the final outcomes as of the PMO start-up date; and documenting the successes and opportunities for improvement in terms of areas in which performance met expectations as well as areas in which challenges were encountered. The results of the review session should be documented and circulated among the team for concurrence as well as to provide an opportunity to include any additional areas of interest, if appropriate, that might have been missed during the formal review session. This deliverable, along with the implementation project plan, status reports, project plan updates, budget analyses, and other relevant project assets should be archived for later use. These deliverables may be among the first items of knowledge that are included in the PMO's project management knowledgebase.

Start-Up Summary

The *PMO Start-Up* section of Chapter 5 has focused on important areas related to the transition from the implementation phase to an operational PMO. There may be other additional relevant areas of focus for a particular PMO that depend on its size, scope, and requirements. Therefore, contemplate and include in the PMO start-up plans, as appropriate, additional areas of need from a start-up perspective.

The remainder of Chapter 5 will focus on the critical first few months of operation in which the PMO will settle into full operation and achieve the initial goals that have been included in the detailed business case. Additionally, a discussion of planning for future phases of PMO evolution and delivery of broader goals beyond the first phase of PMO operations will be included.

THE PMO IN OPERATION

As the PMO begins to operate, attention will shift to delivering the initial goals indicated in the detailed business case. As part of implementation activities, the required action plans for achieving these goals should have already been developed. Now execution of those plans can commence. From an initial operations perspective, several areas are relevant:

- Delivering the initial goals
- Measuring value
- Reporting to management
- Seeking feedback from the organization
- Planning for "what's next"

Each of these areas will be described in more detail in the sections that follow.

Delivering the Initial Goals

Clearly the first priority of the PMO staff should be to deliver the initial results that have been stated in the detailed business case. Each PMO staff member should execute his or her portions of the relevant action plans for achievement of these initial goals through the utilization of the identified strategies in each area. Each PMO staff member should also provide regular feedback to the PMO manager, who in turn should ensure that satisfactory progress is being made toward achievement of each of the goals.

Have a proactive risk-management plan. In the operational mode, the PMO team should meet regularly to review progress and to identify any issues that might affect the ability of the team to meet the initial goals in a timely fashion. When issues do arise, the PMO manager, working with management as needed, should ensure that timely resolution is achieved so that a schedule that has been agreed to is not put at risk.

It is virtually certain that everything will not go according to plan. Without doubt, the aggressiveness of the goals; willingness of the organization to participate in the process of evolving project management practices to meet the intended PMO goals; changes in management priorities; and numerous other factors will create some level of deviation from the plan. Managing this deviation, taking corrective action, and keeping management informed are critical components of overcoming obstacles as they occur.

Unfortunately even the best efforts of the team may not be enough in some cases. When significant roadblocks are leading to a lack of progress, developing a formal plan to identify significant issues, to document the issues and propose corrective action, and to track the issues to resolution will be tremendously beneficial. Developing a formal PMO risk management plan to address these areas as part of the initial phase of PMO operations creates a useful deliverable that can be reused throughout the life of the PMO. A formal PMO risk management plan also provides another important benefit. It provides an ability to systematically track risk areas so that items that might affect the success of the PMO may be reported to management in a timely manner.

Maintain communication. In addition to having a proactive risk management plan, another critical component of achieving the initial PMO goals is maintaining communication and collaboration with areas of the organization outside of the PMO. This may be in the form of informal discussions, brainstorming sessions, periodic reviews of PMO plans with other areas of the organization that will be affected by these plans, or other mechanisms that facilitate ensuring that the broader organization served by the PMO is engaged at an appropriate level as the PMO begins to create its first set of operational deliverables.

Aligning deliverables with the needs of every area of the organization will not be possible in all cases. Without doubt, standardization and adoption of best practices will create some level of change for the organization. Yet, part of the PMO mission should involve encouraging the use of best practices and standardized processes within the organization. As such, the PMO will develop certain standards and practices to deploy to the organization, but it should do so in a way that encourages constructive input and feedback from the organization as these key standards and practices are developed. This is especially true in the early life of the PMO. If the PMO merely deploys one or more of its deliverables for use by the organization without any input from the organization, the deliverables may be viewed as mandates from the PMO. The PMO may be perceived to be operating from an "ivory tower" without due consideration being given to the needs of the organization. Alternatively, another possible outcome may be that deliverables from the PMO are merely ignored if members of the organization perceive that the PMO is not operating in a collaborative manner. Neither of these outcomes is preferable. The preferred approach is to maintain some level of communication and collaboration with the broader project management community as well as with the organization as a whole and, when appropriate, to include constructive feedback and useful practices already in place in the organization as part of the key PMO deliverables.

With these considerations in mind and by ensuring a certain level of due diligence on the part of the PMO staff, the PMO should be well equipped to proactively manage the process of achieving its initial goals. The practices described also help establish a base level of standardization within the PMO itself, in terms of identifying and managing risk, and serve as a starting point for establishing the PMO in its role as a standards organization. Beginning with internal PMO processes is an excellent way to validate approaches and create solutions that are "tested" before being deployed to the organization.

Dimensions of Value

From a management perspective, one of the primary questions of interest will be the extent to which the PMO provides value to the organization. Investment in the implementation and operation of the PMO can be significant. Therefore, management will expect to see value returned to the organization as a means of justifying the investment. Even if the PMO is chartered with an initially small scope—especially if a small initial scope is being used as a means to prove the potential value of a PMO to the organization—it is critical to ensure that mechanisms are in place to measure value and to report the findings to management on a regular basis. There are several components to value.

Explicit value. Explicit value may be achieved through actual, quantifiable cost or effort savings from reducing staff, eliminating rework, consolidating functions to allow staff to focus on other organizational priorities, or other activities that result in real savings to the organization. Although explicit value is often desirable from a management perspective, the role of the PMO should not be limited to providing explicit value alone.

Implicit value. Value created through standardization, providing educational opportunities, growing project management knowledge, establishing a project management culture, and other areas that do not result in directly measurable cost savings, but that serve to improve the level of sophistication and maturity in the organization from a project and program management perspective, clearly provides value to the organization as well. This level of value is often created through the development of "maturity" in which the organization evolves from a lower state of maturity to a higher state of maturity through increased standardization, reuse of practices, and continuous feedback and improvement over time (discussed briefly in Chapter 1). Increased maturity provides additional savings in terms of increased productivity, decreased error rates, and other key factors that, although more difficult to measure in terms of actual dollar savings, still create significant benefit to the organization.

Intellectual capital. Intellectual capital, often created through developing processes that meet the unique needs of the organization or that provide a competitive advantage to the organization, is often not easily measured in terms of true cost savings or increased profits, but it still can be of significant benefit.

The combination of these different value components creates a holistic view of value. From a management reporting perspective, a combination of the different value components should be the preferred means of describing the value provided by the PMO once it is in operation.

Measuring Value

The implementation planning process has already taken the first step toward measuring value. As part of that process, it was suggested that baseline data should be gathered to facilitate an understanding of the current state of operations in the organization. In cases in which hard data in terms of costs to the organization, schedule slippages, increased project risk, or other areas that can be equated to true cost as available, it was suggested that appropriate data should be gathered. If data that has been gathered suggests that the average project cost overrun in the organization is 15% of project cost, that percentage data becomes a starting point for the PMO for measuring improvement and showing value. In cases in which value creation is in areas that have less concrete data, data provided in terms of employee perceptions of process issues or survey results for certain focus areas may be used as appropriate baseline data.

Accumulate existing data. The first step in measuring value is accumulating this available data, preferably prior to the beginning of PMO work to improve these areas, so that the value creation measurement begins with the current state of the organization. Without this existing data, demonstrating value to the organization will be significantly more difficult because any value created cannot be easily contextualized in terms of the initial operational situation that is to be improved.

Identify each goal and its baseline data. From a measurement standpoint, each individual goal and the associated baseline data will determine the level of measurement as well as the measurement time frame. Associated measures have already been defined for each goal as part of the business case process. The initial measurement for gathering the baseline data has likely considered the key measures that have also already been defined for each goal. Therefore, the level of measurement required and the time frame allowed for measuring to determine if the goals have been met and to determine the level of value created will be dictated, to some extent, by the goals themselves. If, for example, one initial PMO goal is to decrease project overruns by 5% within the first 6 months of operations, the measurement for achievement of this goal and the value created would begin only after the associated processes that lead to improved project cost performance are in place and used for a period of time sufficient to allow for meaningful data to be collected.

As another example, if an initial goal of the PMO is to improve the consistency of risk management within the organization, implementing a standardized risk management plan in the organization and collecting data on compliance with the plan, and the associated decreased incidence of risk events, may provide meaningful data that can be used to show how the PMO created value for the organization through the deployment of a standardized risk management plan. In some cases, value can be created immediately. If the organization has no standardized training for new project managers, creating a training offering and delivering it to the organization creates value. The extent of the value created may be determined through surveys of course participants and their managers to understand if the course assisted the new project managers in better managing project assignments.

As the preceding examples demonstrate, often value is not created overnight. In some cases, it may take a number of months before the PMO is able to collect some level of meaningful data that can be used to demonstrate value. However, this does not mean that the PMO is not creating value. In-progress work to achieve an initial set of PMO goals in itself creates value. The difference is that the value is not realized until the deliverables are deployed to the organization and are used to better manage projects and evolve project management processes.

When PMO operations initially commence, and for some time afterward until several of the initial deliverables are delivered to the organization, reporting to management will likely focus on what the PMO is doing to create value rather than focusing on an end value created. As processes are deployed and data is collected to determine the extent of value created, reports from the PMO to management should focus on achievement of milestones that allow the PMO to begin to implement its deliverables. As the deliverables are implemented, the focus of management reporting can shift to measuring and reporting the explicit value created as well as other non-explicit components.

Report the data. In addition to the process of measuring value, the process of reporting value created must also be considered. In some organizations, standardized processes for reporting return on investment data (or similar measures) may already be in place. In other organizations, providing updates on value creation and determination of benefits versus costs from PMO operations will be left to the PMO manager.

An extension of Table 4.4 (see Chapter 4) to include an additional column for "value created" provides one possible means of documenting value creation. Because the goals and measures are already provided, the link to value created is natural. Removing the section related to strategies may be advisable, but an understanding of the specific strategies used to achieve the value created may be of value to some members of management. The key to reporting value in this format (or any other format that the organization may choose to use) is to ensure that the value created is linked to one or more of the goals set for the initial phase of PMO operations. Reporting value in this manner ensures that the progress versus the agreed-to goals is clearly being demonstrated.

The PMO may create value in additional areas as well as a result of other efforts that the PMO may choose to undertake in addition to the initial areas of focus or through extension of one or more of the goals already listed. Additional value created through strategically addressing other areas of concern in the organization should be categorized separately so that value creation in the areas of focus defined in consultation with management and documented in the detailed business case and implementation plan remains clear.

Beyond the reporting format, the content must also be considered. In cases in which data is collected to arrive at conclusions regarding value creation, it is important to provide the results as well as some discussion of the methodology used to determine the value created. In cases in which hard data will not be presented, but instead some of the less tangible areas of value creation are of interest, discussion regarding the efforts undertaken, the outcomes, and how the outcomes have created value will be of primary interest. Most likely, the data presented will be a combination of both. This does not present a significant problem as long as management understands that the value creation measures cannot always be equated to actual monetary savings or profit increases in a meaningful way. If management requires value analysis from the standpoint of funds expended versus funds created alone, an approximation for the value of certain measures may need to be made. In these cases, it is often best to err on the side of underestimating the value created because overestimating can create a situation in which management may request more detailed justification of the data provided.

If the process of determining the value was based on assumptions or estimations in the first place, it is unlikely that any easy answer can be created to justify a seemingly high estimate. In some sense, this situation will be a relatively infrequent occurrence. Assuming that management has been properly educated on the PMO concept and has taken the time to review the business case documents and PMO plans, there should be recognition that the investment made in the PMO creates both tangible and intangible benefits. The intangible benefits, though not easily quantifiable in many cases, represent benefits nonetheless. The value of these benefits to the organization should certainly be considered as part of a holistic view of value creation.

Be proactive. Of course, the possibility exists that the PMO may not be able to initially deliver the value that was expected. Corporate politics, changes in corporate strategy or direction, difficulty reaching consensus with the organization concerning key elements of the PMO's work, and other factors may lead to decreased value creation in the near term. As part of the proactive risk management plan, appropriate steps should be taken to understand the key issues that are leading to decreased value and to devise corrective measures to ensure that these areas of concern are corrected.

Having baseline data on the state of the organization and a set of measures to gauge performance versus the PMO goals, combined with value analysis techniques appropriate for each of the goals, should provide a means to help management understand where factors exist within the organization that are leading to less than expected results. Identifying an area in which value creation is lagging behind plan and reviewing the area in a proactive manner as part of a regular review with management via a PMO progress report will help management understand the factors that are influencing the ability of the PMO to reach its goals and to create an acceptable level of value. Management is thus provided with opportunities to take corrective action and to assist the PMO in reaching its goals.

Although every effort should be made to correct any issues within the PMO itself by working with members of the organization first, keeping management up-to-date on progress and requesting assistance when needed are necessary components of creating and building value over time.

Reporting to Management

Measuring, documenting, and reporting PMO value is only one component of the broader function of reporting PMO activities and progress to management. The PMO start-up has provided an opportunity to transition from *implementation* status reporting to *operational* status reporting.

The PMO steering committee, PMO sponsor, or other key managers who will be responsible for the PMO from an organizational hierarchy perspective will require ongoing communication on some regular basis to obtain the status of PMO efforts, to receive feedback on issues being encountered by the PMO, and to validate that the PMO is operating within its budget and resource allocations. The form and frequency of these communications should be reviewed with management so that an appropriate level of communication is provided.

Scheduling regular PMO review meetings (most often on a monthly or quarterly basis) provides an opportunity to formally update management on PMO efforts. Formally reviewing PMO efforts in a "live" setting will help ensure that management remains engaged in the PMO process throughout its life and demonstrates to the PMO staff that management remains committed to its activities and to assisting with resolution of issues as they arise. Because of the importance of the PMO review meeting, the format and content will now be briefly discussed.

PMO review meetings. The PMO manager will serve as the primary link between the PMO staff and the management team. The PMO manager should have responsibility for coordinating the logistics for regular PMO review meetings, distributing the agenda for the meetings, taking minutes of the meetings, distributing minutes from past meetings for review, and involving other members of the PMO staff as needed to provide reports on specific areas of interest. The PMO sponsor or other key organizational leader who acts as the primary management contact for the PMO manager should have responsibility for ensuring that appropriate members of management are invited to the PMO review meetings.

In the early stages of operation, these meetings will primarily discuss progress toward the initial PMO goals and any issues faced by the PMO as it begins to operate in the organization. As the PMO continues to grow and expand its focus over time, the role of PMO review meetings may shift to reviewing ongoing operations and discussing new opportunities for the PMO. A standard agenda for a PMO review meeting might include the following topics:

- Current operations update
- Operating budget status

- Current issues
- Review of new opportunities

Additional items may be added as needed, but the general topics of interest to management will include a review of current PMO operations (including progress toward agreed-to goals); an update on the PMO's financial situation including any potential areas of budget overspend; discussion of current issues facing the PMO from an organizational, operational, or strategic perspective; and a review of possible additional opportunities for the PMO to begin plans for engaging in new areas of focus.

Note: Although not listed specifically in the agenda, the PMO review meeting agenda should include some level of review of value creation as part of the operations update or budget review in order to give management a sense of where the PMO is providing benefit and some measure of the type and quantity of benefit being provided.

The PMO review meeting is a formal opportunity to discuss PMO operations with interested members of the management team and to gather feedback on PMO operations and opportunities. The use of a PMO status report is another opportunity to provide more frequent status updates and to ensure that management is up-to-date on overall PMO operations.

PMO status reports. Similar to the implementation status report discussed in Chapter 4, a PMO status report provides a summary of PMO operations. It can be distributed on a regular basis (most often bi-weekly or monthly) via electronic mail or paper distribution to provide a high-level view of PMO accomplishments and plans. The status report is not meant to take the place of formal PMO review meetings, but rather it is designed to provide a top-level overview of PMO operations and to keep management informed on a regular basis regarding the status of PMO efforts.

Items of interest in the status report may be discussed as part of the PMO review meetings. Items of interest may also be addressed immediately by management if necessary. Whether or not a PMO status report will be of value will require discussion with management. This discussion should be in the context of providing the status report in addition to, not in place of, a PMO review meeting.

The format for the PMO status report may be based on the implementation status report in Chapter 4, or some other agreed-to format, and should include several components:

- Identification of the time period for which the report is being prepared
- Status of current PMO efforts including:
  - Identification of the project or effort
  - Targeted completion date
  - Status (via the green/yellow/red "stoplight" method or the percent complete versus plan)
  - Summary of issues (if any)
- Identification of upcoming projects or events
- Issues facing the PMO in general

Other areas of interest, including recognition of key staff accomplishments, feedback from PMO customers, or other relevant items may be included in the report as well, but it is critical to ensure that a summary of current efforts is provided along with any areas of concern that may require management attention.

The PMO staff may be involved in creating status reports or reviewing them prior to distribution (potentially identifying additional reporting areas as well). If necessary, the status report can be segmented by staff area of responsibility, with appropriate staff members providing input to the report. The goal of the PMO status report is not to provide a lengthy review of every effort in detail. Therefore, keep the level of detail to a summary level.

Status reports should be distributed in a timely fashion according to a schedule agreed to with management. The specific distribution list may include members of the PMO steering committee, the PMO sponsor, key managers in groups that are directly affected by PMO operations, human resources or finance professionals who have responsibility for the human resource and finance aspects of the PMO, and other leaders as identified by management. Copies of the reports should also be maintained in the PMO archives for future reference. The report may be distributed to the PMO staff as well.

Seeking Feedback from the Organization

An important (and often overlooked or undervalued) component of success for any PMO is seeking and utilizing feedback from the organization. Although regular communication with management will help validate that the PMO is aligned with organizational goals and objectives and that its operations are meeting management's expectations, management is only one segment of the organization that the PMO serves.

Project managers, project staff, future project managers, and other PMO customers are primary constituencies that are also served by the PMO. Depending on the size and scope of the PMO, the extent to which these groups are affected may vary, but it is clear that as the PMO creates deliverables, deploys processes, provides training and development opportunities, and potentially leads major project efforts, there will be interaction with members of the organization beyond the PMO itself. These interactions may be of an educational, consultative, or collaborative nature or they may simply be by virtue of some members of the organization having to follow PMO-created standard processes for certain aspects of project efforts.

Members of the organization that the PMO addresses through standards setting, educational opportunities, knowledge sharing, consulting, or other activities are key customers of the PMO. Feedback from these individuals is critical to ensure that the PMO efforts are aligned with the needs of the organization and to validate that the PMO is adding value to the organization.

Unsolicited feedback. Some feedback may be entirely unsolicited. Unfortunately, much of the unsolicited feedback received will likely be in the form of issues, problems, or areas of concern. Accepting and managing unsolicited feedback, positive or negative, should be factored into the PMO's operational plans. A commitment should be made to respond in a timely manner to all feedback received. The PMO may not be able to provide the answer that the individual providing feedback is seeking in all cases. (*Remember:* The role of a PMO may in some cases be to enforce standards or manage compliance with key organizational project management principles.) Yet, the PMO should be committed to directly answering feedback received and to either providing answers or providing rationale behind the actions that the PMO undertakes.

In some cases, very positive unsolicited feedback will be received. This feedback should also be acknowledged.

A review of unsolicited feedback received may be included as part of regular PMO staff meetings or highlighted in status reports to management as appropriate. Reviewing feedback is an important component of continuous improvement and feedback received should generally not be discredited, even in cases in which the feedback received is not of a positive nature.

Solicited feedback. Ideally, the majority of feedback will be from solicited feedback that is received as part of a concerted effort by the PMO staff to gauge the effectiveness of deliverables, to seek feedback on areas of concern and areas of opportunity, and to proactively identify opportunities to build relationships with the organization so that a two-way dialog is maintained between the PMO and the customers that it serves.

Gathering feedback. There are many potential mechanisms to solicit feedback from the organization. Some common techniques in the PMO environment include:

- Town hall meetings
- Surveys
- Interviews
- Websites or electronic mail

Town hall meetings provide an opportunity for the PMO's customers to come together with the PMO staff (either in person, via audio conference, or via video conference) to receive updates on PMO activities and to provide feedback on PMO operations. Surveys and interviews are another opportunity to gain targeted feedback from certain areas of the organization (or to gather feedback on specific deliverables or PMO opportunities that affect only a portion of the organization). The use of a feedback form on the PMO's website or a specific electronic mailbox for the PMO provides a means for members of the organization to provide feedback in a standardized way that can be tracked by the PMO staff. Other mechanisms can gather feedback as well. The specific combination of feedback mechanisms used will depend on the size and scope of the PMO, the size and scope of the organization in which the

PMO has influence, the types of activities undertaken by the PMO, and other related factors.

Certain opportunities, such as training sessions or other educational activities, provide opportunities to seek feedback based on the nature of the activity itself. For example, at the conclusion of a training session, feedback in the form of a training survey can be administered immediately in order to gauge the perceived effectiveness of the training and the training provider. Follow-up surveys, either via electronic mail or regular mail, can be administered at some point in time following the training to gauge whether or not the participant was able to put the material learned to use in his or her job and to identify additional training needs.

Gathering feedback on other deliverables, such as standardized processes, may be more difficult because the level of use in the organization may be widely varied. For example, if a process for project chartering is put into place, gathering feedback on the process will require understanding when and by whom projects are chartered and then initiating follow-up on the effectiveness of the PMO deliverable through a survey, phone interview, personal interview, or other appropriate means. Determining the target for follow-up is somewhat easier in cases in which the PMO initiates a pilot of a proposed deliverable to a specific portion of the organization for the purpose of gathering feedback and enhancing the effectiveness of the deliverable prior to distributing it broadly.

Determining the frequency and the means of gathering feedback from the organization is an important component of the feedback gathering process that should be assessed as part of the implementation planning for every customer-facing PMO deliverable. It is important to ensure that regardless of the frequency and means of gathering feedback used, the information provided is valuable and can be used to enhance PMO operations. Some feedback mechanisms, such as personal interviews, permit very specific feedback and, by virtue of having dialog, permit the course of inquiry to change based on the responses provided. Of course, personal interviews provide this opportunity at the expense of the additional time and effort required to coordinate scheduling and conducting interviews.

Conversely, surveys provide a means to gather feedback from a broad group of individuals in a very timely and often cost-effective manner. Printed surveys can easily be mailed to a large number of individuals. Web technology has led to the development of a number of Web-based survey products that allow a survey to be sent via electronic mail to a group of individuals and include the ability to automatically gather and summarize survey results. These solutions are very cost effective and can be used to survey a large number of individuals in a very short amount of time.

However, surveys require a significant amount of up-front planning and thought to ensure that the right questions are asked and that the questions are asked in a manner that is impartial and unambiguous. Especially in cases in which a numeric scale is used to allow survey respondents to provide results, it is critical to validate that the right questions are being asked and that an appropriate scale is being used to measure results. Surveys may also have free-form components that allow respondents to write in or type responses or to provide additional detail on a response that is initially provided on a numeric scale. A well-thought-out survey, with appropriate consideration given to the questions that will be posed in the survey, can be a very effective tool to gather information (anonymously if needed) and can be used to quickly gauge performance in various aspects of PMO operations.

Reviewing feedback. Next in the feedback process is reviewing the feedback received and using it to enhance PMO operations and to increase the value provided to the organization. For feedback on particular, unique areas of the PMO, such as a single training course or similar event, the member of the PMO staff responsible for the coordination of the event should be assigned to review the feedback received and take corrective action as needed to address any issues uncovered in the feedback. For broader deliverables or areas that affect the PMO as a whole, the PMO manager, together with the PMO staff, should review the feedback provided and develop recommendations and action plans to address any areas of significant concern.

It is generally not possible to please everyone all of the time. Therefore, it may not be possible to correct every issue brought to the attention of the PMO staff. However, consideration of all feedback received should be included as part of a regular process of reviewing feedback and developing appropriate action plans. As appropriate, management should be kept informed of significant areas of concern in the organization and the plans that the PMO has developed to address these areas of concern.

For cases in which positive feedback is received related to a particular event, deliverable, or other area of PMO influence, use this feedback to recognize exceptional work by members of the PMO team. It may be further used as a means of demonstrating to management the positive perceptions of the PMO in the organization and the value being created by the PMO.

Archiving feedback. Feedback received should be summarized and archived as part of the PMO's records. Survey results may be correlated over time to show improvement trends, interview notes may be helpful in understanding other potential areas of focus for the PMO or for reviewing feedback when certain PMO deliverables are updated or replaced with enhanced versions, and other feedback may be relevant for future review by the PMO staff or interested members of management. Developing a simple database application or other means of collating survey feedback or other forms of feedback that can be easily assimilated may be practical so that a growing repository of feedback history is available for analysis.

At the early stages of PMO operations, likely there will be significant feedback provided, but not over a sufficient time frame to enable detailed trend reporting. However, as time goes on, having easy access to certain key surveys or customer satisfaction results can be beneficial for data analysis purposes.

Planning for "What's Next"

Once the PMO staff is working to deliver the plans set for the initial phase of operations, to seek feedback on current operations, and to maintain communications with the organization and management, a significant amount of the start-up work is well underway. From a PMO management perspective, focus can begin on planning for the next phase of PMO evolution, which is the first of the "what's next" phases. This is also an appropriate time to briefly revisit the topic of maturity.

In most organizations, one of the key goals of the PMO is to bring some level of additional sophistication to the project management practices in the organization. This may come in the form of detailed portfolio management

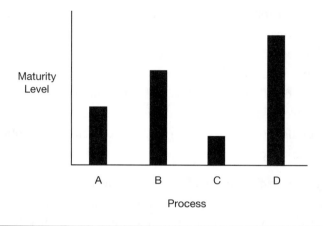

Figure 5.1 Process maturity example.

practices, standardized project planning and execution processes, or any other area of interest to the organization. Likely, there are processes that the organization already does very well from a project management perspective. As well, there are other areas in which significant work is needed in order to bring practices to some level of standardization and repeatability. Therefore, from a project management standpoint, it is often the case that the "maturity" of the organization overall is really an average view of maturity for a variety of processes, with some likely more mature that others. Figure 5.1 depicts this relationship.

As planning for the next phase of PMO work begins, give thought to areas within the project management context in which the greatest value in terms of increased maturity can be achieved through an increased level of *repeatability, standardization,* and *continuous improvement,* which represent some of the key elements of mature processes. Of course, continuing to develop and mature the initial areas of focus in which the PMO is working to achieve its first-phase goals is also important and should not be overlooked.

The preceding discussion has highlighted the dual role of the PMO as it moves forward from the initial start-up phase. In one dimension, the next phase of PMO work should focus on continuing to implement, evolve, and streamline the deliverables from the initial goal set for the first phase of PMO work. Yet, the PMO cannot merely implement a set of deliverables and then expect that they can remain in place perpetually without further evaluation and development. Instead, the PMO must ensure that continuous improvement becomes a key goal of subsequent phases of PMO work.

In another dimension, the scope of the new work that the PMO will undertake, which will allow it to expand its focus and grow additional value within the organization, must be considered. This dimension will likely involve work with management and the organization to identify additional areas of focus and then work by the PMO staff to develop plans to address these new areas of need. Some of these initial areas of focus are already included in the detailed business case document. Therefore, a review of the intended additional areas of focus should be conducted to validate that these areas of focus are still among the highest-priority focus areas for the PMO. Depending on the nature of the additional needs that have been identified by management, a reprioritization of additional areas of focus may be necessary.

The concept of a PMO roadmap for longer-term planning will be introduced in the next section. However, planning for "what's next" from an immediate, next phase of work perspective is very similar to the process of planning for the delivery of the initial PMO goals. An understanding of what will be delivered should be confirmed with management through review of the detailed business case and discussions with management regarding any modifications that may need to be made to the plans documented in the detailed business case. Then, a time line can be developed to guide the PMO team in targeting an appropriate implementation time frame based on the required effort to complete each of the deliverables required to meet the goals that have been established.

If the scope of "what's next" is significant, a new business case may be developed for this work and validated with management. As an alternative, the detailed business case originally developed may be viewed as an evolutionary document and updated as needed to reflect significant new areas of focus not documented in the original detailed business case.

Validating any significant new areas of focus in terms of business alignment is important. Creating a new business case for this new work (or adjusting the original detailed business case to reflect this new work) is an appropriate means because the business case document format contains much

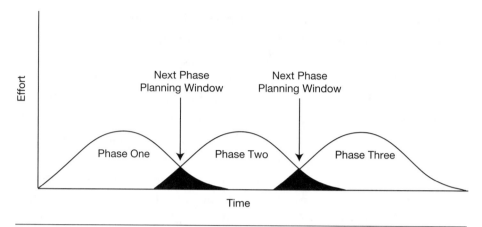

Figure 5.2 PMO phased planning approach.

of the necessary information required to ensure that appropriate consideration is given to the business value of new areas of focus before any work in these areas is undertaken.

This high-level planning is then followed by delivery of a detailed implementation plan for each goal or new area of focus, developed by the PMO staff in consultation with the PMO manager, similar to the process used to define the PMO implementation plan and delivery of the initial PMO deliverables defined for the first phase of operations. This exercise will help to confirm the time lines for delivery and to begin the process of aligning the PMO staff's priorities to the agreed-to targets. This work need not wait for completion of the current initial phase of operations. Ideally, a period of overlap between decreasing effort in the current phase of work and planning for the next phase of work will facilitate a "rolling schedule" of planning, implementation, and further planning. Figure 5.2 depicts this relationship. As shown in the shaded section of the graph in Figure 5.2, the tail end of effort in the current phase provides the opportunity to begin planning for the next phase.

As time passes, support of current operations will begin to play an increasingly important (and time-consuming) role. Therefore, the ability of the PMO to continue to expand its focus into new areas will be constrained by resource capacity.

The PMO roadmap process, which will be discussed in the next section, will assist in planning appropriate levels of staffing to support ongoing operations and new areas of focus.

THE PMO ROADMAP

As the process of determining areas of focus for the next phase of PMO development and evolution progresses, a number of new potential areas of focus or need may become evident. The process of validating existing needs, considering newly identified needs, and developing a plan to address the entire group of needs identified will require development of a high-level PMO time line, or roadmap, that looks beyond the next phase of operations and considers the role of the PMO and areas of focus over a period of years.

Although more detailed planning for the immediate next phase of operations will be required, and should be coordinated by the PMO manager as soon as the scope for the next operational phase is agreed to with management, having a high-level roadmap that identifies the role, scope, and areas of focus for the PMO over a time line of 2 to 4 years can be a valuable exercise from a long-range planning perspective as well as from a management alignment perspective. Advantages of the roadmap from a PMO perspective include:

- Setting expectations with management and the organization regarding when certain key deliverables or goals will be achieved
- Building a framework for ongoing strategic PMO planning
- Assisting with resource planning by identifying new or expanded areas of focus for the PMO

Developing a roadmap also helps the PMO staff to ensure that their efforts are aligned with the long-term areas of focus that the PMO will undertake. It allows the PMO staff to develop plans and strategies beyond immediate project needs and to align those plans and strategies with the intended overall PMO direction. Figure 5.3 depicts the role of management, the PMO manager, and the PMO staff in the process of developing a PMO roadmap and illustrates a standard top-down approach to planning.

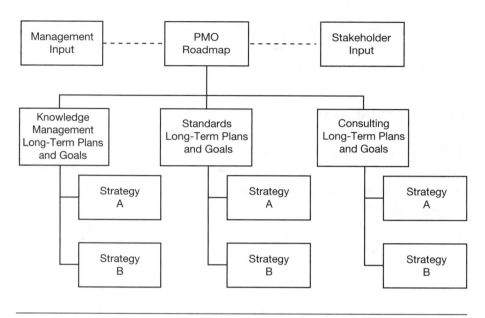

Figure 5.3 PMO roadmap development.

Initially, the PMO roadmap is developed by the PMO staff with input from PMO stakeholders and management to validate that there is alignment with organizational priorities and that an acceptable business case exists for the additional work to be undertaken. Then, with the roadmap complete, individual members of the PMO staff can develop more detailed long-term plans and goals, which can then be transformed into specific strategies that will be used to achieve these goals.

Because the roadmap has a relatively long horizon timewise, the process of developing these goals and strategies should be part of an annual or semi-annual strategic planning session that focuses on the goals for the coming 6 months or 1 year, as appropriate. Attempting to develop goals and strategies for the entire roadmap at the initial stage of development is not a preferred approach because this method does not take into account changes in business climate, PMO priorities, or other factors that may occur in the future that could alter the roadmap's goals, deliverables, and timings. As an example, Figure 5.4 depicts a PMO roadmap for a PMO chartered to primarily engage in standards setting and knowledge management activities.

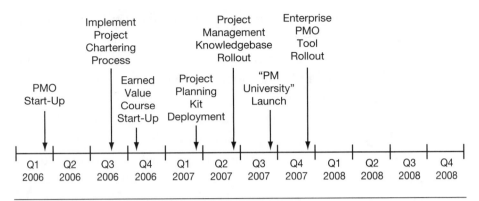

Figure 5.4 PMO roadmap example.

The components of the roadmap in Figure 5.4 include a time scale of some reasonable length (in general, 2 to 4 years is sufficient) and the deliverables that will be completed. As depicted in Figure 5.4, at the roadmap development stage, it is appropriate to place the deliverables within a 3-month time frame because the process of detailed planning, especially for items toward the far end of the roadmap horizon, should take place as part of the annual or semiannual strategic planning process. Firm committed delivery dates should be aligned for near-term deliverables as part of this process. An annual or semiannual strategic planning process also provides an opportunity to review the roadmap with management, to present and validate business cases for completing work identified, and to make adjustments as needed by adding items to or removing items from the roadmap so that the roadmap remains aligned with the needs of the organization.

The roadmap should not be viewed as a firm, committed plan. Yet, frequent significant revision of the roadmap will limit the ability of the PMO to effectively undertake long-term planning. Therefore, revisions should be limited to formal reviews and strategic planning sessions with the PMO staff and management.

SUMMARY

The start-up and ongoing operational aspects of the PMO are important areas of focus for the PMO manager and PMO staff. A smooth transition from implementation to operations is critical, both from the standpoint of ensuring a successful introduction of the PMO to the organization and from an ongoing management and growth perspective. Chapter 5 has considered some of the general aspects of PMO operations related to communication, value measurement, and future planning.

In the remaining chapters, specific functions of the PMO from the standards, knowledge, consulting perspectives will be discussed. These areas of operation encompass a number of important potential areas of focus for the PMO. Although every PMO will address these areas to a different degree, some involvement in each will likely occur. Therefore, the next three chapters are designed to permit the reader to focus on specific areas within these domains that are of interest. The planning, start-up, and operational processes, together with an understanding of the areas of focus within each of these domains, provides a well-rounded view of start-up, operational, and functional considerations within the PMO environment.

THE PMO AS A
STANDARDS ORGANIZATION

INTRODUCTION

Chapter 6 will address the role of the PMO as a standards organization. Standardization may include defining and enforcing uniform project management processes across the organization, utilizing standard tools and templates to perform project management tasks, or maintaining standardized management reporting or project tracking mechanisms to ensure a uniform view of projects, progress, and issues across the organization that the PMO influences. The benefits of standardization are significant. From a project execution standpoint, standardization ensures that a uniform set of practices is available to guide project managers in the delivery of projects, reducing the amount of time project managers spend developing tools to assist with management of projects and ensuring that project managers across the organization are operating within a framework that supports management reporting needs and promotes utilizing best practices. From a management perspective, standardization ensures that uniform data is captured and reported to facilitate summarized management reporting and that mechanisms can be developed to accurately track the status of projects across the organization and to ensure processing uniformity. Four areas of standardization will be examined in Chapter 6:

- Project management standards
- Project management toolsets
- Project portfolio management
- Project reporting

Within each of these areas, an overview of the goals of standardization and expected benefits that can be achieved through implementing change will be discussed, along with practical guidance on developing manageable solutions to address standards challenges within the project management and PMO contexts.

THE STANDARDS CONTEXT

Before considering the specific areas of standardization that will be addressed in this chapter, it is important to understand the standards context from a PMO perspective. For many organizations, the standards role is one of the primary areas of perceived benefit that causes organizational leaders to consider the implementation of a PMO. Typically, the expectations around how standardization will transform the organization and ensure better project outcomes are high. Unfortunately, although the role of standardization and the ability of the PMO to influence standardization within the organization are significant, the process of properly defining, aligning, and deploying standards seldom occurs as fast as the organization's management might prefer. Even in cases in which the organization already has some level of standardization of processes in place (and perhaps more importantly in these cases), it is critical to review and understand the needs of the PMO's stakeholders and to respect the processes currently in place before making significant changes to the way project management is undertaken within the organization. Developing and deploying standards will require significant communication and collaboration with management and the project management community in order to ensure that the standards developed, when implemented, will achieve the intended benefits without creating an undue burden on those who are expected to operate within the standards. Therefore, the transformation from the *as is* state in the organization to the *desired* state from a standardization perspective will take time.

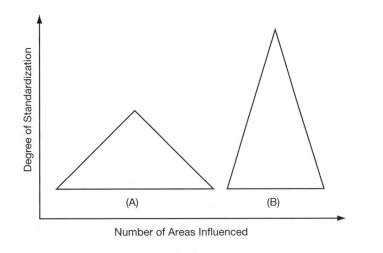

Figure 6.1 Scope of standardization. (A) Far and wide; (B) deep and narrow.

Defining the *desired* state of standardization is a complex proposition in its own right. Will the role of the PMO be to evolve the entire process by which projects are approved, planned, and executed within the organization? If so, where should the PMO start? If not, which specific areas of focus are the most important from management's perspective? Which areas are the most important from the project community's perspective? These are all interesting questions and certainly many more could be posed as well. Standardization means different things to different people and the approach that the PMO takes to undertaking standardization, especially in the process context, will depend on the desired end state. Essentially, there are two approaches to standardization that can be considered—*far and wide* and *deep and narrow*. These approaches are depicted in Figure 6.1.

Far and wide. Triangle A in Figure 6.1 represents the far and wide approach. In this approach, the PMO attempts to influence a number of areas within the project and program management context, but at a relatively low degree of standardization. In the far and wide approach, general standards, guidance on suggested best practices, and mentoring are often used to attempt to steer the project management community toward a more standardized mode of operation. This approach facilitates a more expedient deployment, but at the expense of taking less time to analyze each process that will be influenced and to develop best practices. When useful, standardized processes are already in use within some areas of the organization but not in others, this approach can be used through reapplication of existing processes. Alternatively, if some methodology developed by a third party will be deployed to the organization, it may be possible to affect a significant number of areas of project management practice at once. However, in all situations, caution must be exercised so that the level of change being introduced does not negatively impact the ability of the project community to manage current project efforts or throw the organization into a state of upheaval by introducing too much change too quickly.

Deep and narrow. Triangle B depicts the deep and narrow approach. Although the number of areas influenced is significantly less in this approach, the degree of standardization that can be initially achieved is significantly greater. By limiting the scope of standardization, more time can be spent analyzing current practices in the organization for the key areas that will be addressed; collaborating with members of the project management community on revised, standardized processes; training and mentoring the affected members of the organization on the revised processes; and monitoring and improving the processes once implemented. Unless the PMO staff is large, quite likely the PMO will only be able to consider a few processes at a time, building a significantly more robust set of tools, templates, and techniques for the areas that will be standardized. However, benefits in these areas will come at the expense of other potential areas of focus that will remain in their current state longer due to the additional effort required to focus more deeply on only a few areas of focus that is dictated by the deep and narrow approach.

Achieving a balance. Ideally an appropriate balance between the two approaches can be achieved. Standardization is in many respects an evolutionary process and as such it is not necessary to develop a "perfect" process immediately because, over time, the PMO will evaluate the effectiveness of standards and create updates to reflect organizational needs and further process refinement. Yet, developing standards and then regularly modifying them is not a preferred approach because the organization will continually be in a state of flux as new versions of standards are released. Regularly scheduled updates on a relatively infrequent basis are acceptable; however, monthly or weekly updates are not.

Ideally the areas of focus from a standardization perspective, whether processes alone or some combination of processes, tools, reporting, and other areas, should be mapped and agreed to with management so that it is clear when and how certain standards will be delivered. This process may be achieved using the PMO roadmap itself as described in Chapter 5 or via a separate standards roadmap.

PROJECT MANAGEMENT STANDARDS

In a project context, project management processes such as risk management or development of a project schedule are critical to ensuring successful project delivery. Whether formally documented, informally agreed to, or based on "the way things have always been done," organizations that undertake projects utilize some form of standards or practices to guide their efforts. When these standards or practices are documented, consistently followed throughout the organization, and optimized based on the unique needs of the organization, the benefits can be significant. Documented, repeatable processes ensure consistency and limit process risk throughout the project life cycle.

The concept of a project *methodology* takes the notion of having standardized processes a step further by collecting standardized processes and then creating a framework within which the tasks of project management are undertaken. This framework provides a uniform means of approaching projects, is well understood within the organization, and typically is controlled by a central body or committee (such as a PMO undertaking standards work) so that the methodology meets the needs of the organization and is aligned with project management best practices.

The development and management of project management standards can be a complex undertaking. Numerous project management processes could potentially be standardized. Additionally, development, alignment, and deployment of a complete methodology that encompasses a significant number of project management processes can take years. Therefore, the role of the PMO in a project management standards context for an organization that has no existing formal project management methodology will likely be to develop and deploy a common set of project management standards through focused effort on a few project management process areas at a time, leading to a complete project methodology at some point in the future. Chapter 6 will discuss the process of developing project standards in the context of development of a single standard. The process can then be repeated for each area of focus to be addressed.

Instead of the PMO undertaking standards development, the PMO staff may choose to investigate purchasing a standardized project management methodology from a vendor. These "out-of-the-box" solutions provide standards, templates, processes, and associated deliverables to assist organizations in achieving some level of process standardization. If this approach is considered, it is critical to understand the extent to which the organization will be capable of adapting to a set of standards that were created without the organization's context in mind. If the agreement with the vendor permits modification of the product, it may be possible to adapt an out-of-the-box methodology to the organization. Yet, the time and expense spent performing this modification work may offset the time savings that are purported to be achieved through the adoption of a vendor-provided product. Certainly, there are cases in which these products may be very appropriate. If an organization has no base standards, it may be possible to merely adapt a pre-built solution and move forward. However, due caution is suggested, and a thorough review of the costs and benefits of a prepackaged solution should be thoroughly considered before investing in such a product, especially if the product must be purchased and used out-of-the-box only, with no means for the organization to modify the solution to meet its own needs.

If a number of standards or a methodology already exists in the organization, the PMO's role in the project management standards realm may involve improving the existing standards components, increasing the utilization of the existing standards, or identifying new areas of focus for standards development that are not already addressed by the process assets that are in place. Additionally, the PMO may assume ownership for the existing standards, allowing the PMO to take the role of standards manager and evolve the standards already in place over time. The existing standards in the organization may not represent best practices or align with generally accepted project management practices. In these cases, the PMO may choose to significantly overhaul the standards currently in place. A review of the current standards and analysis of potential improvement areas by the PMO staff will assist in determining areas of focus for improvement to existing standards.

The project management standards development process, which will be discussed next, is equally relevant for PMOs that are building an initial standards set as well as those that will supplement or improve an existing set of standards or integrated methodology.

The Project Management Standards Development Process

The first step in a standards development process is to determine the specific process that will be standardized. This step defines the scope of what will be delivered. The process could be a small area of focus such as delivering a project status report or a complex process such as project risk identification and quantification. In order to provide a consistent example for use in this discussion, a general project process of project status reporting will be used. Thus, the specific process that will be standardized could be titled "Monthly Project Status Reporting," "Weekly Management Status Report," or something similar.

In addition to identifying the process, the specific set of deliverables that will define the standard should also be considered. In some cases, a simple definition of the standard and associated process steps may be sufficient. In other cases, additional supporting items may be required. These may include templates, forms, or other items that, together with documentation of the standard itself, create a complete package that can be delivered for use by the organization. In the case of the project status report, a process document explaining the project status reporting process and a supporting standardized project status report template are appropriate.

Much like the benefits that can be achieved through the development of project management standards, having a standard methodology for standards development provides benefits as well. Figure 6.2 depicts the standards development process that will be discussed in the remainder of this section.

Beyond the phases themselves, it is important to note that Figure 6.2 represents a continuous loop. Because standardization is an evolutionary process, in general it is unreasonable to expect that a completely optimized process will be built as part of the initial standardization efforts. The initial standards that

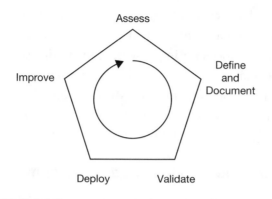

Figure 6.2 Project management standards development process.

the PMO deploys, which will be based on significant feedback from the organization, should be subject to periodic review based on feedback from the organization and updated as part of a regular standards review process. Therefore, because the PMO is setting out to develop and deploy an initial standard in the organization, perfecting the standard at this time is not necessary. Instead, over time, a set of solid, well-thought-out standards that represent the needs of the organization can be deployed, evaluated, and improved through a regular process of updating and managing the set of standards that the PMO develops. Therefore, as the process of initial standards development begins, the focus should be on establishing a baseline set of expectations about standards use and deploying standards that, while likely imperfect, will create a foundation of uniformity that can be built upon over time. When considering the next few sections related to the steps shown in Figure 6.2, keep in mind this general guideline and avoid the temptation to develop a "perfect" standard initially.

Assess

Determine processes in place. As noted earlier, the first step in the standards development process involves performing an assessment to determine the processes in place in the organization that address the process or procedure that will be revised as part of the standardization process as well as the current state of standardization (if any) within the organization from the perspective of the process or procedure to be standardized.

Determine business needs. Additionally, an assessment of the business needs that must be satisfied as part of the revised process should be conducted. Some important areas of consideration in this phase include:

- Gathering information on any existing processes in the organization that are currently used to facilitate the process to be standardized, including current benefits provided and challenges encountered through use of the existing processes
- Gathering business requirements that represent the needs that must be met in the new, standardized process
- Defining the individuals or groups in the organization that will be affected by the new, standardized process

The outputs from this exercise should include sample process documents, templates, or other information related to representative processes in use in the organization, a set of minimum requirements that must be met within the context of the standardized process, and a list of individuals or groups that will be affected (directly or indirectly) by the deployment of the standardized process. In the case of the project status report, status reports that are currently used within the organization to provide project status could be gathered and reviewed to determine areas of commonality. Discussions could also be held with project managers and members of management who receive status reports to determine the benefits of the reports currently in use as well as additional areas that could be addressed and improved as part of the development of a standardized project reporting process and template. This is also closely tied to the need to gather business requirements that must be met so that the revised process meets the needs of the process's stakeholders, which are defined as part of the process of determining individuals or groups that will be affected by the outputs of the standardization process.

At the assessment phase, it is not necessary to determine the specific requirements that must be met in the final standard. The assessment is intended to determine what is currently in place, what changes would benefit stakeholders who are affected by the process being standardized, and what elements of the existing process (or processes) in the organization provide benefit to the organization currently. The process of determining what should be included in the standardized process will be discussed in the next step.

Define and Document

With assessment data in hand, the process of defining a standard and documenting the standard can be undertaken. As a starting point for designing the standard, consider the existing process examples that were collected as part of the assessment process. (If no examples of existing processes were located, this step may be eliminated.) *Note*: Merely combining all of the elements of all of the examples that have been collected for inclusion in the final standard, in an attempt to "please everyone" through addressing every need represented in the examples (and perhaps others as well if additional elements beyond what is represented in the examples are determined to be relevant as part of the assessment process), is not advisable. Instead, first gain an understanding of what is "required" to be included in the standard. Any remaining potential items for inclusion should be discussed separately.

Determine requirements. The process for determining "requirements" should start with a review of the examples and documentation collected in the assessment. ("Requirements" is in quotation marks to note that a requirement for one constituent may not be a requirement for all constituents—another reminder of the danger of trying to please everyone). The review process is fairly straightforward. For each example provided, note the level of commonality between the example and other examples collected in terms of the elements of the examples that have full similarly (cases in which all examples contain some similar element) or partial similarity (cases in which some examples contain similar elements but not others). Figure 6.3 depicts the full and partial similarity cases. In the completely filled region, all process examples share some common traits. In the partially filled regions, two of the processes share some common elements. The unfilled regions represent uniqueness within each example.

Consider full-similarity elements. Elements within the completely filled region should be strongly considered for inclusion in the draft standard because these elements will likely provide some level of value to a number of

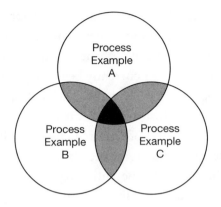

Figure 6.3 Process similarity.

different constituents (at least those represented by the samples collected). Therefore, development of the draft standard should begin by documenting these elements. Using project status reporting as an example, areas of full similarity might be related to the process of status reporting itself (e.g., all groups report monthly, all groups base reports on a calendar month reporting period, etc.) as well as to the areas related to the particular format of status reports reviewed (e.g., all examples include percent complete and percent spent data, all examples are distributed via electronic mail, etc.). These areas of full similarity create a skeleton upon which further development of the standard can be based.

Review remaining elements. The remaining elements represent either elements of partial similarity within the examples collected, elements unique to one of the examples collected, or elements collected through the process of discussion with relevant stakeholders which are not included in any of the examples collected. Potentially the list of these elements could be quite long, and, as previously mentioned, it is not advisable to merely include all of them in the draft standard. Instead, the PMO staff, in consultation with management and other relevant stakeholders, should determine the set of these remaining elements that will provide the most value to the stakeholders.

In some cases, one or more of the elements may be very specific to a particular stakeholder group. These elements are likely not candidates for inclusion in the standard and may be relegated to the stakeholders affected to manage through a process that augments the developed standard. In other cases, elements may represent opportunities to provide a better process, better reporting, better control, or some other benefit to the organization as a whole. Although these elements may not currently be in use by the organization as a whole, these "best practices" may be worthy of wide deployment and thus should be included in the draft standard. Because inclusion of these elements may create some additional level of required effort for those groups that do not currently include the elements in their process, the benefits should be carefully considered in light of the potential costs.

In other cases, the required additional process changes or time requirements may represent an unreasonable level of risk within the context of the initial standard. In these cases, it may be necessary to postpone inclusion until a later revision of the standard. For example, if the organization is considering a standardized project status report process and does not currently use earned value management as a technique throughout the organization, training on earned value management techniques and collecting earned value data may represent an unacceptable level of additional effort within the areas of the organization in which earned value data is not currently captured. However, if part of the PMO roadmap includes eventual training on and deployment of earned value management techniques, inclusion of the earned value data within the project status report may be postponed until such time as the training and deployment for the earned value process is complete. Those groups who capture earned value data can continue to do so as an activity that is separate from the project status report in the interim until earned value management is fully deployed and then report relevant data on the revised status report once the earned value management deployment process is complete and the status report template is updated.

Create a draft template. Through review and negotiation within the PMO staff and with consultation with relevant stakeholders, a draft document representing the proposed standard should be created. From a process perspective, this draft might include process flow charts, documentation defining process steps, key contacts for questions regarding the process, and so forth. Additionally, draft templates (such as a draft project status report template using the project status report as an example) or other supporting deliverables should be included as well.

Develop a standard template. Because the PMO may create a number of standards over time, a standard template for documenting project management standards should be developed to ensure that all standards delivered have the same general "look and feel." If a template already exists in the organization for process documentation, it should be considered for use and, if necessary, adapted for the unique needs of the PMO. If no template currently exists, the process that the PMO undertakes to deliver its first standard or sets of standards provides an excellent opportunity to draft a template format and gain feedback on the proposed format as part of reviewing the proposed standard with the PMO's stakeholders. Some common elements that should be included in a standards template include:

- Standard name
- Standard owner
- Version number
- Release date
- Validity date
- Goal
- Processes and/or procedures
- Supporting documents

Each standard should be given a name that is representative of the process being described. *Owner* represents the primary contact person (typically a member of the PMO staff) who is responsible for the maintenance of the standard. Appropriate contact information for the owner should also be provided. A version number is used to track revisions of the standard. Additionally a version number may identify the document as a draft or a final standard. *Release date* defines the effective date when the standard is available for use in its final form. *Validity date* defines the period of time when the standard is in effect (typically some finite period of time or "until superseded"). The remaining sections define the goal of the standard, the process steps and/or procedures that define how the standard is used, and any supporting documents that are relevant.

Once a template format is created and agreed to by the PMO staff, the draft standard can be formatted within the template to create a draft of the proposed standard that can be circulated within the organization for feedback. The template itself should become part of the PMO's standards assets and should be used for the development of all subsequent standards that the PMO will create. Although standards may change over time, maintaining a consistent template format is advisable. As the number of standards that the PMO manages grows, the PMO may choose to create and publish a concise methodology document that brings together a number of standards along with associated discussion and guidance. Ensuring that all standards follow a consistent format and maintaining that format over time will assist with transitioning to an integrated methodology document. Additionally, the organization will know what to expect in regard to how standards are documented and presented, which aligns with the general principle of a standard as a uniform method of operation.

Validate

This step involves ensuring that the proposed standard is aligned with its intended goals and validating that the standard will meet the needs of the stakeholder groups that will be impacted by the standard.

Validate internally. The first validation that should occur is an internal validation within the PMO team to ensure that the proposed standard is aligned with PMO goals and objectives, that it considers the feedback received as part of the assessment step, and that it is documented in sufficient detail to allow the standard's users to operate within the spirit of the standard without significant ambiguity. This step serves as an internal quality assurance measure to validate that the standard is in suitable form to be presented to a broader audience.

Gather feedback from stakeholders. Following the internal review, the proposed standard should be distributed to a limited group of project managers or other members of the organization who represent the standard's intended audience. The purpose of this step is to gather feedback on the proposed standard from the organization to ensure that the standard created meets the needs of its intended audiences. (Using the project status report as an example, the draft standard process and template for project status reporting should be distributed to a number of project managers within the organization who are currently responsible for project status reporting for feedback.) A survey, feedback form, or other mechanism of gathering feedback should be distributed along with the proposed standard and a time line established and communicated for returning feedback to the PMO staff. Once all comments have been forwarded to the PMO, feedback received should be reviewed by the members of the PMO staff who are responsible for the development of the standard and, as appropriate, incorporated into an updated draft. In some cases, feedback received from different individuals may be contradictory and require the PMO staff to find a compromise solution, keeping in mind the general goals and benefits of standardization.

Review updates with management. The next step in the validation process involves reviewing the updated draft of the proposed standard with appropriate members of management to ensure that the standard aligns with management needs. This step serves as a final validation point and also provides an opportunity to conduct a final review of the standard and gain valuable feedback from management. For example, the project status report may be reviewed to validate that the frequency of distribution, format of the report, and other relevant areas defined in the standard are appropriate to meet management needs. Feedback received from management can then be incorporated into a final version of the document that can be deployed to the organization. Assuming that the development and validation processes that occurred prior to the management review were conducted with due diligence, there should be no significant changes as a result of the management review. However, if significant modifications are proposed, these changes should be reviewed within the PMO staff and with relevant additional stakeholders and, if appropriate, incorporated into an updated revised draft.

Produce the final standard. A thorough and thoughtful validation process will help to ensure that the standard, once implemented, is well received by the organization. Once complete, a final version of the standard should be produced and prepared for distribution. This version should not be modified except as part of a regular standards review and update process (to be discussed later in this chapter).

Deploy

From a deployment standpoint, the PMO must consider the scope and intent of the standard being deployed, the method of deployment, training requirements, and the means of support for the standard during and after deployment.

Scope. The scope aspect includes determining the appropriate areas of the organization that must be included in the deployment in order to ensure that all parties for which the standard is relevant are reached as part of the deployment. For a small organization or a PMO with a scope limited to a single division, group, or region within the organization, the affected parties may be relatively small in number. For a PMO with a larger scope, the required communication may need to be significantly broader, with particular attention paid to ensuring that all relevant parties are reached.

Intent. Within the standards context, intent refers to the expected level of compliance with the standard being deployed. Some standards may be *advisory* in nature and intended to provide the organization with a suggested technique or best practice in some relevant project management area. Other standards may be *compulsory* in nature, representing required practices that must be followed by the organization and which, by nature, will likely be monitored for compliance. In some cases, a standard may be determined to be advisory in some situations and compulsory in others. For example, development of a formal risk response plan could be *suggested* for projects below some project cost threshold and *required* for projects above the threshold. It is critical that the intent be discussed and agreed to with appropriate management prior to deployment so that appropriate expectations can be set with the organization. In the case of compulsory standards, a communication from management may be helpful so that the areas of the organization affected by the standard being deployed have a clear understanding that compliance with the standard is expected. Additionally, an *effective date* should be established to ensure that there is a clear understanding of when compliance with the standard is expected to begin. For the project status report example, deploying the standard as a compulsory standard would be most appropriate if management's intent is to achieve standardized status reporting throughout the organization.

Deployment and training. Determining the method of deployment and considering the training requirements that must be met in order to ensure that affected individuals understand the standard being deployed should be considered together. If the standard being deployed is fairly small in scope and the required processes and templates to support the standard are well documented, simply providing the standard to the organization via electronic mail along with appropriate instructions for use and expectations for compliance may be sufficient. For standards of greater scope or standards in which some level of complexity exists, formal training opportunities such as Web-based training, instructor-led sessions, or audio conferences may be required. These activities provide an opportunity to explain specifics of the standard in greater detail. Of course, providing formal documentation is still a requirement and is most appropriately provided in advance of any scheduled training sessions to allow for review by training participants.

Support. Beyond initial deployment of the standard, which will take place either via a communication announcing the standard or some coordinated training and deployment effort, the standard must be available in some readily accessible form that allows members of the organization to access the "official" standard on-demand. As new members join the organization, as members assume new roles, and as other factors change the parties that are affected by project management standards, ensure that parties not already familiar with these standards have easy access to training and official standards documentation. A standards repository such as a website or other collaboration technology that allows the PMO to post published standards in a form that is available on-demand is highly advisable.

Improve

The final stage of the standards development process includes the processes of gathering feedback on the effectiveness of the deployed standard and improving the standard to better meet the needs of the organization. This is best achieved through the development of a standards review cycle that defines how and when feedback is solicited from the users of the deployed standards, how this feedback is incorporated into a revised standard, and how and when standards revisions are deployed. Standards should be used in the organization for a significant period of time (at least 6 months) before feedback is formally solicited, although informal feedback may be received from members of the organization much sooner. This time frame ensures that users of each standard have sufficient time to operate within the context of the standard and assess the benefits and drawbacks of the standard prior to providing formal feedback.

Solicit feedback. Feedback may be solicited through surveys, interviews, or informal discussions. Feedback should focus on the strengths, weaknesses, and potential areas of improvement for the standard under review. The feedback gathered provides a starting point for determining if any changes in the standard are warranted.

Create a draft revised standard. If changes to the standard are determined to be beneficial, these changes should be made in the form of a draft revised standard and should be reviewed within the PMO staff, with appropriate stakeholders, and with management to validate that the proposed changes as appropriate.

Deploy the revised standard. The final revised standard should then be deployed, along with additional training or guidance if required. The newly revised standard should become the official standard in the PMO's standards repository as of the time that it is deployed to the organization. Standards updates should occur no more than once yearly. Optimally, updates should occur less frequently in order to provide some level of stability. Constantly changing standards often creates confusion for the members of the organization that must comply with the standards and the PMO alike. Limiting changes to a relatively infrequent basis will help to avoid this difficult situation.

Transitioning from Standards to Integrated Methodology

As more standards are deployed and the organization's standards repository becomes larger, the PMO may consider bringing together all of the accumulated standards into a single methodology that encompasses one or more of the major project management processes that are in use in the organization. For example, if standards have been created for estimating activity duration, documenting work breakdowns for projects, and related scheduling activities, a single concise scheduling methodology can be developed that encompasses all of the standards that have been developed for this domain of project management knowledge. Additionally, best practices and other detail beyond the standards themselves may be included as part of a complete methodology. In some cases, it may be practical to develop a complete methodology initially rather than merely deploying a few standards at a time, but from an effort and organizational change standpoint, it is often easier to start with a small subset of a major process such as scheduling, introduce a few key standards to address critical needs, and then grow the number and scope of standards over time, eventually encompassing all of the relevant processes in the domain that the organization wishes to standardize.

Over time, the number of standards that the PMO must track and update will grow. Having varying schedules for updates and their deployment can create the impression of virtually constant change. To avoid this situation, grouping standards into a logical methodology component such as "project risk management" or "project scope management" and then addressing changes to the component as a whole on a common schedule is suggested. If the variety of standards created and deployed does not support easy grouping, a suggestion is to make, at a minimum, a single deployment of standards updates at a fixed time (e.g., once a year, once every 18 months, or some other reasonable time) so that the organization receives only one communication regarding updates that reflects changes to all PMO-defined standards. This consistency provides the opportunity to gather consistent, integrated feedback on the standards in general and on how the standards process overall is operating. Once the number of standards deployed within the organization reaches a point at which project managers, team members, or other constituent groups are required to operate within more than just a few standards, this type of methodology is strongly suggested, and it should be integrated with the standards improvement process.

The concept of an integrated methodology takes the concept of grouping standards a step further by ordering sets of standards (also called methodology components) into a complete, unified process of managing projects. Integrated methodologies typically document the complete project life cycle, from initiation to completion, and define a set of processes that are followed within each phase of a project, such as an integrated risk management process that includes risk identification and response planning in the project planning stages; risk monitoring and response as the project is executed; and review of risk management practices and documentation of risk events and lessons learned as part of the project closeout. When a number of these project management processes are standardized and integrated together, the result is a complete set of processes for managing a project. The benefits of this approach are clearly significant in terms of providing project managers with a complete toolset to guide their project efforts. The integrated project methodology not only contains the accumulated set of standards, but it also provides methodology guidance, expectations, and best practices to completely define the project processes for the organization.

Developing an integrated project methodology does not occur overnight, but if the PMO wants to eventually deploy a completely integrated methodology, considering how developed standards are logically related and grouped at the standards development stage will be helpful. Once a complete set of useful standards is in place, combining these standards into a complete methodology can be undertaken. In some organizations, it will take a significant amount of time to achieve an integrated methodology. Building a foundation through the creation and deployment of standards will still provide significant benefits even if an integrated methodology is not available. Therefore, considering such a methodology as a long-term goal may be appropriate.

Managing Standards Compliance

The process of ensuring compliance with compulsory standards is often a difficult task at best. The PMO, if empowered by the organization to undertake standards activities, may be faced with situations in which standards compliance mangement is expected. Yet, the PMO may have limited authority to influence business leaders and project managers in diverse parts of the organization that are outside of the direct reporting lines of the PMO.

Noncompliance. In some cases, standards noncompliance may be obvious. If expectations are that every project manager will submit a project status report on a monthly basis, and if these reports are consolidated into management reports, missing reports can easily be identified and noted on the consolidated report. In this instance, the PMO may choose to individually follow-up with project managers who are not complying with the reporting standards to validate that the process is understood, providing feedback to management if compliance does not improve.

A potentially significant number of standards may be compulsory in nature yet quite difficult to track and report. If, for example, a formal risk analysis process must be followed for certain categories of projects within the organization, the PMO may not be able to easily determine if this process is being followed if the PMO does not have any direct involvement in the management of projects within the organization. Certainly, the PMO may play the role of central project portfolio manager and thus have visibility to all projects in the organization, but tracking individual deliverables such as risk management plans may be a level of effort that the PMO does not wish to undertake. The PMO may choose to track only certain compulsory standards deliverables or leave tracking and management of compliance to the areas of the organization in which projects are undertaken. Although this reduces the level of control over ensuring that standards are being followed, it also limits the amount of project administration that the PMO must undertake.

Tracking compliance. Determining the level of compliance tracking, methodologies for tracking compliance, and related factors should be considered as part of the standards development process and reviewed with management. When significant deviations from agreed-to standards occur and are noticed by the PMO, the PMO should be proactive in ensuring that individuals or groups circumventing the standards understand the important role that standards play in the organization as well as the benefits that are achieved through standardization. In some cases, management involvement may be necessary if significant, repeated violations of standards occur. The role of the PMO should not typically be that of a standards enforcement body. If the intent of the standards is clearly defined, the standards developed are created with input from the organization and are easy to use, and the method of disseminating the standards is sufficient to ensure that the standards reach the appropriate members of the organization, then there should be few cases in which significant, repeated violations of the standards occur.

Minor, occasional deviations from the standards may require some level of reeducation or additional auditing, but these cases can usually be handled by the PMO staff itself without the need for management involvement.

PROJECT MANAGEMENT TOOLSETS

In addition to managing project management standards, identifying and implementing useful toolsets such as software packages, project models and templates, and other items that make the practice of project management easier may be included within the scope of the PMO's responsibilities. The process of implementing these toolsets follows the general process that has been depicted in Figure 6.2. In addition to the general considerations related to implementing project management standards that have been discussed previously, there are several important considerations unique to the implementation of toolsets that are worthy of mention.

Supports processes or a methodology. Toolsets such as project management software packages are best used to support a well-defined set of processes or methodology rather than as the methodology themselves. Standards development, training, and mentoring of project managers and project staff in the practices of project management are critical components of developing successful project managers. They should not be shortcut because a tool implements a particular set of functionality. For example, purchasing a software package that assists with project risk management can certainly assist with the documentation and analysis of potential project risks, but it would not be reasonable to expect that the software would somehow be able to discern every relevant risk for a given project. Training in risk management practices and the development of a set of risk management standards provide the *foundation* for successful risk management. Software provides a *means* to simplify certain aspects of the process.

Has acceptable training requirements. When considering the selection of a toolset, one of the most important considerations that must be taken into account is the amount of time and effort required to train the members of the organization who will implement and use the tool. Implementing any tool, whether a simple application for calculating earned value or a complex project management application, will require an investment in the development and deployment of training to support the individuals in the organization who will use the tool. In some cases, prepared training guides may be available or training may be available from vendors who specialize in training on the particular product being deployed. Although these options provide opportunities to reduce the effort that the PMO must expend on training to support the toolsets being deployed, standardized training opportunities are limited in the sense that many do not have an inherent ability to be customized to the unique needs of the organization.

As a part of the assessment and validation processes that takes place before a tool is implemented, certain benefits will likely be identified and key areas of exploitation of the tool's functionality will be defined. In order to ensure that these benefits are achieved, special attention must be given to the unique features, capabilities, or processes within the tool that provide value within the organization's unique context in any training provided. To merely deploy a tool, provide some level of general training, and then expect to see significant improvement in whatever areas the tool is to improve is a formula for failure. Processes, training, and related items must include some level of focus on the specific use of the tool in the organization and the expected benefits that will be achieved. Although this may require the development of specialized training, user manuals, or other documentation, each of which is a time-consuming task in its own right, it is critical for ensuring that the benefits of the toolsets being implemented are exploited and that the maximum level of benefit from the toolset is achieved.

Additionally, consideration must be given to the post-implementation training and support requirements for any tool selected. As new members join the organization and require training, opportunities must be provided to support allowing these individuals to gain an appropriate level of knowledge on the toolsets in use. Although some level of informal training may be available from peers within the organization, the PMO must have some opportunities for formal training available.

Invariably there will be questions regarding the use of any tool deployed. The PMO must have a role in addressing questions regarding the functionality and use of any tool deployed. For a simple tool, the level of support required may be extremely low and can likely be handled by a member of the PMO staff as part of his or her responsibilities. However, for a larger tool such as an enterprise project management software package, the support requirements can be significant. Support for installation of the package on an individual's computer may be provided by computer support personnel within the organization, but functional training and consulting will likely need to be directed by the PMO. The PMO could hire a devoted resource to manage administration and training for such a package. If the PMO has the resources to support hiring an individual to be the in-house expert on a tool of significant size and scope, this option should certainly be considered, but in many cases the PMO may find value in investing funds in other areas. An alternative option could involve recruiting and training a number of "expert users" within the organization who spend a portion of their time assisting users within their particular groups, divisions, or geographies with questions related to the use of the tool as well as providing some level of basic training. These individuals may be supported by the PMO and have a designated contact within the PMO who can address issues that they cannot resolve individually. The designated PMO contact will provide information to the in-house expert users regarding product updates, advanced training opportunities, best practices, and so forth. This ensures that the expert users remain well trained and up-to-date on the tool and its features. This model involves a smaller investment of time and effort on the part of the PMO, but its success hinges on the willingness of individuals in the organization to serve in the expert user role as well as the level of support that these expert users receive from the PMO to allow them to do their job effectively.

Supports project management standards. Consideration must also be given to how the toolset, either through its existing functionality or through customization, will support the organization's project management standards. The benefits of a toolset that the entire organization relies on for supporting its project management processes can be significant, but these benefits often require that the organization either adjusts its processes to the toolset's processes and methodology or that the toolset be customized to meet the needs of the organization. If customization is simple within the toolset itself, the amount of time required to implement changes to address the unique needs of the organization may be minimal. However, if the toolset requires extensive knowledge of the toolset itself, programming experience, or vendor involvement to ensure that the toolset can be properly customized to meet the needs of the organization, the required commitment of time and money may be significant. It is, of course, possible to adjust the organization's processes to the preferred processes supported by the toolset. If the organization chooses to take this approach, the appropriate standards documents and toolset training documents must be aligned to ensure a consistent understanding of how the toolset will be used.

PROJECT PORTFOLIO MANAGEMENT

Another important area within the standards context in which the PMO can provide value to the organization is through the coordination of processes that support management in selecting and monitoring projects that are under their control. A particular member of the organization's management team may have multiple project managers within his or her organization, each potentially managing multiple project efforts. From the individual project manager's viewpoint, the projects under his or her direct control are of primary interest. From a unit or group manager's viewpoint, a consolidated view of projects currently being undertaken as well as scheduled future projects is required. Additionally, a cross-division or enterprise view of projects may be required by senior management.

The concept of the *project portfolio* represents the collection of all projects either being executed in the organization (or appropriate subunit of the organization) or approved for execution but not yet started, along with relevant detail on each project such as resource utilization, cost and schedule performance, budget information, or other relevant data. For small- to medium-sized organizations, a single project portfolio representing all of the projects in the organization may be developed. For larger organizations, portfolios are often maintained at the unit, division, or regional level and may be consolidated to an enterprise level as needed.

The responsibility for the portfolio from the standpoint of ensuring that projects undertaken are aligned with business objectives, are appropriately prioritized, are completed successfully, and so forth rests with the manager

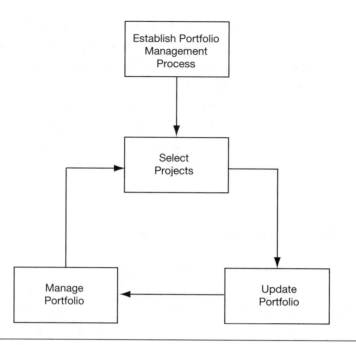

Figure 6.4 Project portfolio management process.

who has oversight for the particular segment of the organization in which the projects within the portfolio are undertaken.

The role of the PMO includes developing and implementing a process for project portfolio management and working with management to develop and maintain their project portfolio(s). Additionally, the PMO may serve in a consulting role to advise management on issues related to the portfolio, an area of focus that will be discussed further in Chapter 8.

From a standards viewpoint, the PMO should play an active role in development of a portfolio management process that meets management's needs and that can be supported by the PMO. If the scope of the PMO is only a particular division or unit, the process should be aligned with the enterprise-level PMO as well if one exists. The general portfolio management process is depicted in Figure 6.4.

Establish a portfolio management process. The portfolio management process begins with establishing a project portfolio management process for the organization (or the part of the organization) that will be served. This process includes defining standards for selecting projects, defining the roles of business leaders and the PMO in executing the portfolio management process, and creating process documentation and templates to ensure that a consistent project portfolio management process is followed.

Select the projects. The project selection process includes validating project business needs and ensuring that projects meet the organization's business and financial objectives before they are approved and placed on the portfolio.

Update the portfolio. The process of updating the portfolio includes maintenance of the master project portfolio, such as updating statuses on existing projects, adding new projects, and removing completed or terminated projects, to ensure that the portfolio remains an accurate representation of the projects being undertaken within the business scope that the portfolio serves.

Manage the portfolio. Managing the portfolio includes providing updates to management on the status of the portfolio and evolving the portfolio process and tools over time to enhance the value of the portfolio as a management tool. There are a number of advantages to the portfolio management approach:

- A consistent methodology for maintaining an accurate view of projects being undertaken in the organization helps management to make better business decisions and ensures that the organization's resources are being used efficiently.

- Consistent project status reporting and regular project portfolio updates provide a "dashboard" view of project work that enables management and portfolio managers to identify at risk projects and take proactive measures to correct these underperforming projects.

- The portfolio view of projects waiting to commence assists managers with planning resources and setting project priorities.

- The portfolio management process provides an opportunity for the PMO to create noticeable value to the organization and facilitates developing and implementing processes to ensure that consistent, uniform project selection and status reporting processes are in place.

- Managing the project portfolio process gives the PMO an opportunity to gather and analyze frequent feedback on project successes and challenges, enabling more refined and effective processes for managing future project efforts.

The project portfolio management process also has some challenges. The critical factors that will affect the success of the project portfolio management process are found in two major categories—standards and organizational alignment, both of which have been discussed previously.

Standards alignment. From a standards perspective, an effective portfolio management process will require that standards be developed for key portfolio processes such as documenting project needs and business plans to assist in the project selection process, scheduling projects that the organization will undertake, providing project status reporting on in-progress projects, and providing portfolio status reporting and review to management. Consistent, uniform processes in these relevant areas are critical to success because the project portfolio must represent a consistent view across projects. For example, having certain projects reporting data on a dollar basis and others reporting on a percentage spent basis will only create confusion. Uniformity ensures that the management view of the portfolio is consistent.

Organizational alignment. From an organizational alignment perspective, a critical factor that will affect the success of the project portfolio management process is ensuring organizational commitment to the portfolio process. Effectively executing a portfolio management process requires commitment and effort from management, the PMO staff, and the project managers and staff within the organization that the portfolio will serve. Management will be expected to set expectations regarding the portfolio management process, actively participate in managing the portfolio, and guide further development of the portfolio management process, in line with business needs. The PMO will have day-to-day responsibility for gathering inputs to the portfolio process such as project proposals and project performance data, maintaining the portfolio on an ongoing basis, and conducting portfolio reviews with management. Project managers and project staff will be required to provide project performance data and to proactively identify significant project issues so that the portfolio remains an accurate representation of the position of projects within the organization. Aligning these diverse groups and ensuring continuous communication and collaboration is critical, and significant thought should be given to how to develop and deploy effective processes to ensure consistency. The PMO will play the role of facilitator of the process, but management and affected members of the organization will have critical roles in the overall success.

Establishing the Portfolio Management Process

The components of the portfolio management process will now be addressed individually, beginning with establishing the portfolio process in the organization. As previously discussed, the scope of the portfolio may be a single business unit or division or the scope may represent the enterprise as a whole. For a single division (or group or region) portfolio with no further "roll up" to an enterprise-level portfolio, establishing the portfolio management process may occur at the division level. However, for smaller organizations with only one or a few divisions and a centralized PMO, a single portfolio for the entire organization may be appropriate even if several divisions undertake projects. This "enterprise" portfolio view provides benefits to management in terms of visibility to the status of all projects within the organization by aggregating all project efforts within a single portfolio. Figure 6.5 depicts this arrangement.

As Figure 6.5 depicts, the enterprise project portfolio represents a single portfolio, which aggregates many projects into a single view. For a single division or region PMO, the simple enterprise view may be entirely appropriate, with all projects undertaken in the division or region being reported on a single portfolio for use by management. If multiple divisions or regions undertake projects and individual control is required at the division or region level, a single view such as Figure 6.5 may be limited because the enterprise portfolio will represent the totality of all projects, perhaps separated by division within the portfolio itself, but with no intermediate view available to support more localized management.

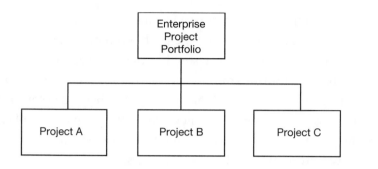

Figure 6.5 Enterprise portfolio view.

In organizations in which multiple divisions or regions will undertake more than a few project efforts, individual portfolios for each division or region may be maintained and the results can be integrated into an enterprise portfolio that contains data from each division or region portfolio. In some organizations, each group may have its own PMO as well as a central enterprise PMO. In other organizations, a single PMO may exist at the enterprise level that provides guidance to all of the divisions or regions within the organization. If each division or region will maintain a portfolio of its projects, which has significant advantages in terms of ability to effectively manage projects at the division or region level and also facilitates gathering data on projects at the group level that may not be relevant at the enterprise level, an integrated rollup to the enterprise level will require consistent information to be maintained within each division- or region-portfolio. This information must align with the enterprise portfolio requirements in addition to any division- or region-specific data. Figure 6.6 depicts the concept of the integrated enterprise portfolio, with each division within in the organization maintaining a portfolio along with a centralized, enterprise portfolio maintained at the organization level to capture relevant project information from across all projects in all divisions.

Determine approach. The first step in the process of establishing a portfolio management process is to determine which approach to portfolio management the organization will take. The *single enterprise* portfolio view has advantages in terms of having to maintain only one portfolio, but if the number of projects in the organization is large, maintenance of a single portfolio

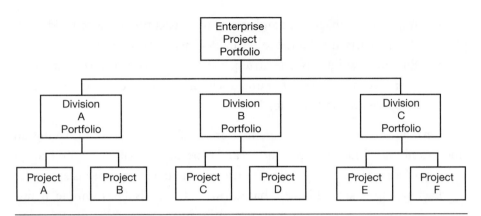

Figure 6.6 Integrated enterprise portfolio view.

can be a time-consuming task. The *integrated enterprise* portfolio decentralizes the administration of the portfolio, allowing lower level management to have greater visibility of projects and statuses, but a rollup to the enterprise portfolio requires that each division or region portfolio maintains enough consistency to facilitate an easy rollup. For these larger, cross-division integrated portfolios, software products are often used to enable consistent reporting and aggregation of data to the enterprise level. Organizations considering an integrated rollup may wish to consider investing in a software product, especially if hundreds or more projects are to be integrated as part of the portfolio process.

Understand management needs. The second step in the process involves understanding management needs and expectations regarding the portfolio. Initially, this step may require socializing the portfolio concept within the organization's management so that management is aware of the goals of portfolio management and the potential benefits of developing and maintaining a project portfolio.

Typically, benefits of the portfolio management process include:

- Consolidated tracking and reporting of project cost, schedule, and quality performance data to enable management to identify at risk projects
- A consistent view of resource utilization across projects

- Improved management and review of project proposals to validate that projects are aligned to business goals prior to approval
- Enhanced ability to prioritize projects as a result of a consistent, overall view of project status, including project completion and resource availability dates

Certainly there are other potential areas of benefit as well. Having an understanding of management's needs and expectations will help guide development of a portfolio process that ensures that management needs are met.

Each potential area of benefit has its own set of costs. For example, maintaining an accurate view of resource utilization across the organization requires that project resources are identified and linked to project tasks consistently throughout all portfolio projects, a task that can be time consuming in general and that can also be a significant challenge if it must be done without the assistance of integrated project management software. As another example, reporting project budget status may be a simple task if budget management standards are in place in the organization, but ensuring that data which may potentially be provided by many project managers is consistent (in terms of representing the same reporting period, etc.) may still pose a challenge. Consulting with management and identifying the top few priorities that must be addressed as part of the portfolio management process is critical. It may not be possible to address every management need as part of the deployment of the initial portfolio process, but laying a solid foundation provides an ability to grow the scope of the portfolio process over time.

With an understanding of management needs in mind, the process of addressing the three key areas of portfolio management—project selection, updating the portfolio, and managing the portfolio—can begin. In the following sections, the important elements to be considered within the context of each of these areas, from the perspective of establishing the portfolio management process, will be addressed.

Project Selection

The process of selecting which projects the organization undertakes is an area in which many organizations could benefit from improvement. Ensuring that projects are aligned with business objectives, validating cost and effort estimates for the projects themselves, and making appropriate project prioritization decisions in light of organizational constraints are critical components of success from the standpoints of project selection and delivery. Developing a uniform standard for project review and selection ensures consistency across the organization and also sets expectations regarding the required criteria that must be met in order for a project to be undertaken.

Although it is possible to implement the portfolio process without using the process of project selection, e.g., with the requirement that a project be approved through some other mechanism in the organization as the entry point into the portfolio process, the benefits of a consistent process that is aligned with management's expectations, which occur when a project selection process is an integrated component of the portfolio process, are often lost. Critical steps in establishing the project selection process are:

1. Determining management's expectations
2. Determining project selection criteria
3. Documenting a project selection process (see *The Project Selection Process* in this chapter)
4. Creating a project selection standard (see *The Project Selection Process* in this chapter)

Determine expectations. The first step is to determine management's expectations. This involves identifying any *key criteria* that management will require in order to consider a project. These criteria could include measures such as degree of alignment with corporate strategy, forecast achievement of a certain minimum level of return on investment, documentation of an acceptable level of risk to the organization, or a combination of these and other criteria. Understanding the criteria that must be met in order to meet management expectations helps guide development of the remainder of the project selection process. The PMO may have additional criteria specific to project management practices and standards as well. Completion of a standard risk management template, identification of a project sponsor or project board, validation of project budget and schedule estimates by the PMO or peer review, or other such factors may be required prerequisites to considering a project for approval. Documentation of these expectations, along with those of management, is the key output of the first step in the process.

Determine project selection criteria. The second step involves considering management's expectations and the requirements of the PMO that have been determined in the previous step and then developing a set of project selection criteria that can be used to assist in determining which projects the organization will undertake. A number of models may be used. One of the simpler, and more effective, models is a *weighted* ranking model. Developing the weighted ranking model is fairly straightforward. First, the relevant criteria that will be used to gauge project suitability are defined. Second, a ranking or scoring scale is established to permit individuals conducting project reviews to score projects based on the identified criteria. A simple scale is often appropriate:

5 = Very high degree of compliance
4 = High degree of compliance
3 = Compliant
2 = Minor deficiency
1 = Major deficiency
0 = Noncompliant

Other scales may be used as well. For example, if one factor being considered in the selection criteria is the type of contract that will executed as part of any contractual aspects of the project, a scale that assigns rank based on contract risk may be appropriate:

5 = Firm fixed-price contract
3 = Cost plus fixed-fee contract
1 = Time and materials contract

In this example, more points are awarded for the contract type that represents the least risk to the organization.

Another methodology may be a simple binary relationship. For example, consider the criteria of having an identified project sponsor:

5 = Project sponsor recruited and in place
0 = No project sponsor

Table 6.1 Project Ranking Model with Preference Score

GOTPMO Corporation
Project Selection Score Sheet

5 = Very high compliance, 4 = High compliance, 3 = Compliant, 2 = Minor deficiency,
1 = Major deficiency, 0 = Noncompliant

Factor	Score	Weight	Total
Project aligns with business unit goals	3	2	6

Project ROI
   5 = Positive ROI
   0 = Negative ROI
	5	2	10

Project sponsor identified
   5 = Yes
   0 = No
	5	1	5

Project risk analysis represents acceptable risk to the organization as defined in project risk management standards	3	2	6
Project Preference Score			**27**

As the previous examples demonstrate, likely no single scale will be applicable for all situations. However, having a consistent range of scale values (e.g., 0 to 5) is important.

Another component of interest in the weighted ranking model is having a "weight" value that is used to factor some criteria with a greater level of importance than others. The weight will be multiplied by the score to determine a weighted score for each criterion identified. A criterion with a score of "5" and a weight of "1" would yield a weighed score of "5." A criterion with a score of "3" and a weight of "2" would yield a weighted score of "6." Taken in sum, the weighted scores can be used to create an overall "project preference score." This score, when compared to the scores of other projects, can be used to rank project alternatives, with higher scores representing more preferable projects. As an example of the process of developing the project preference score, consider Table 6.1.

Table 6.1 contains only a small sample of project criteria and is provided only as an example of a general format of a project ranking model. Every relevant factor that the organization wishes to consider as part of the project selection process should be included in a list that the PMO has developed and then weighted appropriately based on the organization's needs and priorities. When constructing a table, provide a general scoring scale along with a number of factors to be scored. In some cases, factor-specific scoring criteria will be provided as well. The "Score" column is populated by the reviewers who are tasked with reviewing project proposals. These reviewers may include members of the PMO staff or other qualified members of the organization who can objectively assess project proposals according to the developed criteria. The scores are then multiplied by the weights to yield the line totals, which are in turn summed to determine the overall project preference score.

With project preference score data, projects can be compared on a highest-to-lowest score basis. This facilitates identifying projects with major deficiencies that may represent an unacceptable level of risk to the organization. Projects may be reviewed that absolutely must be completed (e.g., projects undertaken to comply with legal requirements). If these "must do" projects receive low overall project preference scores, further definition and planning may be required for these projects before any work begins. This situation highlights the dual role of determining a project preference score. In one aspect, the score can be used to compare project alternatives to select the most preferable projects. In the other aspect, the preference score can be used to highlight projects that, although critical to the organization, may not yet be sufficiently defined and documented at a level to ensure success. A project that scores low based on a review by impartial reviewers should be seriously evaluated to determine if it is well defined, if it has significant benefits, and if the costs of the project to the organization are merited.

The Project Selection Process

This step brings together management's needs and the project selection criteria from the previous section and creates the process steps and documents that will be required to implement a project selection process in the organization. The deliverables from this step will include a project proposal document, a project selection process standard, and a project proposal review process.

The Project Proposal

The first component is the project proposal. A uniform proposal document that guides members of the organization in defining and documenting project needs, benefits, costs, and other relevant factors must be developed. Creating a single template for providing project proposals ensures that all project proposals contain sufficient information to allow proposal reviewers to assess project options using the project scoring mechanism developed previously. Numerous elements may be included in the proposal document. A review of the base or detailed business case documents that were developed earlier to guide the PMO proposal process (in Chapter 1 and Chapter 3) may be helpful for determining relevant project assessment areas that are beyond the scoring criteria themselves. Some relevant types of information in the project proposal include:

- Project name
- Project sponsor's name
- Project description/overview
- Summary of project's business need and benefits
- Return on investment, net present value, or other benefit calculations
- Anticipated project time line
- Required budget allocation or cost summary
- Required resources
- Review of major assumptions and risks

There may be other relevant areas that should be included in the project proposal form as well. A critical factor that must be considered is whether or not the form provides sufficient information to allow projects to be judged based on the evaluation criteria that have been identified.

The proposal document should be created as an electronic template in a word processor or spreadsheet format to facilitate easy completion and submission. In some cases, a website with an electronic form that can be completed online may offer some convenience versus a template document that must be centrally stored and distributed for use. *How* the project proposal is submitted is less critical than *what* is contained in the form. Significant thought should be given to the proposal form to ensure that it captures the essential data that is required to allow the individuals reviewing project proposals to judge projects effectively. Likely the organization will not be able to undertake every project proposed. Therefore, ensure that sufficient data is provided in the project proposal to allow project reviewers to gauge projects and make informed assessments.

The Proposal Review Process

The proposal review process provides an opportunity to review project proposals and make decisions regarding which projects the organization will undertake. The proposal review process will be facilitated by the PMO, but it will also include business leaders and other key stakeholders. In most cases, the PMO will not directly decide which projects are undertaken, but it will facilitate the process of reviewing project proposals from administrative and "center of expertise" standpoints.

The success of the proposal review process will, to a large degree, be based on the extent to which the process is fair, impartial, and timely. A review process that strongly favors one type of project or area of the organization will quickly lose credibility within the organization as a whole. A process that is unduly long will create the impression that it will be an administrative burden and may lead individuals to bypass the process or to attempt to circumvent it. Important considerations that must be addressed as part of developing the project review process are:

- Who will review project proposals?
- When will proposal reviews be conducted?
- Who will determine which projects will be undertaken?
- When will project selection decisions be made?

The proposal review process begins with a complete review of project proposals. Determining who will review proposals is an important step that should include members of the PMO staff along with other senior project managers or qualified individuals. This "review team" should represent a wide cross section of the organization. Its function is to review the proposals submitted, consider them within the context of the project scoring criteria that have been identified and business needs, gather additional information as needed from the project submitter or other parties, and score the project according to the proposal scoring criteria. Note that this review does not make a decision regarding which projects will be undertaken, but rather gathers data that will be used as part of a formal proposal review. The reviewer makes an assessment based on the information provided and may represent the proposal at the formal project review. Alternatively, data from the reviewer may be made available to organizational decision makers in advance to help guide them in preparing to make project selection decisions. At the inception of the process, reviewers should be provided with training on their role as a reviewer, the review process, the review form, and expectations regarding impartiality, timeliness, and thoroughness.

Because this step provides critical data to management that will be used in selecting projects, ensure that the process is impartial. Reviewers should not review projects that they themselves have submitted nor should they review projects in which they have a close relationship with the group or division within the organization that is submitting the proposal. Utilizing the PMO staff to conduct reviews is one approach to ensuring impartiality because the PMO staff should not be tied to any particular project, group, or constituency and therefore is often an appropriate impartial third party.

Another approach, which is useful if sufficient resources exist, is to review each proposal multiple times, using two or more different reviewers. If the reviewers return similar reviews, multiple points of validation may provide additional assurance that a thorough and impartial review has been conducted. If several reviews return widely different results, additional reviews or a consensus average review may be used to determine an appropriate "score" for the project. In all cases, every proposal review that will be submitted for consideration by management should be reviewed by the PMO manager or the member of the PMO staff who is responsible for coordinating the review and selection process to validate that the review process was properly followed and that the results appear reasonable.

With a number of proposal reviews completed, the process of determining which projects the organization undertakes can begin. Approval of project proposals should rest with an "executive review committee" that includes key members of the organization's management team who are authorized to expend funds and charter projects. The members of the executive review committee should be determined by management and may include corporate management such as vice presidents or division presidents, finance and budget officers or directors, or senior members of group or division staff such as division vice presidents or division directors. Ideally, these individuals will also serve in the role of the "portfolio review committee," responsible for overall management of the portfolio, but this is not a requirement. Although the makeup of the executive review committee need not be large, ensure that the members of the committee are authorized to make decisions regarding project proposals and that the committee members represent a sufficiently broad cross-section of the organization to be able to balance the interests of the group that the PMO managing the portfolio process serves.

The executive review committee will review all project proposals within its designated scope. Activities of the committee should be coordinated by the member of the PMO staff who is responsible for the project selection process. The task of representing project proposals may fall with the proposal reviewer, the proposal submitter, or some combination of the two. The committee should meet regularly (likely monthly or quarterly depending on the average number of proposals submitted and required decision time frame) and should be tasked with several general responsibilities:

- Understanding and validating project proposals in the context of:
  - Business direction and strategy
  - Competitive direction and desired competitive positioning
  - Availability of funding and resources
  - Soundness of the project proposal and benefits
  - Legal, regulatory, or other statutory requirements
- Making project approval and funding decisions
- Allocating resources to approved project efforts

The project proposal document and project review results (including project preference score), along with supporting comments from the proposal reviewer(s) and/or the proposal submitter, provide the base information required to allow the committee to make informed project decisions. In some cases, the decisions will be quite easy. Proposed projects that are required to meet legal requirements will likely be approved with little difficulty. In other cases, however, weighing probable business value and available resources will be extremely difficult and may lead to situations in which a number of well-qualified projects cannot be funded. The committee may choose to "defer" some of these projects to a later review cycle and revisit the proposals at some later date based on anticipated changes in business conditions or other factors. In other cases, projects may be denied outright. The critical role of the committee is to make decisions regarding projects. Therefore, at the conclusion of each committee meeting, ensure that a firm decision has been made as to which projects are approved for execution.

For approved projects, the task of allocating resources may fall within the authority of the executive review committee or this task may be delegated to other management. At the project approval stage, resource allocation for an entire project effort will often not be possible because detailed planning that will occur within the project planning processes will determine detailed project resource needs. However, the assignment of a project manager to take charge of the detailed project effort following approval is appropriate. In some organizations, approval from the executive review committee signals business approval to proceed with a project under the general responsibility of a division or group within the organization. Management of that division or group is authorized to proceed with the project effort upon concurrence of the executive review committee and works as a business unit to allocate appropriate resources, including a project manager, to complete the project. In other organizations, the executive review committee will review and approve projects and assign a project manager to lead the project effort, considering the current utilization of project managers and the skill sets required to complete the project effort. In either scenario, it is clear that an immediate next step following project approval is the appointment of a project manager to guide the project effort.

The Project Selection Standard

The final step in this process brings together the processes of project proposal, proposal review, and project decision making into a single standard that, when deployed to the organization, clearly outlines the process by which proposals are submitted, reviewed, and approved or denied. This document should be created and managed in the same manner as any other project standard. Therefore, a complete review of the standards creation process will not be provided here. However, it is important to note a few points regarding the information that should be included within the context of a project selection standard.

The proposal time line. The first important component that must be considered is developing a time line that defines the entire lifecycle of a proposed project, from submission of the initial project proposal document through disposition of the proposal via the executive review committee (referred to as the "proposal review cycle"). This time line will serve as the basis for the project selection standard, ensuring that members of the organization understand not only what *documentation* is required to submit a project proposal, but also within what *time constraints* this documentation must be submitted in order to ensure timely consideration of the project proposal. The specific time frame required will vary from PMO to PMO based on the frequency of executive review committee meetings, anticipated number of proposals to be reviewed per review cycle, size of the PMO staff, and other factors.

The review cycle. A typical review cycle for an executive review committee meeting that occurs monthly may follow the time line depicted in Figure 6.7. Notice that the starting point for the review cycle is 4 weeks prior to the meeting of the executive review committee: 1 week is allocated to processing proposals received, addressing any administrative issues related to the proposals received, and assigning reviewers; 2 weeks are devoted to conducting reviews and preparing review results and proposal documentation for submission to members of the executive review committee; and prior to the executive review committee meeting, a final week is devoted to allowing sufficient time for members of the committee to review proposals and proposal review findings. This final week also allows the PMO staff to have time to prepare for the

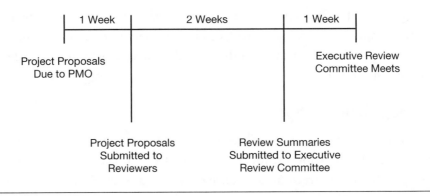

Figure 6.7 Proposal review cycle.

executive review committee meeting. For smaller PMOs or organizations in which the number of submitted proposals is expected to be low, this time line could be compressed and still have sufficient time included to allow for a thorough review and decision-making process. In an organization in which the executive review committee will meet less frequently than monthly, a deadline of 4 weeks prior to the meeting may still be appropriate. It is important to ensure that members of the executive review committee will have sufficient time to review proposals and reviewer feedback prior to the executive review committee meeting. Therefore, the final week prior to the meeting should be reserved for this review regardless of whether other areas of the time line are compressed or not.

The selection process standard document. With a time line, a standard proposal format, and a set of guidelines for evaluating project proposals complete, development of the project selection standard involves bringing these items together into a single, consolidated document that addresses the following major points:

- Overview of the project selection process
- Project proposal format and required supporting documentation
- Method of proposal submission and required submission time line
- Overview of the proposal review process (including key evaluation criteria)
- PMO contact for process questions

The final standard, once reviewed and approved by the PMO manager and the organization's management, can then be deployed to the organization and put to use as the remainder of the portfolio management process is developed and deployed.

Developing the Portfolio

The project selection process will determine which projects the organization undertakes. The portfolio will then document the projects the organization has undertaken and track performance of these projects. However, reporting every project in the organization on the portfolio is not necessary. Small projects or projects that do not meet some minimum threshold criteria defined by management (e.g., in terms of scope, cost, or schedule) may be tracked through internal processes within the organization and therefore may not require visibility on the portfolio. In general, the tradeoff between placing a project or category of projects on the portfolio or leaving the efforts to some other process lies in the administrative overhead required by the PMO to manage the portfolio. More projects represent more effort on the part of the PMO to gather performance data and keep the portfolio up-to-date. A portfolio with fewer projects is more convenient from a portfolio management perspective, but results in less visibility to the overall project situation in the organization. Some organizations will choose to present only "key," "critical," or "high-priority" projects on their portfolios. This is perfectly acceptable as long as the definitions of key, critical, and high priority are clear. The portfolio is designed to be a management tool. Like most management tools, developing it in a manner that creates the most net benefit to the organization and its managment is preferred.

As projects are approved and meet the criteria for portfolio reporting, they will flow onto the portfolio and be tracked over their lifetime. As projects are completed or terminated, they will be removed from the portfolio. The portfolio should be viewed as a "living" document, subject to review and update at regular intervals. Even though "alive," updates and reviews should be conducted in a systematic manner so that the portfolio remains accurate. Establishing the position of portfolio manager within the PMO (or, for a smaller PMO, utilizing an existing resource on a part-time basis to serve in the role in addition to other duties) is the most appropriate means of ensuring that consistency of reviews and updates is maintained. The general duties of the portfolio manager include:

- Defining and documenting portfolio standards in terms of:
  - Data reported on the portfolio
  - Method of obtaining required portfolio data
  - Update process for managing portfolio additions and attrition
- Maintaining and updating the project portfolio
- Briefing management on portfolio contents, issues, and other relevant items
- Working with the PMO staff to ensure that other relevant standards are aligned with the portfolio process
- Serving as the first point of contact within the PMO for questions regarding the portfolio, portfolio process, and related standards
- Other duties as assigned by the PMO manager

Define the portfolio format. One of the first tasks for the portfolio manager is to define the portfolio format that will be used by the organization. The general goal of the portfolio is to provide an overview of projects being undertaken in the organization along with key cost, schedule, quality, risk, and other relevant data in order to allow management and other interested parties to understand the overall status of project efforts within the organization. Specific portfolio formats can vary widely and are typically based on management's data needs. Therefore, a review of the key performance indicators or other relevant data items that management requires should be included as part of the process of developing the portfolio format. In general, the types of base project data reported on the portfolio include:

- Identification data
  - Project name
  - Portfolio project number (or some other unique identifier that is assigned to each project on the portfolio)
  - Project manager name
  - Business unit, division, or region in which the project is being undertaken

- Project data
  - Inception date
  - Anticipated completion date
  - Current phase
  - Major phase or milestone completion dates

- Performance data
  - Percent complete, percent spent
  - Total spending versus budget
  - Cost variance, schedule variance
  - Cost performance index, schedule performance index, estimate at completion, or other earned value metrics (if earned value management is being used)

As required by management or the PMO, other data may be included as well. One area that is often of particular interest is tracking resource utilization on project efforts. In all but the smallest of PMO scopes, the process of tracking resource utilization at a detailed level, allowing management to understand who is working on which particular project efforts at any point in time and to identify when resources might be available to assist with other project efforts, is a complex task, especially without the assistance of project management software. Therefore, caution should be exercised before actively pursuing this area of focus. The portfolio management process should be viewed as an area in which benefits will be built over time. Initially developing and implementing a basic, fairly straightforward portfolio tracking and reporting process builds a foundation upon which further improvement can be built. Unfortunately, the tendency to want to do great things, fueled by the prospect of many benefits from advanced portfolio management, often leads to initial portfolio implementation efforts that are seriously hampered by complexity or that fail complete. Therefore, due caution should be exercised when determining the scope of an initial portfolio development effort.

Capture data. As long as a standard template is used and it is organized in a manner that is easy to read, update, and understand, capturing the data on the portfolio document should not be a tremendously difficult task. As a general guideline, starting small and including only a subset of all possible data that could be reported is desirable. For a larger PMO or a PMO with significant data needs, commercial templates and software tools are available to assist with managing large portfolios, but it is generally possible to develop and deliver a useful portfolio using only a spreadsheet format. Although some of the advanced features of software-based solutions such as advanced resource management, rapid summarization of large amounts of project data, and so forth are lost, the cost of a spreadsheet is also significantly less than the cost of an advanced commercial product. Over time, the PMO may choose to invest in software to assist with the portfolio management process, but starting with a simple solution is certainly possible and will pay benefits. Assuming this data is captured in a fairly consistent format, a significant amount of the data collected can likely be transferred to a software package at a later date.

Manage data collection and reporting. Developing the portfolio format is not a particularly daunting exercise as long as there is clear alignment with management as to the types of data that should be reported on the portfolio. The far more difficult task is gathering data on projects being undertaken in the organization and ensuring that this data is transferred to the portfolio in a timely manner. As part of the portfolio management process, the portfolio will be made available to management as part of a regular review of projects in the organization. Therefore, it is critical that the portfolio be up-to-date as of these review dates, which are typically scheduled on a regular basis. Ideally gathering project status data would be included in a project management standard related to project status reporting, with a requirement that data be provided in a format that can be transferred to the portfolio with reasonable ease. If project status reports are scheduled to be provided to the PMO by project managers on a monthly basis, portfolio reviews that occur on a monthly basis as well (ideally shortly after the submission deadline for project status reports) are ideal. Alignment of (or development of as needed) the standard for project status reporting, and compulsory compliance for projects reported on the portfolio, is a critical step in establishing a portfolio process. Without consistent data and a consistent means of data acquisition, the portfolio will begin to develop significant "holes," representing project data that is not current or not available. If a consistent process for reporting project status is in place and understood within the organization, any "holes" in the portfolio will usually represent individual projects in which the project manager is not meeting his or her obligations to report on project progress. Management visibility to these situations will likely be sufficient to correct these deficiencies over time.

Define the data collection starting point. With a defined process for gathering project performance data aligned with the organization, the initial work to develop the portfolio can begin. For the initial version of the portfolio, project data on all relevant projects will need to be captured from a common starting data point. This will require all project managers to report on the project(s) that they are managing and provide the current status of each. Filling out the initial project status report form with all of the required data for ongoing status reporting will create a useful template that project managers can reuse from reporting period to reporting period, changing the appropriate data as needed for reporting purposes. Submission of this data with an appropriate "as of" date (universally aligned within the organization for all projects being reported on the initial portfolio) will facilitate creating an initial portfolio view. If software, a website, or other electronic means of submitting data will be used, providing a document with data input standards and expectations may be required to ensure that quality initial data is provided.

Highlight projects of interest. Once all project data is captured on the portfolio, the process of highlighting items of potential interest to management can begin. Typically, these would include projects in which significant cost or schedule deviations are evident as well as any projects that have been prematurely terminated or suspended. If a uniform methodology of determining status is required for all projects, a "stoplight" format can be useful for highlighting project issues. In this format, threshold values for "green," "yellow," and "red" status are determined and each performance criteria of relevance is compared versus these status criteria and an appropriate stoplight value is assigned (perhaps by highlighting certain data points on the portfolio in green, yellow, or red). For example, if project cost and schedule performance are the relevant criteria to management, criteria similar to the following may be used:

Green   =   Actual cost or schedule ±5% of planned value

Yellow =   Actual cost or schedule greater than ±5% and less than or equal to ±10% of planned value

Red   =   Actual cost or schedule more than ±10% of planned value

In some organizations, significant variances that represent under-budget or ahead-of-schedule conditions may always represent a green status (e.g., management does not view significant favorable variances as being of interest). In other organizations, even significant favorable variances will require review. The threshold values should be agreed to within the PMO staff and with management so that projects are reported in yellow and red status only when the variances are of interest to management. Other criteria beyond cost and schedule, such as project risk level or customer satisfaction measures, may be included as well with appropriate threshold values assigned.

If evaluation of individual project criteria is not desired, an overall status may be subjectively assigned by the PMO staff based on a combination of cost, schedule, risk, quality and other measures. However, the best systems are those that are rooted in a consistent, documented, and repeatable process that ensures that the determination of a red, yellow, or green project is the same from project to project and reporting period to reporting period. As appropriate, PMOs may also choose to use additional color coding to designate on-hold, terminated, or other project conditions.

Managing the Portfolio

With a portfolio in place, the remaining process that must be addressed is ongoing maintenance of the portfolio. Four key portfolio maintenance tasks must be undertaken as part of the portfolio management process:

- Performing regular project status updates
- Adding projects to and removing projects from the portfolio
- Reporting the status of the portfolio to management
- Validating and improving the portfolio over time

Perform Regular Project Status Updates

Performing regular project status updating is the most frequent portfolio task, and it involves ensuring that the portfolio remains current with respect to project status. A current copy of the portfolio should be made available to the organization on a regular basis as well. Although portfolio review meetings will provide an opportunity to formally review the portfolio with portfolio stakeholders, it is advisable to have an additional mechanism such as a website or an electronic file "store" where the most current version of the portfolio is available on-demand to authorized members of management, the PMO staff, and other relevant portfolio stakeholders. Performing portfolio updates should be the responsibility of the PMO staff to ensure consistency and should be performed on a regular basis based on the frequency that project status updates are received from project managers. Alternatively, if automated tools are available to project managers that permit direct updates, the PMO may wish to perform some validation of the data entered to ensure accuracy and conformance to standards.

Frequency of updates to the portfolio will also be driven by management needs and the capacity of the PMO staff and the organization's project managers. Although having day-to-day updates to project status would certainly provide near "real time" data on projects, the administrative overhead required on the part of both project managers and the PMO staff often makes this level of frequency burdensome. A more preferable option is to have updated project status reported for inclusion on the portfolio on a weekly or monthly basis. If a means exists for project managers to update their own projects on the portfolio without involvement of the PMO staff, weekly updates may be feasible. If the PMO staff wishes to maintain direct control over the portfolio itself, receiving weekly updates for all projects on the portfolio and making those updates on the portfolio itself can be time consuming unless the portfolio is small. In this case, monthly updates may be advisable as long as receiving updates once a month meets the needs of management. Philosophically, by nature the portfolio is not designed to be an up-to-the-minute view of project activities. Instead, it is designed to be a useful tool that allows management to understand what projects are being undertaken in the organization and the status of these efforts, thus allowing management to have useful data that will assist in prioritizing project efforts, proactively addressing issues, and effectively utilizing organizational assets.

Add and Remove Projects from the Portfolio

Adding and removing projects from the portfolio is an important portfolio management task and is a key responsibility of the PMO from a portfolio management standpoint. In order to ensure portfolio consistency and control, only the PMO should be authorized to add or remove projects from the portfolio. Projects should be included on the portfolio only upon project approval by management as part of the project selection process. If the portfolio is intended to include only projects that meet certain criteria set by management, new projects should be included only if these criteria have been met. Once included on the portfolio, the project manager responsible for executing the project should be briefed on expectations with respect to project status reporting and should begin to provide regular updates to the PMO on the status of the project for inclusion in regular portfolio updates.

Removing a project from the portfolio should occur either when a project is successfully completed and "closed out" or when, per management direction, a project is terminated prematurely. In either case, part of the regular portfolio review should include determining which projects will be removed from the portfolio and documenting the reasons for removal. For historical data and knowledge management purposes, it is helpful to remove projects from the portfolio and to maintain their relevant portfolio data in an archive, either as a separate portfolio of archived projects or as one component of a complete project archive maintained by the PMO.

Report Portfolio Status

Regular formal portfolio status reporting provides a link between the PMO's portfolio management activities and the organization's management. Although the portfolio can provide a significant amount of important information regarding the state of projects in the organization, additional relevant context may not always be available in the portfolio itself. Therefore, a review of items of interest within the portfolio is best achieved through regular meetings to review portfolio status and discuss relevant items. The member of the

PMO team responsible for portfolio management should coordinate these sessions, set the agenda, and ensure that appropriate portfolio stakeholders are in attendance and that other individuals such as project managers managing key portfolio projects are invited as needed. The occurrence of these meetings should be tied to the frequency of portfolio updates, ensuring that up-to-date portfolio data is available prior to each meeting. If project managers provide project updates on a monthly basis, a monthly meeting shortly after these updates are due (allowing time for updates to be reflected on the portfolio) is advisable. If project updates are provided to the PMO more frequently, opportunities for more frequent portfolio review may exist, but should be coordinated based on stakeholder need.

The agenda for a portfolio review meeting should include the following items:

1. Current status of portfolio projects
2. Discussion of troubled projects
3. Portfolio additions
4. Portfolio attrition
5. Summary and action items

Provide the current status of projects. The review should begin with a high-level update of portfolio status, provided by the PMO portfolio manager, which is designed to provide stakeholders with a view of the portfolio status in terms of number of projects that are "green," "yellow," or "red." The review should highlight any portfolio project efforts whose status has improved since the last portfolio review. This is in keeping with the general principal of starting meetings with good news and then progressing to bad news. There may not be a significant amount of bad news to report, but it is important that stakeholders are alerted to the status of any projects that have either remained in yellow or red status since the last portfolio review or moved from green to yellow or from yellow to red status.

Discuss troubled projects. The second agenda item for the portfolio review is a discussion of potentially troubled projects. The discussion should focus on identification of the key issues that are facing the projects, corrective actions taken to date, and proposed further actions to bring the project back into green status. This is also an appropriate time to request management involvement as needed to assist with ensuring the success of these projects. In some cases, the PMO may be able to provide a report on these projects based on status reports received from project managers, but it is preferable to have the project mangers responsible for projects that are not in green status available to provide input on the current state of their projects and proposed actions to resolve project challenges.

Add or remove projects. The next two agenda items involve adding projects to the portfolio and removing projects from the portfolio. All projects approved since the last portfolio review should be briefly outlined and noted as new projects that will be tracked as part of the portfolio management process. Recommendations for removing projects based on efforts that have been completed, placed on hold, or terminated should be made to management and concurrence should be obtained before the projects are removed. This step ensures that projects are not removed that still have relevance to management from a tracking and reporting perspective. For example, if a project is placed on hold for a period of time, management may still want this effort reflected on the portfolio even though no work is actively being completed. In other cases, it may be appropriate to move the project off of the portfolio until work resumes.

Validate and Improve the Portfolio

The process of validating the portfolio is an ongoing effort coordinated by the PMO to ensure that the portfolio remains accurate and reflects the true position of projects within the organization. Validation activities may include follow-up with project mangers who fail to meet project reporting requirements, documenting out-of-compliance projects within the portfolio, or periodic audits of project status reports to validate that the data being reported is timely and accurately reflects the current status of reported projects.

As part of the portfolio process it is critical to build an expectation with project managers and other individuals who provide project status reports that status reporting is expected on a regular, timely basis in compliance with the relevant project reporting standards deployed to the organization. One of the areas in which portfolio management tends to quickly lose effectiveness is in terms of data provided on the portfolio becoming out of date. Missing or out-of-date data must be promptly dealt with to ensure that portfolio reviews can be conducted with a complete, current status for all relevant projects. Missing data often causes individuals reviewing the portfolio to make assumptions regarding the status of project efforts. These assumptions can have serious consequences if decisions are made based on assumptions. Setting expectations with the organization regarding project reporting requirements and providing appropriate management follow-up when issues of compliance arise will help limit the amount of missing or old data reported on the portfolio and ensure that it remains a useful tool.

In addition to having data reported regularly, steps must be taken to validate that the data is reported accurately. Merely having data on the portfolio is clearly not sufficient. If a project is reported on the portfolio at 75% complete yet the project is actually only 50% complete, a clear gap exists with respect to the reporting of the project and reality. There are numerous reasons why data reporting anomalies may occur, many of which represent honest mistakes rather than intentional efforts to mislead the PMO or management regarding project status. In some cases, poor data collection practices may lead to incorrect data being reported. In other cases, a rush to comply with reporting deadlines may lead to project managers creating estimates regarding certain required reporting elements rather than taking the time to provide accurate, data-based estimates. Translation errors between status reports and the portfolio may cause erroneous data to be reported. In order to minimize the effects of these and other potential reasons for inaccurate data appearing on the portfolio, standards for project data collection and reporting should be in place and consistently used.

Additionally, it may be beneficial to perform periodic project audits or high-level reviews of project status as part of the PMO portfolio data collection and reporting process to validate that data being collected fairly represents the status of projects. The intent of these reviews is not to painstakingly sift through detailed project data in an attempt to identify every area within a project in which potential data collection or reporting errors could be occurring, but rather to perform high-level periodic reviews with project managers to ensure that data collection practices within the project environment are in compliance with project status reporting standards and to encourage project managers to continually improve their status reporting processes. When deficiencies are identified, additional training may be required on reporting standards and practices to ensure that future status reports are accurate. Adjustments to the portfolio data may be needed in some cases to restate the status of a project, reflecting revisions that may be necessary due to reporting gaps identified in certain projects.

Project audits represent an opportunity to perform continuous improvement activities as part of the portfolio process. Over time, additional continuous improvement activities should be undertaken as well so that the portfolio process continues to meet management needs. The starting point for identifying appropriate continuous improvement activities is a periodic review with management of the portfolio process. This review, conducted every 6 to 12 months, provides a formal opportunity to discuss the strengths and weaknesses of the portfolio process and to identify improvement areas. The initial deployment of the portfolio process is a first step in an evolutionary process that includes determining how to best exploit the project portfolio over time. As the PMO matures and additional processes, tools, and best practices are deployed to the organization, opportunities to improve the quantity and quality of relevant data reported on the portfolio will undoubtedly be identified. Close coordination among the PMO staff will ensure that as these opportunities present themselves, a coordinated effort to improve portfolio reporting is undertaken.

A NOTE ABOUT PROJECT REPORTING

The development and deployment of project management standards serves many useful purposes, not the least of which is facilitating standardized processes for capturing project information. As the previous section has noted, project reporting from a portfolio perspective is a key part of the portfolio process. Beyond the portfolio process itself are numerous other project reporting activities that serve the purpose of providing useful project information to a variety of stakeholders. Customers may require frequent updates on project progress, issues, and plans. The PMO may have additional reporting needs beyond the portfolio itself for the purpose of tracking additional data on projects being delivered within the organization that the PMO serves. Members of the organization's finance division may require specific information on project spending to meet budget forecasting or other needs. As the scope of the PMO grows and the information needs of the organization expand, the need for timely reports for a variety of stakeholders will increase as well. In order to ensure that the information needs of the organization are met in a manner that does not create an excessive burden for project managers, project reporting needs should be considered throughout the standards development process.

Ideally the PMO will develop and implement a consolidated project reporting strategy that considers the needs of many project stakeholders. Over time, this may represent an area of focus that the PMO undertakes as part of its long-term goals. Initially, unless project reporting is among the most pressing project management issues facing the organization, it is likely that other areas of focus will initially be addressed. This does not preclude the PMO staff from considering reporting needs as part of the development of standards in other areas. For example, if a project budget estimating standard is being developed, the PMO staff may consider how budget data and subsequent actual spending data are combined and reported as part of tracking estimating accuracy. Alternatively, the development of a risk scoring standard for assessing project risk may lead to an additional data field being added to the project portfolio, representing the assigned risk score for each project on the portfolio. In these and other cases, the important step is to consider how relevant data will be captured and retained in a form that is easy to access and summarize as needed. Although the final storage location and summarization may not be in place initially, a foundation is built for gathering the data that may be required for future reporting by considering the means in which relevant data can be captured and reported as part of the development of every standard that the PMO creates.

If the resources exist to support developing or purchasing software tools to track project data such as budget, schedule, risk, and other relevant areas and to retain this data over a number of reporting periods and a number of projects, the PMO should strongly consider implementing such a system. The data captured is useful for trend reporting and exception reporting and can be used as baseline data to support process improvement efforts. Although some very sophisticated software exists in the market that is appropriate for large organizations that undertake many projects, it is not necessary to invest a large sum of money in order to achieve benefits. Most basic project management software supports tracking key project metrics, establishing baselines, and exporting data for use in reporting. Although these packages may not have the level of integration and sophistication that exists in an enterprise tool, the required investment in money, training, and support is often significantly less. If resources do not exist to deploy an integrated enterprise tool to track key project data for the entire organization, the PMO may wish to consider any tools that can be used within the PMO itself to ease consolidation and tracking of key project metrics.

SUMMARY

Having effective standards represents a critical component in the success of any project organization. Consistent, proven processes that include best practices from throughout the organization and beyond the organization ensure that critical project management processes are consistently followed and benefit the organization significantly in terms of ensuring that projects are delivered in a quality manner. The PMO, as the central organization responsible for project and program management practices, should serve as a leader in the development and deployment of quality project and program management processes. Whether leadership is in project delivery processes or project selection and portfolio management activities, the PMO has the greatest potential to influence and guide management and the organization toward evolving the level of project delivery maturity and ensuring that repeatable processes are designed, deployed, consistently followed, and improved over time to track and provide useful data to management and for the betterment of the organization overall.

THE PMO AS A
KNOWLEDGE ORGANIZATION

INTRODUCTION

As a project is undertaken within an organization, information is created that documents many interesting aspects over its life cycle. Scope statements, project plans, budgets, and related items document the planning that takes place as part of beginning a project effort. Project status reports, issue reports, budget and schedule updates, risk logs, and other deliverables document the project as it is in progress. Upon closeout, contract closeout reports, lessons learned, copies of final budgets and schedules, and so forth document the end result of the effort from a number of different perspectives. When the project is fully completed, closed out, and resources have been assigned to other efforts, these knowledge assets remain, even as resources come and go. As such, these knowledge assets (also referred to as project "artifacts") offer valuable insight into the planning, progress, and delivery of past projects and allow interested individuals to gain knowledge about past successes and challenges in the project environment, hopefully facilitating better project delivery in the future through the reuse of past practices that have worked well and through avoiding issues that have previously created challenges within the project environment.

The PMO is in a unique position to serve as a knowledge manager for the organization from a project and a program management perspective. The PMO has visibility to the project efforts of the organization, even if the PMO does not actively manage projects beyond internal PMO projects, and also has a primary role in standardizing the way project processes are undertaken. As such, the PMO has a tremendous ability to influence the knowledge assets that are created (through standardized processes), how knowledge is captured and cataloged (through processes, portfolio management, etc.), and how knowledge is distributed throughout the project organization (through knowledge management, education, and training). Through its ability to reach beyond just a single project or program, the PMO can capture broad representative knowledge from a variety of different projects, representing numerous different areas of operation within the organization. Even in small department or group PMOs, capturing and maintaining knowledge can, over time, lead to a large catalog of project knowledge. Therefore, the role of the PMO as a knowledge organization is an important and central role that, when properly developed and executed, can create tremendous value in terms of improved organizational knowledge and project delivery.

THE KNOWLEDGE PROBLEM

All projects create relevant knowledge assets. Project plans provide important data on the work required to complete a particular effort, which could be of use as a reference document if the organization is faced with planning a similar project in the future. Project budget and actual cost data provides valuable insight into areas in which a particular project under- or overspent, data which could be used to improve estimating accuracy in future projects. These examples (and numerous others that could be listed) demonstrate areas of potential value that can be achieved if the required project plans, budgets, schedules, and other knowledge assets are systematically documented, collected, cataloged, and made available for use.

Unfortunately, for the most part, the systematic documentation, collection, cataloging, and presentation of knowledge assets are areas in which organizations face significant struggles. Lack of standards for documenting project processes and relevant project knowledge assets creates disparate knowledge assets that cannot be easily compared. Undocumented knowledge, representing "just how we do things," creates pockets of expertise in the organization and stifles knowledge sharing. Many other relevant examples exist. Therefore, a key dimension of the "knowledge problem" in most organizations is not a *lack of knowledge*, but rather a *lack of a process* for dealing with knowledge. When knowledge is not easily accessible and sharable, its value to the organization is severely limited. Overcoming the knowledge problem requires establishing processes and procedures to manage the collection and dissemination of knowledge and establishing systems (manual or computerized) to catalog and retain relevant knowledge assets.

Another dimension of the knowledge problem relates to relevance. Even with systems in place to capture, store, and disseminate knowledge, the organization must still be concerned with the relevance of the knowledge that is captured. Due to advances in technology, perhaps more knowledge is being captured today in organizations than at any other time in history. Project management software supports capturing detailed project data from planning to project completion. Word processing, spreadsheet, and database applications support documenting tremendous amounts of information, from meeting minutes to advanced databases of project documentation. Although theoretically all of the project-related data in the organization could be captured and made available for use by the organization, having vast quantities of information creates the potential for significant frustration on the part of the organization if the data is not cataloged or searchable in such as way that *relevant information* is easily available. (*Note*: The concept of relevance relates to the knowledge captured being relevant to the work of the PMO in general, i.e., project- and program-related knowledge, as well as being knowledge that is available and relevant to the needs of individual knowledge seekers.)

From the standpoint of capturing knowledge, the PMO may play a role in ensuring that information on project- and program-relevant topics is stored as part of the organization's knowledge capture activities and that irrelevant material is excluded from capture. From the standpoint of ensuring that knowledge seekers can find results that are relevant to their individual knowledge requests, the specific methods of presenting knowledge to the organization and the means by which knowledge is made available to be searched by knowledge seekers will determine how effectively members of the organization are able to obtain relevant search results. These topics will be discussed in greater detail later in this chapter, but it is important to note here that without a coordinated effort to manage the knowledge available to the organization, the organization risks creating a situation in which quickly locating relevant knowledge is difficult for its members.

The validity of knowledge assets must also be addressed. Although large amounts of knowledge assets may be available, it is possible that not all of these knowledge assets will represent standards and practices that the organization wishes to repeat. A certain percentage of knowledge assets may contain erroneous data, antiquated processes, or inconsistencies that do not align with current best practices within the organization. Left unfiltered, the organization's knowledge catalog may make these items available to the organization, thus introducing unintended erroneous knowledge. A certain level of vetting must occur as part of the knowledge management process to validate that only appropriate knowledge assets are included in the knowledge made available to the organization.

KNOWLEDGE MANAGEMENT OPPORTUNITIES

If implemented with due diligence, knowledge management offers an organization many advantages. Capturing and maintaining organizational project knowledge in a consistent manner builds an archive of information on past project efforts, standards, and best practices. Identifying and cataloging relevant knowledge assets and making these assets available to the organization facilitate reuse and encourage organizational learning. Readily available access to knowledge resources ensures that project managers and project team members have useful information at their disposal when needed, decreasing project life cycle time and ensuring that access to relevant information useful for making project decisions is available as needed.

Two important dimensions of knowledge management will be addressed in this chapter. The *Project Management Knowledgebase* section will address capturing, maintaining, and distributing relevant project knowledge through the concept of maintaining a project management knowledgebase. The next section, *Education and Training*, will discuss the role of education and training as vehicles for building and sharing knowledge. Together, these two areas of knowledge management create many opportunities for the organization to better utilize knowledge for the benefit of project managers, project team members, and other stakeholders, increasing the likelihood of project success.

THE PROJECT MANAGEMENT KNOWLEDGEBASE

In general, a knowledgebase is a collection of knowledge assets that are organized and made available for use by one or more individuals. A knowledgebase may take the form of a collection of physical assets that are cataloged and stored with an appropriate index or reference catalog. Alternatively, a knowledgebase may be an electronic collection of knowledge assets that are available on-demand through the use of a computer interface. In either scenario, the knowledgebase houses relevant knowledge assets and includes a means of accessing the accumulated knowledge. The management of the knowledge assets themselves as well as the cataloging of new knowledge and maintenance of the knowledgebase typically falls to one or more individuals within the organization who are tasked with oversight of the knowledgebase.

In some cases, especially in the case of the electronic knowledgebase, it may be possible for members of the organization to submit knowledge assets directly, minimizing the amount of time required for maintenance of the knowledgebase by facilitating a process that eliminates the need for additional human intervention beyond the work of the person submitting the knowledge. Over time, what may start as a small collection of knowledge assets may grow to a large and complex collection of related, relevant knowledge assets that, if used effectively, can enhance the organization's capacity to leverage organizational knowledge.

The goal of building a project management knowledgebase is to create a repository for relevant project knowledge assets that is organized, useful, and available to the organization for reference. Depending on the size of the organization, the number of projects undertaken, and the availability of technology, the form that the knowledgebase takes may range from a simple paper library of information on past projects, project management standards, educational materials, and other relevant knowledge assets to an electronic repository that includes many knowledge sources and that is readily available and easily searchable by many members of the organization at any time. Although the latter case might represent an "ideal" state of knowledge management, i.e., on-demand access to numerous well-organized knowledge resources at any time from many possible locations, it is representative of a goal for many PMOs. Limited resources, lack of appropriate technology, and many other factors may affect the ability of the PMO to create an ideal knowledge management environment, but it should not keep the PMO from taking the initial steps to organize and maintain project knowledge. Knowledge management is an evolutionary activity and as such it is reasonable to expect that initial implementations in the knowledge management domain will likely be of a relatively small scope. As with many other areas of PMO implementation and focus, the concept of starting small and growing over time is suggested.

The subsections that follow will provide guidance about building a foundation for the PMO's role as a knowledge organization from the perspective of the project management knowledgebase. The primary items of interest include discussion of the types of knowledge that the PMO might consider capturing as well as guidance on the mechanisms of knowledge capture, storage, and access that may be used to initially build a knowledge foundation for the organization. With these concepts in mind, the PMO may then begin the process of capturing and organizing knowledge assets as well as building a knowledge management strategy and plans for further developing the project management knowledgebase. (*Note*: Although knowledge management is a broad subject that can potentially have a significant positive impact on the entire organization, the process of developing an enterprise knowledge strategy is beyond the scope of this chapter and a PMO in general.)

A project management knowledgebase is a project management-relevant repository for knowledge that seeks to achieve the following general goals:

- Assemble and make available to the organization a catalog of useful best practices, templates, tools, and techniques for project processes within the organization.

- Build a foundation for growth in knowledge management by defining processes for the capture, organization, and dissemination of knowledge.
- Create a "knowledge culture" within the PMO and the project management community within the organization through a focus on sharing relevant knowledge.

The project management knowledgebase also serves as a useful tool for providing additional resources to project managers and team members within the organization as well as a practical starting point for building a knowledge framework within the PMO.

Knowledge, Knowledge Everywhere . . .

There is no shortage of information in most organizations. In fact, many project managers would contend that the amount of information produced, disseminated, and analyzed in support of projects today is significantly greater than what was produced even 10 years ago. The first step in the development the project management knowledgebase is determining what knowledge is relevant to the organization. Given the number of categories of project information available, the question of what specific information the PMO may wish to capture as part of its role in maintaining knowledge assets is very relevant. Although the desire to err on the side of caution and capture as much knowledge as possible may be appealing, the practical constraints in terms of time and resources required to support this endeavor may be a significant limiting factor. Thus, it is advisable to give significant thought to the types of knowledge that, if captured, organized, and disseminated, would provide the most value to the organization from a reuse, knowledge-building, or some other relevant perspective.

From a knowledge asset perspective, the possibilities for types of knowledge assets to capture are numerous. Some examples of relevant project management knowledge assets include:

- Schedules
- Budgets
- Status reports

- Risk logs
- Standards
- Lessons learned
- Articles and case studies
- Training guides
- Presentations

The question that must be addressed related to the knowledge that should be captured is a not a question of what knowledge *can be* captured, but what knowledge *can provide* the most value to the organization that the PMO serves. Insight into this question requires contemplation of the project management needs that the PMO was chartered to address as well as the additional areas of influence that the PMO hopes to address as part of its long-term mission. This level of analysis will help to validate that, from a knowledge capture perspective, the PMO remains focused on addressing the key areas of influence in which the project management knowledgebase can provide value. Therefore, two alternate viewpoints must be considered as part of determining what knowledge will be captured in the project management knowledgebase.

Limited categories. One viewpoint suggests that only relevant knowledge that will be vetted, organized, and disseminated should be collected. Under this premise, if using knowledge management as a vehicle to improve project scheduling were a goal, the PMO would collect examples of project schedules and scheduling practices, review them to identify strengths and weaknesses, and publish example project schedules along with associated commentary, as appropriate, as part of the PMO knowledge management strategy. Knowledge assets in other areas, such as risk management, would not be collected or considered until such time as the PMO decided to undertake risk management as an area of focus from a knowledge management perspective.

Broad categories. An alternate viewpoint suggests that many categories of knowledge assets created by the organization should be captured. It also suggests that the process of determining which knowledge assets should be considered and presented as part of the project management knowledgebase is an exercise in analyzing the knowledge assets received, determining which are relevant to the current area(s) of focus from the PMO perspective, assimilating those into the project management knowledgebase, and retaining additional assets received for future use. This viewpoint creates an opportunity to "revisit" knowledge assets received in the future, but at the cost of additional overhead, storage space (physical or virtual), and effort to maintain a broader scope of potentially useful knowledge assets.

The decision. Deciding which approach to take is a fundamental decision that must be considered as part of planning for implementation of the project management knowledgebase. In general, the principle of "more is better" may be applicable in this situation. If the organization has the capacity to capture and retain knowledge assets for a variety of processes, even those not initially within the areas of focus for the project management knowledgebase, capturing these assets can be valuable and will provide a basis for expansion of the knowledgebase in the future. If the organization faces resource constraints that limit the quantity of knowledge that can be captured or the amount of time that can be devoted to reviewing, cataloging, and disseminating knowledge, it may be necessary to initially limit the focus of knowledge asset collection to the PMO's immediate priorities. The role of knowledge capture can be expanded over time. For example, the organization can later be encouraged to submit a broader range of knowledge assets as the PMO expands its knowledge focus. The specific planning for and communication of how the organization will determine which knowledge assets should be submitted to the project management knowledgebase as well as the methods of collection and presentation will be discussed later in this chapter. At this stage, it is important to keep in mind the *intended* scope and goals of the project management knowledgebase in the organization as these topics are addressed.

Developing a Knowledge Management Action Plan

Developing and documenting a plan that will facilitate building the project management knowledgebase is important. Having an action plan ensures that a time line and a task list are in place to guide the implementation of the project management knowledgebase. The components of this plan should include:

- Determining who will be responsible for establishing and maintaining the project management knowledgebase

- Identifying the relevant knowledge assets that will be collected
- Documenting the process for collecting knowledge assets, including expectations of organizational involvement
- Determining how knowledge relevance and validity will be addressed
- Determining an appropriate facility for cataloging and disseminating accumulated knowledge
- Presenting the project management knowledgebase to the organization

In the following subsections, each of these important components of planning for the project management knowledgebase will be discussed.

Finding a Knowledge Leader

The process of collecting, organizing, and distributing knowledge to the organization will require a commitment of time from the PMO staff regardless of the size and scope of the effort undertaken. For a pilot project or a relatively small implementation of the project management knowledgebase, an existing PMO resource working on a part-time basis on knowledge management activities may be a viable option. For large PMOs or PMOs considering a knowledgebase of more significant scope, a dedicated resource may be required. Because systematic knowledge management from a project management standpoint represents a unique, new undertaking for many organizations, appointing an existing member of the PMO staff to perform the initial work required for beginning to capture, organize, and disseminate knowledge is advisable.

Choosing the appropriate resource for the job, whether an existing member of the PMO staff or an additional hired position, is important. Although prior experience in knowledge management would be helpful, it may be difficult to find resources who have this experience within the existing PMO (even within the organization). If an external candidate will be considered, including experience with developing knowledge management solutions, working with knowledge management software, and effectively working with an organization to develop a knowledge management strategy are desirable traits. If an existing member of the PMO staff will be utilized to lead the project management knowledgebase effort, a member who has capacity to devote at least one quarter of his or her time to the effort should be selected. For an external candidate or a PMO candidate, experience with project management practices and techniques, experience collaboratively working with an organization to design and implement processes, and strong organization and communication skills are desirable.

Determining Knowledgebase Scope

As the PMO begins to engage in the knowledge domain, ensure that a clear scope exists to govern the types of knowledge management activities that are undertaken. This scope should focus on the types of knowledge assets that will be captured and managed by the PMO. As previously discussed, there are many possibilities and attempting to capture and retain a broad scope of assets, at least initially, can dilute efforts to ensure that a strong foundation for the project management knowledgebase is built. Therefore, focusing on a few key categories of knowledge assets, and linking the capture, organization, and dissemination of these assets to the PMO's goals and strategies, is crucial. If the PMO is tasked to focus on developing standardized processes to produce better estimating and schedule tracking, knowledge assets in the general category of project scheduling, including examples of project schedules, estimating templates that have been used within the organization with good results, best practices from external organizations that address scheduling topics, and other relevant types of scheduling knowledge assets should be sought out and collected.

A general scope statement for the project management knowledgebase should include categories of knowledge that will be captured as well as specific types of knowledge assets within these categories. At this stage, it is not necessary to consider the method by which these assets will be collected or the manner in which they will ultimately be made available to the organization for use. These issues will be addressed as part of the additional planning that will be undertaken once the scope of knowledge to be managed is finalized. For capturing this scope data, a simple format may be used:

- Category
  - Knowledge asset
  - Knowledge asset
  - Knowledge asset

Determining the appropriate scope of knowledge categories to be captured and the specific knowledge assets within these categories should be undertaken as a brainstorming exercise within the PMO team, relying on additional input from other project management stakeholders as needed to validate that a complete list is developed. The list may be focused only on immediate knowledge management needs or it may include additional areas of knowledge that will be captured as part of the long-term knowledge management strategy. If the latter approach is taken, a clear distinction should be made between areas of initial focus and other areas of focus beyond the initial development and deployment of the project management knowledgebase.

Once developed, the list should be reviewed with the PMO manager or another appropriate member of management to validate that the list is aligned with PMO and organizational goals. Upon review and concurrence, the final list becomes an input to the process of determining how to capture relevant knowledge in the approved categories that will be addressed by the project management knowledgebase.

Collecting Knowledge Assets

Now that the knowledgebase scope has been identified, the process of determining how to collect knowledge assets can begin. As a starting point for this process, an understanding of how knowledge in the relevant categories identified as part of the knowledgebase scope is currently captured and maintained within the organization should be obtained. This process may involve consulting project managers and project team members within the organization, identifying current project management practices (and PMO practices if the knowledge management process is being initiated after initial PMO rollout is complete) from a project reporting and management standpoint and identifying any systems in place within the organization to capture project management data. If systematic processes are in use for any of the areas identified in the knowledge management scope, these processes should be understood and examples of process outcomes (reports, templates, etc.) should be obtained. If processes are primarily ad hoc, this may represent an opportunity to undertake a standardization effort as well as to capture relevant knowledge assets.

With an understanding of the knowledge that will be captured in the project management knowledgebase and how it is currently captured in the organization, the next step is to determine knowledge assets within each category identified that should be captured from the currently available knowledge as well as the knowledge asset gaps that exist from a knowledge acquisition perspective. It is important to link the capture of knowledge to organizational needs. If useful knowledge assets are available within the organization and they align with the categories and related assets that have been identified as areas of focus, these assets can be used as the basis for knowledge capture to address the identified areas of focus. If no relevant knowledge assets are systematically captured in the organization for one or more of the areas of focus identified, a process must be developed to capture knowledge in these areas. Ideally, this process will be linked to one or more standards within the organization, thereby making a process for submitting relevant knowledge assets to the PMO a component of the standard. For example, one component of a risk management standard might include submitting project risk mitigation plans to the PMO for use as knowledge assets relative to risk mitigation practices.

Any knowledge management standards, whether developed separately for knowledge management purposes or integrated into existing standards, must address not only the type of knowledge that should be captured and submitted, but also the method of submission and expected frequency of submission. Some knowledge assets, such as status reports or other compulsory submissions required as part of the PMO's standards work will come to the PMO by virtue of these standards processes. However, others will require development and deployment of a knowledge-capture process to facilitate easy submission of requested knowledge assets by members of the organization. Submission may be compulsory in some cases and optional in others. Therefore, the submission process, frequency, and other expectations must be clearly defined for the organization. An electronic mailbox, website, or another electronic means of submission can provide an effective vehicle for making it easy for members of the organization to submit knowledge assets. Electronic submission also facilitates electronic storage, which in many cases is preferable to maintaining large quantities of paper documents. These items should be considered and a standard should be developed to guide the organization and set appropriate expectations regarding submission of knowledge assets in support of the project management knowledgebase.

Additionally, consideration must be given to how knowledge assets are evaluated prior to being cataloged and made available to the organization for use. Introducing inaccurate knowledge assets or assets that are not consistent with organizational policies and standards into the project management knowledgebase would be undesirable. Ideally the first point of knowledge quality assurance will be determined by the submitter, who should understand the expectations regarding knowledge submission via either documentation or training. Beyond the submitter, the PMO staff member responsible for the knowledge management process should perform a review of submitted items to determine compliance with PMO policies and standards as well as to ensure that the submitted items are suitable for inclusion in the project management knowledgebase. As needed, the PMO may consult with other experts within the organization to determine the applicability and accuracy of certain knowledge assets. The extent to which this process is undertaken will depend on the types of knowledge being captured. Routine items such as project schedules from completed projects or actual cost data for particular projects may require only a limited amount of validation. Unique items such as project costing models, complex risk-analysis tools, or other items that, if used broadly, could have a significant impact on one dimension (or more) of project outcomes should be reviewed more thoroughly to provide an assurance that a flawed tool, technique, standard, or process is not introduced into the organization.

Capturing External Knowledge

Although thus far the discussion of capturing knowledge has been focused on internally created knowledge that results from PMO or project processes, external knowledge is another dimension of knowledge that may be relevant and worthy of capture and dissemination. External knowledge could include case studies, articles, websites, books, or other sources of knowledge that are produced and distributed outside of the organization. Acquisition and dissemination of external knowledge should strongly be considered as a part of the knowledge strategy of the PMO. Inclusion of external knowledge in the project management knowledgebase can provide the organization with an external perspective that often provides a unique view of the project and program context as well as access to best practices beyond the organization itself.

Distributing external knowledge may be as simple as providing website links to relevant project and program management websites or obtaining electronic case studies, articles, or other relevant documents and placing them on the PMO's website or in some other suitable location (with proper permission). Obtaining subscriptions to relevant magazines, newsletters, or other publications in the fields of project and program management may be beneficial as well, but from a distribution perspective, there are additional logistical challenges that must be addressed because these items may not generally be available in electronic format. A PMO "library" may be a viable option if the PMO serves only one geographic location. For a PMO that spans multiple geographies, the use of electronic books or electronic access to relevant printed content may be preferred.

Cataloging and Distributing Knowledgebase Contents

The next step in building a project management knowledgebase requires considering how knowledge assets will be cataloged and distributed. Cataloging and distributing knowledge can be a particular challenge because of the diverse nature of knowledge assets, which could potentially include databases, spreadsheets, electronic project plans, paper documents, presentations, and other items. Fortunately, technological advances have created tools that make storing and sharing information easy (e.g., via electronic means rather than relying on paper files and systems to store relevant knowledge assets in a single physical location). The advantages of an electronic approach include wide availability, near continuous availability, and ease of access via common tools such as Web browsers. Potential drawbacks to the electronic approach include needing to make additional investments in required technology, needing to standardize formats for electronic information to ensure availability to a wide range of computer users with different hardware and software platforms, and needing to develop expertise within the PMO to catalog and make knowledge available electronically. Electronic options range from a simple website to the purchase of commercial knowledge management software. Because the scope of possible options is broad, the investigation of these tools should include a survey of several different products as well as seeking advice and consultation with the organization's information technology department to ensure compliance with corporate technology policies.

Cataloging content requires developing a system that supports easy access to the types of knowledge that users of the project management knowledgebase will require. Developing appropriate categories and subcategories of knowledge assets (likely in line with the structure developed to document the relevant knowledge categories that are captured as part of building the knowledgebase) and ensuring that knowledge assets are correctly cataloged within these categories is critical. If users do not find the structure of the knowledgebase easy to use, use will begin to trail off significantly over time. An electronic knowledgebase with search capability would be ideal, but if this option is not feasible, a simple hierarchical structure of categories and subcategories can be used as long as the navigation within the structure is simple to follow and users can quickly find the types of knowledge they are seeking.

Dissemination of knowledge is best accomplished via some electronic means. Making the project management knowledgebase available on-line provides significant benefits both in terms of ease of use for the organization and in terms of reduced work effort for the PMO. Maintaining a paper-based knowledgebase and tracking knowledge assets that are available or in use by members of the organization could be a significant undertaking that should be avoided if possible. If technology permits, electronic mail communications that summarize new additions to the knowledgebase or other improvements may be used to ensure that users are informed of new items that have been added to the knowledgebase. Many commercial knowledge management products support this functionality, but such a product is certainly not necessary to obtain the intended effect. Alternatively, a PMO newsletter or some other routine communication to the project management community can be used to keep the organization up-to-date on PMO activities in the knowledge management domain, including new knowledge assets added to the project management knowledgebase.

Rollout and Critical Success Factors

Introducing the project management knowledgebase to the organization is the final step in the initial implementation process. The rollout of the knowledgebase should be handled much like the introduction of any other PMO deliverable, with a coordinated effort and sufficient communication. In the case of the project management knowledgebase, the communication process will be particularly important. Availability of the project management knowledgebase should be widely communicated in order to ensure that members of the organization are aware of its existence and are able to take advantage of the knowledge available.

Before considering the knowledgebase "ready to deploy," the PMO staff should validate that it is easy to use and contains a sufficient quantity of relevant knowledge. A sparsely populated knowledgebase will provide limited value to the organization and may make members of the organization reluctant to access it frequently. Yet, having a well-populated knowledgebase that contains largely irrelevant knowledge or knowledge of questionable integrity will likely suffer the same fate. A well-balanced knowledgebase containing relevant knowledge that is logically arranged and easy for the organization to access will quickly gain a reputation as a useful tool. The use of a pilot version of the knowledgebase, involving the PMO staff and other individuals who will likely be knowledgebase users, can assist with validating ease of use. A pilot version also provides an opportunity to gain early feedback on strengths and potential improvement areas.

Monitor use. In order to gauge the effectiveness of the knowledgebase, regularly monitor its use to gather data on the frequency of use and areas of the knowledgebase that are most often referenced. For a knowledgebase that is managed through commercial knowledge management software or through an electronic format such as a website that supports usage tracking, tracking data should be collected to determine the number of users who access the system as well as the types of knowledge assets that are being accessed or requested. For a largely paper-based or manually maintained knowledgebase, statistics on specific items checked out of the knowledgebase or the number of requests for knowledge assets may be maintained. The data collected can be used to further develop the knowledgebase, to identify the need for additional communication to the organization, and to identify areas of the knowledgebase that may require further development. Additionally, a feedback mechanism such as a survey or electronic comment mechanism should be considered to assist the PMO in understanding perceptions of the knowledgebase within the organization and in identifying improvement areas. The feedback process and further acquisition of relevant knowledge as part of the PMO's knowledge management efforts are critical to the long-term success of the knowledgebase. Continuous monitoring, feedback, and improvement will ensure that the value of the knowledgebase grows over time.

Update assets. Another key success factor is the extent to which the knowledgebase is continually "refreshed" with new or updated knowledge assets. The PMO will have certain areas of focus from a knowledge management perspective and will continue to acquire and make available relevant knowledge assets that are aligned with the PMO's knowledge management strategy. This process must occur continuously so that the knowledgebase grows over time. In addition to the PMO's focus, members of the organization may be encouraged to submit useful knowledge outside of the direct scope of the PMO's focus areas, potentially growing the knowledgebase in additional relevant project management domains. Although some level of control must be exercised over the types of information presented in the knowledgebase, members of the organization should be encouraged to be active contributors of knowledge, both within the identified domains of knowledge captured within the knowledgebase and in additional relevant areas as well.

Integrate knowledge. The extent to which the knowledgebase integrates internal and external knowledge in a manner that supports the development and presentation of best practices for use by the organization is another critical success factor of interest. Although many knowledge assets may represent useful internal knowledge, many users will want to seek out external best practices to help them understand how to improve their own project management practices. Linking internally created knowledge that reflects the unique needs of the organization with external practices that represent broad best practices within the project management community provides a powerful vehicle for utilizing knowledge for the benefit of projects. The key factor that must be considered is how internal and external knowledge is brought together within the knowledgebase framework. This may require effort on the part of the PMO to assimilate internal and external knowledge assets in a particular domain into a meaningful construct or set of knowledge assets that, when viewed in whole, bridges the gap between internal processes and external best practices. As an example, an internal process for earned value management may specify that value is recognized on a "50/50" basis, a common practice in some organizations. An external knowledge resource may suggest a best practice for reporting earned value data, providing sample templates and data acquisition spreadsheets to facilitate data gathering that feeds a reporting mechanism. Ideally the internal practice of recognizing value on the 50/50 basis would be presented along with the reporting best practice to help a knowledgebase user understand both the organization's process of recognizing value and how that process is used in the context of the reporting mechanism. Drawing these parallels is extremely powerful, but requires more complex cataloging and referencing of knowledge assets.

Maintain. Maintenance of the knowledgebase is another critical success factor. Over time, as the scope and size of the knowledgebase grows, the accumulated knowledge will begin to contain knowledge assets that are out of date or that represent non-preferred practices in the organization. For example, data such as project cost data will begin to lose significance over time because material costs and labor rates vary. Changes in organizational standards, adoption of revised practices and policies, and other factors may cause items in the knowledgebase to be representative of old practices. The knowledgebase must be occasionally reviewed for outdated knowledge assets and purged as appropriate. These purged assets may be retained in an archive to provide for their availability in the future if needed, but only currently relevant knowledge assets should be presented to the organization. In a review of knowledge assets, also appropriate are determining if the assets contained in the knowledgebase are appropriately cataloged and reviewing aspects of the knowledge collection and dissemination processes to identify potential areas of improvement. Conducting periodic reviews of the knowledgebase contents and knowledge management procedures ensures that the project management knowledgebase remains a useful tool. These activities should be included as part of the responsibilities of the member of the PMO staff that has responsibility for the project management knowledgebase.

Beyond the Knowledgebase

The participatory nature of knowledge management, encouraging those with knowledge to share knowledge for the benefit of the organization, is an intriguing concept that extends beyond the project management knowledgebase. The broader concept of knowledge management as a cultural factor within the organization is worthy of mention. The project management knowledgebase creates a foundation for making relevant knowledge assets available to the organization, but the knowledgebase is only one mechanism that the PMO may facilitate to foster effective knowledge management within the organization. Although the general concept of knowledge management is broad and beyond the scope of this discussion, from a PMO perspective, two additional components of knowledge management are important.

Interaction. The first component relates to the role of the PMO in facilitating knowledge management through interaction between members of the organization. Although the project management knowledgebase provides the opportunity to make knowledge assets available to the organization, the relatively static nature of the knowledgebase is not conducive to bringing together those with knowledge and those with knowledge needs. A logical extension of the PMO knowledgebase, if technologically feasible within the organization's information infrastructure, would be to include facilities that permit members of the organization to post knowledge "requests." Members of the organization possessing knowledge in the topic requested would respond and in turn provide guidance, advice, or relevant knowledge assets related to a particular request. This interactive facilitation requires a commitment from the PMO to implement the required technology to facilitate this process and to publish knowledge requests in a manner that is visible to the organization as well as a commitment from members of the organization to monitor these knowledge requests and provide timely feedback. In some organizations, the appointment of knowledge experts or subject matter experts to serve as knowledge moderators and actively foster communication within this question-and-answer framework can be used to facilitate this process. If requesting volunteers to serve in this capacity is not desirable, place knowledge requests in a conspicuous place on the PMO's website or in some other area that is easy to find and that can be used to facilitate ensuring that knowledge requests receive appropriate attention. Additionally, the PMO must perform advertising activities so that the organization is aware that this facility exists.

Communities. The second component is the concept of "communities of practice." The communities of practice concept extends the idea of bringing knowledge seekers and knowledge holders together by forming communities of members (virtual or live) within the organization who have similar interests to address topics within a particular knowledge area. For example, a community of practice on the topic of scheduling might meet regularly to discuss difficulties in building effective project schedules, alternate scheduling techniques beyond the critical path method, or tools to assist with project scheduling. The members of the communities themselves set the agenda for the range of topics addressed and encourage knowledge sharing through collaboration and professional development within the community.

Although communities focused around live, in-person meetings may be possible within certain organizations, organizations that are widely dispersed may still facilitate communities of practice through virtual meetings, audio conferences, or occasional in-person gatherings to discuss timely topics within the realm of the community. Using tools such as electronic mail, websites, and collaboration software, community members can share knowledge, ask questions, participate in discussions, and leverage the collective knowledge of the community to improve project results.

The PMO can play a role in community development by identifying areas of need within the organization that might logically foster a community, seeking out members of the organization to serve as leaders of particular communities, and encouraging the formation of communities within the organization at large. Additionally, the PMO may provide limited funding to support community development, offer meeting space to community members to facilitate discussion and knowledge sharing, or maintain membership rosters or other community documents that may be useful in marketing the communities to the organization and recruiting members. Ideally the communities will exist in the organization as largely self-sustaining groups, by the active involvement of the members of the communities themselves and with appropriate encouragement from management and the PMO.

The benefits of bringing together members of the organization in terms of knowledge sharing and knowledge growth, whether in forums to address specific questions on topics of relevance in the project management domain or in more formalized communities of practice, are significant. The PMO can play a role in the coordination of knowledge management activities, but the majority of knowledge to be managed is within the organization itself and as such the members of the organization represent significant knowledge assets. Bringing these individuals together and encouraging knowledge sharing and collaboration is an important step in developing a knowledge-sharing culture, which is critical to the success of any knowledge management effort. From the simplest knowledgebase to the most complex knowledge management system, the power is in the people.

EDUCATION AND TRAINING

In addition to capturing and organizing knowledge for use by the organization, the PMO should play a primary role in another key dimension of knowledge—education and training. The terms "education" and "training" are often used interchangeably, but in a PMO context these terms represent two distinct roles. The *education* role refers to providing opportunities for members of the organization to gain knowledge or skill in relevant topics related to project and program management. For example, the project management knowledgebase provides an opportunity for project managers to gain additional knowledge through reviewing best practices contained in the project management knowledgebase. The *training* role refers to providing opportunities for members of the organization to improve their knowledge and skills through instruction. Training opportunities may include formal courses on project management topics or access to computer-based training or training manuals and represent one possible method of educating members of the organization. Although the areas of education and training are both important areas of focus for the PMO, this section and its subsections will primarily discuss developing the training role.

Many organizations have training departments to manage corporate training curriculums for topics of interest to the broad organization, yet far less have dedicated resources with sufficient knowledge of project- and program management-specific training needs to establish and maintain effective project management training for the organization. Often, education and training departments will rely on external vendors or training providers that do not focus primarily on project training to help define and deliver project management training opportunities to the organization. Alternatively, these training departments may purchase computer-based training packages that provide a general overview of topics of interest to project managers, but in such a general fashion that the specific needs and processes of the organization cannot possibly be addressed. These situations lead to diluted training opportunities that do little to truly build mastery in the project management discipline within the organization.

Training represents a tremendous opportunity for the PMO. As the center of expertise for project management, the PMO should be actively engaged in defining and delivering quality training opportunities that meet the specific needs of the project management community. In organizations with education or training departments, the PMO may be a valued partner, relying on the experience of these training and education professionals to coordinate training activities, but providing significant input into the types and formats of training opportunities provided. In organizations without an education or training department, the PMO may take the lead role in defining and delivering all aspects of project management training. In either scenario, the PMO acts as a valuable contributor to the process of ensuring that adequate training opportunities are available to members of the project management community (project managers and project staff members) from a foundational level to advanced training offerings.

The benefits of PMO involvement in training activities, beyond the inherent benefits of building project management knowledge within the organization, include ensuring that training offerings are aligned with organizational best practices and standards, defining training opportunities that meet the unique needs of the organization, and influencing training curriculum models to encourage participants to grow their skills over time.

In the following subsections, the process of developing a project management training curriculum and training plan will be discussed. Additionally, the benefits of different methods of training delivery will be introduced as well the process of evaluating training effectiveness.

The Project Management Training Plan

Identify opportunities. Before considering the individual training offerings that will be available to the organization, the PMO staff should evaluate the training needs of the organization in terms of the training opportunities that are currently available, the effectiveness of these opportunities, and training gaps that, if addressed, would provide additional educational value to the organization. This analysis, combined with the PMO areas of focus defined as part of the PMO business case, forms the basis for determining the training needs that the PMO should address in the near term. These needs, along with training offerings currently available in the organization, should be organized according to some logical division such as skill level or area of focus:

- Foundational
  - Introduction to Project Management *
  - Team Building
  - Fundamentals of Estimating
- Intermediate
  - Managing Project Risk
  - Earned Value Management
  - Negotiating Contracts *
  - Project Estimating Workshop
- Advanced
  - Six Sigma for Project Managers
  - Project Portfolio Management

---

* Training is currently available in the organization.

This example provides only a sample of potential training opportunities. It is intended to demonstrate a possible format for delineating logical groups of opportunities rather than for the purpose of providing an exhaustive list of potential project management training topics. Identifying training opportunities that are in line with the organization's needs and grouping them in terms of relative skill area or knowledge area provides a simple means to create a list of training needs. Not all of these training needs will be addressed by an organization, and even among those that are addressed, there may be different requirements in terms of method of delivery, frequency of delivery, and other logistical factors. This exercise is to identify *what is needed*. The determination of *what will be delivered* is considered next.

Analyze opportunities. The previous exercise is designed to be a brainstorming exercise to identify current training opportunities and relevant areas of need. The next step in the development of a project management training plan is to analyze the developed list and to prioritize the identified opportunities based on organizational need. For this exercise, the list developed previously will be expanded to include relevant detail such as training priority, intended audience, and linkage to PMO objectives. A table such as Table 7.1 may be used to capture this information.

For the purposes of this example, Table 7.1 contains only the training opportunities that have been previously identified as foundational opportunities. In addition to the training opportunities themselves, the table indicates if the particular topic is currently presented in the organization, the format of presentation, and a statement regarding the effectiveness of the training. This ensures that part of the development of the training plan considers the currently available opportunities and identifies those opportunities that are effectively serving the needs of the organization and those that are not. Past course evaluation data, feedback from training participants, or other mechanisms may be used to determine the relative effectiveness of these opportunities.

Consider currently available training opportunities and document the effectiveness of these opportunities as part of developing the training plan. The PMO may find that some of the currently available opportunities will ultimately be changed or discontinued, but the process of determining the role of current training opportunities in the PMO's training plan must begin

Table 7.1 Training Opportunities Grid

GOTPMO Corporation
Training Opportunities Review

Topic	Currently Presented?	Audience	Development Priority	PMO Objective
Introduction to Project Management	Yes: 2-day seminar; highly effective	New project managers	C	Provide consistent introduction to PM practices for new project managers
Team Building	No	Project managers and project team members	B	Build more effective project teams
Fundamentals of Estimating	No	Project managers	A	Increase project estimating accuracy

with a review of the need for and effectiveness of these currently available opportunities. As the PMO training plan is being developed and implemented, continue current course offerings so that the organization has access to project management training opportunities while the transformation to a curriculum that aligns with the PMO training plan is carried out. Over time, opportunities that do not align with the PMO training plan can be discontinued as new offerings are implemented.

Identify audiences. The next column identifies the intended audiences for each topic. Information in this column will be used in later planning activities to validate that an appropriate mix of opportunities is being provided to meet the needs of project managers (both junior and senior), project team members, and other relevant PMO constituents. In some cases, it may be beneficial to distinguish between "primary" and "secondary" audiences, identifying those who will be the primary users of the training, but also recognizing that additional groups within the organization may find value in certain opportunities as well. This information can be useful as part of marketing training to the organization from the standpoint of ensuring that appropriate audiences receive notice about opportunities that may be of interest to them.

Prioritize opportunities. The final two columns are used to ensure that the topics presented are aligned with PMO objectives and to assist with prioritization of the list. Documenting each topic's connection to one or more of the PMO's objectives validates that the topics included are consistent with the objectives of the PMO. Creating a prioritization is important because it clearly identifies the areas of focus that the PMO should undertake first and assists with planning a time line for implementing the PMO training plan. A straight numeric prioritization in which the single highest training priority is identified followed by the second highest priority, etc. may be used if a relatively small number of topics are listed. Alternately, a relative priority scheme such as the "A," "B," "C" priority scheme used in Table 7.1 may be used, with "A" representing the highest priority topics, "B" representing the second highest priority topics, etc. When a large number of topics are listed, a grouping such as this is often beneficial. Once the groups are agreed to, further numeric prioritization within the groupings may be used as needed. The important aspect of prioritization is to focus on prioritization from the perspective of development of the topics listed. In Table 7.1, the "Introduction to Project Management" topic is listed with a priority of "C," which reflects that development of this topic is a low priority for the PMO (likely because an effective training offering on this topic already exists).

The development of a prioritized list of training opportunities is not a trivial task. A significant amount of time will likely be required to consider the training needs of the organization, to determine and analyze the currently available training opportunities, and to discuss within the PMO staff and with relevant stakeholders the training requirements that should be met as part of the training plan. Input from a variety of stakeholders should be considered and included as part of this process so that the needs of the organization are adequately represented in the plan. Additionally, input from management should be obtained. Management should review the final, prioritized list of training topics to ensure that the prioritization is aligned with organizational strategy. Once complete, the grid provides the required scope of work that the PMO must address as part of its knowledge role from a training standpoint.

Like project planning, training planning begins with *what* must be accomplished and then proceeds to *how* the work will be accomplished. This includes considering how training offerings will be developed, when training will be made available, how training will be presented, and a variety of other considerations. The PMO should begin by focusing on a few of the identified highest-priority items and then developing a plan to address these key areas. In the following sections, a review of some of the important considerations from a training development and delivery perspective will be addressed, along with a process for creating a PMO training roadmap to guide the PMO's training development and implementation efforts.

Training Logistics

As an organizational entity, typically the PMO is not primarily tasked to develop and deliver training, but rather to coordinate project and program management training opportunities. Developing and delivering quality training opportunities are time-consuming tasks which may draw attention away from the PMO's other areas of focus such as standards setting or organizational consulting. Therefore, consider how the PMO will support the development and delivery of training opportunities while still maintaining a focus on the broader goals of improving project outcomes in the organization.

Developing and delivering quality training opportunities that effectively meet the needs of adult learners is a complex undertaking. Expertise in instructional design and teaching techniques is typically not within the skill sets of most project managers. Therefore, the PMO may have limited capacity internally to support developing and delivering training in a quality way. This is especially true within the context of training development. Although the PMO staff or other experts within the organization may have significant expertise in the project management disciplines, this does not imply that they can adequately translate this expertise into a format (written or oral) that is conducive to adult learning. For this reason, serious consideration should be given to involving outside experts in the development and delivery of training. Within larger organizations, a corporate training division may be a viable starting point for finding this expertise. In organizations without dedicated training experts, engaging outside consultants or trainers may be required. If the PMO will develop and deliver training internally, a review of adult learning models and methodologies for developing quality instructional materials should be undertaken by the members of the PMO staff who will be responsible for developing and delivering training.

The following subsections will address a few of the key questions that must be considered as part of developing and deploying project management training. The guidance is, by design, general enough to be applicable for those who will internally develop and/or deliver training as well as those who will partner with resources outside of the PMO to assist with these tasks. Regardless of approach, it is important to realize that development of inadequate training opportunities has the potential to do as much, if not more, "damage" within the organization as doing nothing at all. Taking time to thoughtfully consider each of the following areas and then to develop quality training products is crucial to gaining the maximum benefit from the process of developing and delivering training programs.

What Form of Delivery Will Be Required?

The first important consideration is the method of delivery that will be used for each training offering. Common methods of delivery include:

- In-person courses
- Web seminars
- Audio conferences
- Computer-based training
- Training manuals

Each of these categories offers its own unique set of relative advantages and disadvantages.

In-person courses. In-person courses, in which attendees meet in person with an instructor or instructors, encourage a high degree of personal interaction between students and instructors. In-person courses offer the most opportunities for active learning exercises such as role-playing exercises, group discussions, case study reviews, and problem-solving exercises. Because participants are centrally located and fully devoted to the training experience, it is possible to convey a significant amount of information to participants in a reasonably short time frame. In-person courses also facilitate gauging student learning and adjusting the pace and flow of the course accordingly to meet the needs of the participants. Although in-person courses are preferred for many situations, they tend to not work well for largely dispersed organizations because the cost of travel to enable training in a central location is often prohibitive. Additionally, because in-person training requires a time commitment on the part of the participants that is not particularly flexible, scheduling in-person training may be difficult.

Web seminars. Web seminars provide training via an Internet platform that allows an instructor to share training slides or other materials with participants via a Web-based application. They also provide live commentary to participants via a Web-based audio feed or via audio conference. Web seminars can be presented live or prerecorded for use in playback mode. In the live mode, students follow along with the instructor. The instructor provides occasional opportunities for students to provide feedback, ask questions, or participate in learning exercises. In the prerecorded format, the instructor records the training material and the material is subsequently made available on-demand for student use. Web seminars overcome the geographic barriers that may hamper the ability to conduct live, in-person courses through the use of technology, but at the expense of personal interaction between students themselves and between students and the instructor. The ability to make these offerings available on-demand also helps to overcome scheduling and coordination issues that occasionally hamper in-person courses. These offerings only require participants to have access to a computer with network access for the duration of the training. For relatively short-duration courses, a Web seminar session or series of several 1- to 3-hour sessions provides an adequate means to deliver training. However, for training offerings in excess of 1 day in total duration, Web seminars can be troublesome because maintaining participant interest without significant personal interaction is difficult, even if the training is divided into several sessions.

Audio conferences. Although audio conferences are similar to Web seminars, they lack the Web technology components that facilitate sharing training slides, computer applications, or other electronic information. Also similar to Web seminars, participants may join an audio conference live at a pre-set time or an audio conference may be recorded and made available for playback at a later date. If training materials such as slides are presented, they are typically provided to participants in advance. The instructor can "walk through" the relevant materials as part of the conference and address questions or concerns as time permits. The lack of a mechanism to dynamically support sharing documents, training slides, or other information as the training is being conducted limits the degree of interaction possible through audio conferences, but it may also decrease the cost. Live audio conferences require participants to be available at a predetermined time, but they do not require any travel or special arrangements beyond access to a telephone. For relatively short-duration training offerings, audio conferences provide an effective means for sharing information, but typically they are relatively ineffective at providing significant opportunities for participant engagement.

Computer-based training. The previous methods of training delivery have all included some means of engagement between the instructor and the participants, albeit perhaps limited in the case of audio conferences and Web conferences. Computer-based training is designed to present material that does not require any significant degree of instructor engagement. It is typically used for "push" scenarios in which information must merely be presented for consumption by the participant. Computer-based training may be presented via the Internet or a CD-ROM or some other physical computer media. It is typically provided on-demand. The primary goal of computer-based training is the presentation of content. Although some interaction in the form of participants responding to questions posed by the training program or participating in short exercises may be available, this interaction is not designed to mimic an instructor-student interaction. Answering questions or completing exercises is primarily used to simply assess learning or validate that participants are following along with the material and understanding key concepts. Certainly the on-demand nature of computer-based training is desirable for many participants, but the limited interaction and relatively bland presentation of many computer-based training programs may limit effectiveness.

Training guides. Using training guides or manuals may be an option for training delivery. These manuals are typically electronic or physical guides that present information, much like a college textbook. Students read the material presented, comprehend the topics, and perhaps answer a set of questions relative to particular topics that is designed to gauge learning. Training manuals offer significant flexibility in terms of when and where students can access the materials, but the training manuals must be well developed and presented in order to ensure that learning actually takes place. Additionally, when students have questions about material presented in manuals, knowledgeable resources must be available to assist with answering questions and clarifying the material presented in the manuals.

Choosing a method. Determining which method of delivery is appropriate for a particular training offering requires consideration of several factors. First, the required degree of engagement must be considered. For presenting simple, relatively straightforward topics, a significant amount of engagement may not be required to support learning. For more complex topics, or topics that by their nature lend themselves to interactive forms of instruction such as role playing, simulation, or other similar techniques, in-person training may be a requirement. Additionally, the length of the training must be considered. For short sessions of several hours or less, scheduling an in-person course may be impractical if all required participants are not centrally located. In this case, the use of Web seminars or audio conferences may be appropriate. For multiday sessions, the use of audio conferences or Web seminars may be impractical because participants can become easily distracted when not in a dedicated training environment such as a classroom.

In addition to the previously mentioned factors, the cost of developing and providing training must be considered. Training offerings designed for a large portion of the organization, such as a required training on project time-tracking practices that must be attended by all project resources in the organization, may be impractical to facilitate as an in-person course due to travel requirements or the number of participants that must be trained. The use of computer-based training or audio conferences may provide a more cost-effective means of providing the training because these methodologies do not generally incur travel costs and more easily accommodate varying schedules. For specific training that addresses a small number of participants, such as an introductory course for new project managers, the use of in-person training may be justified from a cost perspective based on a limited number of participants who will

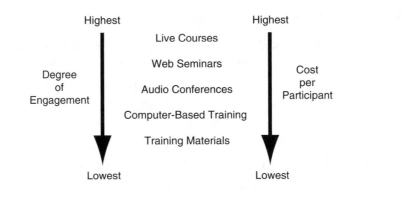

Figure 7.1 Training delivery mechanism comparison.

need to make travel arrangements and the importance of significant interaction between the instructor and students in an introductory project management course. In general, the degree of engagement and cost of providing training, per method of delivery, can be depicted as in Figure 7.1.

In Figure 7.1 degree of engagement and cost are generally related—more-engaging training typically involves more cost. The tradeoff between engagement and cost must be considered by the PMO staff as part of the process of assessing the appropriate means of presentation for each training offering. This aspect must be considered in terms of cost of training delivery over time as well as the cost of developing the training that will be presented. There is no single answer. The type of training, length, desired student outcomes, and other factors will all weigh into the decision. Additionally, organizational expertise in designing and delivering training in the various methods described must be considered. Availability of Web or audio conferencing technology, the ability to create and distribute training manuals or computer-based training products, and other such factors will be critical considerations. In some instances, the procurement of "off-the-shelf" computer-based training products or other materials from external vendors may be necessary to bridge the gap between the cost of producing training materials in house and not having any training at all.

What Is the Scope of the Training?

Determining the scope of training offerings requires developing a training breakdown structure that elaborates the major topics that will be addressed by each training offering. (*Note*: PMOs that outsource training content may eliminate this step because the content provider will be responsible for providing appropriate content.) If the PMO staff is developing training materials, a simple outline list of topics may suffice because the purpose of this exercise is not to develop a detailed plan to produce the training content, but rather to confirm that the scope of the training experience is well understood. This exercise will also help the PMO staff consider what form of training will be most appropriate as well as the types of training materials (training assets) that may be needed to support the training. An outline format such as the following provides a useful means for capturing the training scope:

- Learning objective
  - Content area
    - Topic
    - Topic
  - Exercises and/or assessments
    - Exercise
    - Assessment

This format outlines the scope of the training in terms of major learning objectives that the training should achieve, the specific content areas and topics that will be addressed in order to support each learning objective, and the relevant exercises and/or assessments (if any) that will be used to further encourage student learning or assess understanding. Focusing on learning objectives ensures that the training topics are aligned with the overriding goals of the training experience and helps frame the topics within logical domains. Much like a work breakdown structure, a training breakdown structure such as the one presented here does not attempt to specify the *order* in which topics will be presented, but instead focuses on *what* will be presented. As an example, a portion of a training breakdown structure for a course on project cost estimating is provided:

- Learning objective: Participants should be able to explain the advantages and disadvantages of several major categories of project estimating techniques.
  - Types of estimates
    - Analogous estimates
    - Bottom-up estimates
    - Parametric estimates
  - Exercise
    - Computer simulation: comparison of analogous and bottom-up estimating techniques

Defining a complete set of learning objectives and expanding these objectives to include major topics to be covered within each, as well as suggested activities and assessments to enhance student learning, creates a meaningful foundation for further detailed development of training materials. This exercise is best undertaken by the PMO staff or other members of the organization who are knowledgeable in the categories of material that should be presented. This work is not for training experts, but rather for project management experts—defining what should be covered within a particular training activity, not the detailed form of how the final training materials will be presented.

What Training Assets Must Be Developed?

Determining the training assets that must be developed to support a particular training course will be necessary. For an in-person training activity, a written participant training guide, presentation slides, student exercises, quizzes or other materials to gauge student learning, and other assets may be required to support a particular course. For remotely delivered training such as Web or audio conferences, appropriate training scripts, presentation slides, follow-up materials, or other relevant assets may be required. Structuring a useful set of training assets is best accomplished with the assistance of an experienced trainer who is knowledgeable about the development and delivery of quality training. An experienced trainer can not only provide guidance on what training assets may be appropriate for a particular type of training activity, but can also guide the PMO staff so that the assets are developed in a way that encourages learning.

If retaining the services of such an individual is not possible, a few general guidelines should be followed:

- Every training course should have a participant guide or other written materials that support the material being presented.
- Every training course that includes a presentation should include presentation slides with appropriate slide notes for use by the instructor.
- Any presentation slides used should be included within the participant training materials.
- Instructor materials and course notes should be created for every training course that will be presented.
- Training developers should consult references on adult learning practices and techniques to ensure materials are developed in a way that facilitates learning.
- Every newly developed course should be piloted before being presented to a general audience.

Although many of these guidelines may appear to be common sense, nonetheless it is important to note them as a reminder of the importance of allowing sufficient time in the training development process so that all necessary training materials are developed in a quality way.

As a starting point for determining the needs for a particular course, review the training scope statement developed previously. Because this scope statement identifies the major learning objectives and activities that will support achievement of the learning objectives, it contains the necessary base information required to begin developing a list of required training assets. The development of these assets is a critical activity in the training development process. Beginning with a complete list of needed assets helps to ensure that sufficient time is budgeted to complete development of the required training materials.

Who Will Develop the Training Materials?

To a large extent, the method of delivery chosen, scope of the training, and time constraints will guide determining who will develop the training materials needed to deliver a particular training course. Two dimensions must be considered—*creating* the actual materials that will be presented (the knowledge) and *formatting* the materials that will be presented into a set of training assets that can be used to support training delivery.

Creating materials. Creation of the relevant material must be undertaken by individuals who have a reasonable degree of expertise within the domain of the topics that will be included in the training. A number of potential sources exist for this expertise:

- Members of the PMO staff
- Project managers within the organization
- Subject matter experts from other areas of the organization
- External consultants
- External knowledge providers

Using internal staff, such as the PMO staff or project managers within the organization, is often an appropriate choice, especially when dealing with topics that include training on unique organizational standards or practices. Unfortunately, unless resources are primarily dedicated to the development of training materials, a time-consuming task in its own right, it is quite likely that the required time to deliver the necessary training materials could be significant. Utilizing knowledgeable external consultants can alleviate this issue by allowing internal staff to continue to focus on other organizational initiatives, but the unique perspective of internal staff and the detailed knowledge of internal practices and policies may be lost when external resources are contracted to produce training deliverables.

For fairly standardized training, eliminating the content creation step and merely purchasing training materials from external knowledge providers may be possible. These providers may have complete training courses, computer-based training products, or other similar materials that are already prepared and ready to be delivered to the organization for use. In some cases, a simple license can be purchased that permits the organization to use the materials as it wishes, within the terms of the license agreement, including presenting the materials to internal audiences. In other cases, the materials and presentation may be bundled together as complete externally sourced

Web seminars or in-person training courses. External knowledge providers often have standardized offerings that do not lend themselves to training on organization-specific practices or processes unique to the organization, but which may be perfectly appropriate for general topics of interest such as team building or negotiating skills.

Formatting materials. Determining who will format the training materials into a complete set of training assets that can be used to deliver the training is the second component of training development. If external consultants or external knowledge providers will be engaged, this step will be handled by the provider. However, if the organization will create the relevant training assets internally, validating that they are developed in a form that facilitates learning will be necessary. If available, instructional designers, members of the organization's education or training department, or senior trainers within the organization should be consulted for this important step. Ideally they should also be actively engaged in developing the final training materials that will be used. Relying on experts in the field of education and training helps ensure that the final materials are highly effective in encouraging participant learning. If the PMO staff or other members of the organization will produce training assets directly, minimally these assets should be reviewed by several other members of the organization prior to presentation to confirm that the materials are concise, clear, technically accurate, and appropriate for the intended audience. This quality assurance exercise may require several iterations of review and correction before a final set of training materials is ready to be presented. Taking the time to perform this validation activity prior to the training being presented to a full audience of participants will pay significant dividends in terms of participant learning and training success.

Who Will Deliver the Training?

Perhaps the most important task that will be undertaken as part of developing training opportunities is determining who will present training offerings to the organization. Although content development is certainly a crucial step, the effectiveness of even the best content can be limited by ineffective trainers. In the case of training manuals or computer-based training, i.e., when learning is not primarily guided by instructors, the content of the training will certainly be the key to success. However, for in-person training as well as

Web and audio conferences, one or more individuals will be responsible for guiding students through the training material and facilitating student learning. In these cases, there must be significant consideration given to who will provide the instruction. There are two options—internal resources and external resources. Internal resources, including the PMO staff and other experienced project managers or other members of the organization, are likely to be available within the organization. Internal resources require minimal cost to utilize. External resources such as consultants or outside training organizations offer the advantage of supplementing the organization's staff and leaving internal resources to focus on other efforts, but at the expense of significant additional cost. In some cases, external resources may provide the content as well as delivery of the content. Thus it is possible for the organization to completely outsource training. In other cases, it may be possible to retain the services of external resources to present material that the organization has created internally, utilizing the external resource as a contract trainer rather than as a content developer and presenter.

Whether internal or external resources are used, the person or persons conducting the training must be well qualified to present the material and must be adept at teaching adult learners. Mastery of the material being presented is clearly a must, but other considerations are important as well. A few of the important questions that must be addressed as part of selecting a trainer include:

- Does the candidate have sufficient experience with and mastery of the concepts that will be presented?
- Does the candidate have sufficient communication skills and experience in public speaking?
- Is the candidate engaging? Will the candidate be able to keep an audience's interest?
- Does the candidate have prior experience teaching adult learners?
- Does the candidate possess any relevant professional credentials related to the material being presented, public speaking, or teaching?
- Does the candidate have sufficient time to adequately prepare for teaching (especially important with internal resources that may have multiple priorities)?

Figure 7.2 Trainer skill dimensions.

In general, three dimensions must be considered when selecting a trainer. As Figure 7.2 depicts, knowledge, experience, and presentation skills represent these three key dimensions of interest.

The PMO should select trainers who possess an acceptable balance of knowledge, experience, and presentation skills. A presenter with significant knowledge, but limited presentation skills is not desirable nor is a presenter with excellent presentation skills, but no experience in the area being presented. The triangle of knowledge, experience, and presentation skills must be balanced for maximum likelihood of success.

Figure 7.2 also provides strong criteria for assessing potential trainers. Candidates, whether internal or external, should be assessed in terms of each of these three dimensions as part of the instructor selection process. This assessment may take place by reviewing an application, by conducting a personal interview, by assessing a demonstration of presentation skills, or through a combination of these methods. Perhaps the best of these methods is to assess candidates through a demonstration. Asking candidates to give a brief presentation on a topic relevant to project or program management in a simulated course environment allows those who are responsible for selecting trainers to see how well the candidates conduct themselves in a presentation setting. This process, combined with information on the candidate's professional skills and experience, creates a full picture of a candidate's potential as a trainer.

If internal candidates are being considered, the process of assessing candidates and selecting trainers is fairly straightforward and can typically be conducted within a reasonable amount of time. The process may be slightly lengthened if external candidates must be considered because locating qualified candidates and conducting interviews with individuals outside of the organization can be time consuming. However, the process is largely the same.

The use of contract training providers is a slightly different matter. Contract training providers will likely provide both training materials and presenters. This greatly simplifies that PMO's task from a training development and delivery perspective, but requires the PMO staff to take due diligence to validate that the material and the instructors provided by the contract provider are adequate to meet the organization's needs. Two important considerations are of interest—material content and trainer professionalism.

Materials. An external training provider should not be considered unless the provider is willing to provide, as part of the selection process, a complete copy of all materials that will be presented (with completion of a nondisclosure agreement by the PMO manager or other staff reviewing the materials a potential, and perhaps reasonable, request) or to provide complimentary admission to an actual course presentation for one or more members of the PMO staff who will be responsible for selecting the training provider. The responsibilities of the PMO in the selection process should also include ensuring that the material that will be presented is aligned with project management best practices and is consistent with the desired state of operations in the organization. Determining if these conditions are satisfied will not be possible unless the PMO has the ability to completely review the training content.

Trainers. The trainers that will provide the training are a second area of consideration. External training providers often engage multiple instructors to present material. Minimally, the PMO staff should review the provider's instructor selection process or request copies of past course evaluations for a variety of instructors to determine the degree of professionalism that can be expected from the training provider's staff. Ideally a review of the credentials, past course evaluations, and references for the specific instructor that will be responsible for presenting training to the organization should be conducted to ensure that the instructor is well qualified. If possible, the PMO should ensure that this level of detail is provided when negotiating with all potential training providers. (If a specific instructor cannot be identified because the training provider utilizes multiple instructors and schedules each according to need, the minimum information mentioned previously related to qualifications of instructors and past evaluations for a variety of instructors should be obtained.) Additionally, professional references should be checked in all cases to gauge other organizations' experiences with the provider.

A combination of reviewing the material that will be presented by the training provider, the credentials or evaluations of the provider's instructors, and the references provided by the provider ensures that an appropriate level of due diligence is conducted when making a provider selection. Initially, it may be advisable to contract with external training providers on a course-by-course basis in order to verify that quality training is being conducted prior to entering into any agreement of significant length or breadth. Clearly, the provider should be closely monitored and training effectiveness should be measured to ensure that high-quality training is being given throughout the provider's relationship with the organization. This topic will be discussed next. It is equally relevant for internal and external instructors and courses.

How Will Training Effectiveness Be Measured?

Delivery of training is the conclusion of the process of selecting appropriate courses, developing training materials, and selecting instructors. Ideally, one or more pilot sessions of each course will have been conducted in order to gather detailed feedback and make improvements prior to making the course generally available. Once a particular course "goes live," continuous monitoring of the course must be conducted to validate that the course is meeting the intended learning objectives and resulting in positive student outcomes. A feedback mechanism should be developed to monitor all training offerings. The mechanism of gathering feedback and the specific types of feedback gathered may vary from offering to offering, but as a general principle, the PMO must consistently gathering feedback on training effectiveness.

For computer-based training or similar training offerings in which an instructor does not guide learners, a simple survey may be implemented that addresses the effectiveness of the material presented and the effectiveness of the technology used to deliver the training. Using a survey also provides an opportunity for participants to offer suggestions for improving the course material. For instructor-led courses, additional feedback on instructor effectiveness should be obtained. Development of a standard course evaluation form that is used for all training courses is suggested. This form will ensure consistent feedback across all offerings (whether internally or externally provided). The evaluation form should include quantitative measures as well as opportunities to provide qualitative feedback and comments. The quantitative measures may be used to establish a training effectiveness "score" that can be tracked over time while the qualitative comments provide opportunities for the PMO staff to understand specific needs and limitations in the current course offering, a key to consistently improving courses over time.

The content of the evaluation form should be tailored to the specific needs of the PMO from the data gathering and course improvement standpoints. In general, include the following items:

- Course number and title
- Date(s) of course
- Instructor name(s)
- Participant name (optional)
- Course content
  - Effectiveness
  - Practicality
  - Applicability to job
  - Appropriate course length
- Instruction
  - Appropriate variety of learning techniques
  - Presentation materials easy to understand
- Instructor
  - Knowledge of subject matter
  - Effectiveness of presentation
  - Appropriate use of time
  - Ability to respond to questions
- Logistics
  - Training facilities (if applicable)
  - Technology facilities (if applicable)
  - Scheduling/registration process

- Comments
  - Content
  - Instruction
  - Instructor
  - Logistics

Within each of the major evaluation areas (e.g., course content or instruction), a series of specific topics and directed questions should be included along with a rating scale to allow students to provide responses. A rating scale using descriptive ratings such as "excellent," "very good," "good," "fair," and "poor" or a simple numeric scale such as a "1" to "5" scale may also be used as long as the relative values of each numeric within the scale are defined (i.e., it is clear whether a "1" represents a good score or a bad score). Sufficient space should also be provided within the evaluation form to allow students to provide comments on the major evaluation areas.

Gathering feedback is only effective if the feedback gathered is used to improve the training offering. Therefore, the PMO should consistently gather and analyze feedback on courses and course presenters to ensure that high-quality training courses are being delivered. Tracking course and instructor effectiveness over a number of course presentations is most effective because a single data point, such as one instructor's presentation or one delivery of a particular course, may not be representative of the overall strength or weakness of the course or the instructor. Over time, as feedback is gathered and analyzed, course designers and presenters can be coached on the strengths and weaknesses of courses and presentations and appropriate actions can be taken to improve the training offerings. From a content perspective, revised course materials, presentation slides, exercises, or other training assets may be developed in response to participant feedback. From an instructional perspective, instructors can be provided with feedback on areas of improvement or, as needed, replaced with other instructors if consistently marginal or poor feedback is received.

Continuous improvement in both the content and delivery domains are important components of effective training delivery. Having data to support the quality of materials and instruction will facilitate presenting data on training effectiveness to management and, as needed, will justify additional investment in resources to support ongoing training improvement.

Before leaving this topic, note an item of relevance pertaining to utilizing external training providers. Often, these providers will have standard training evaluation forms that are used to gauge the effectiveness of their content and presentation and which are used to uniformly track training effectiveness within their organizations. These forms should not be viewed as substitutes for the PMO's standard training evaluation form. If a training provider requires a particular form for their own purposes, this form should be provided to students in addition to the PMO's standard evaluation form. This provides consistency of evaluation and feedback from the PMO perspective and also ensures that specific, unique evaluation criteria that the PMO may have included as part of the PMO evaluation form is consistently gathered.

The Training Abstract

As the previous sections demonstrate, a number of areas must be considered when developing a training offering. Bringing all of these components together into a single document, a "training abstract," may be a useful part of the planning process. The training abstract serves as a single vehicle for documenting course goals, learning objectives, form of delivery, development process, and time line for development. A training abstract can also serve as a planning document for each training deliverable that the PMO wishes to implement. Additionally, the abstract can be used over time to track changes to the training objectives and deliverables once the initial training content is delivered. Major components of the abstract include:

- Training topic/title
- Staff member responsible for training development or sourcing
- Training goals
- Intended audience(s)
- Learning objectives
- Content outline
- Form of delivery
- Proposed subject matter experts or content designers
- Proposed content reviewers or quality assurance agents

- Major training deliverables/assets
- Time line for development

Ideally the abstract will be created as part of the planning process by the individual who will be responsible for owning the training from a PMO perspective. A single point of contact should be identified for each training opportunity that the PMO will deliver, whether internally or via external providers. This individual should have responsibility for all decisions related to development and ongoing delivery of the training, in consultation with the PMO manager and other resources within the organization as needed. This ensures that there is clear accountability for each training opportunity and that an individual is identified and tasked with coordinating development, delivery, and continuous improvement of each training opportunity. If a number of training deliverables are anticipated, a PMO training manager may be required to coordinate the entire training curriculum. If only a few offerings will be required, members of the PMO staff may divide these offerings based on area of expertise and supervise the development and delivery of the offerings directly. By starting with the training abstract, the responsible member of the PMO staff has a guiding document that, once agreed to with the PMO manager and, as appropriate, organizational management, can be used so that the final deliverables for the training experience are aligned with PMO and organizational goals.

Developing a Training Roadmap

If the number of training programs that the PMO will coordinate exceeds more than a few offerings, it is advisable to align the training offering list that has been created as part of the training plan process with a time line for development and delivery. Developing a training roadmap for this purpose is a useful way to plan the development and implementation of training deliverables and to track progress versus plans for each training deliverable. Because the training plan prioritizes training deliverables according to organizational need, the training roadmap can be developed in such a way as to ensure that high-priority training offerings are included in the early phases of the roadmap. The speed with which training deliverables can be produced and made available to the organization is a function of many factors including

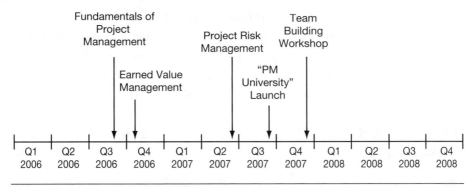

Figure 7.3 Training roadmap.

method of delivery for each, length of training, resource availability, and other factors. As such, the roadmap may represent a best guess based on the collective belief of the members of the PMO staff responsible for training development and deployment rather than a firm plan for delivery. As training abstracts are developed, a preliminary understanding of the required work to develop and deliver each training deliverable will be obtained. This data can be used to appropriately map training deliverables to the training roadmap.

The roadmap should be formatted in a time line of reasonable length. Because the purpose is to map completion of training deliverables, items placed on the roadmap should be placed at the point at which the PMO believes the training will be generally available to the organization. Figure 7.3 provides a possible format for a training roadmap.

A training roadmap can serve as an excellent vehicle not only for internal management of PMO training priorities, but also for discussions with management regarding training prioritization and deliverables. If the roadmap is based on the PMO's best belief regarding when training can be made available based on organizational resource commitments and PMO priorities, discussions with management can be undertaken to either gain management alignment to the plan or to discuss methods of adjusting the roadmap if the schedule provided does not meet management expectations. The criticality of a well-trained project management staff as a vehicle for improving project success may require adjustment to the time lines and considering options such as engaging external resources to deliver one or more of the training courses. Another option is considering adding additional PMO staff to accelerate the pace of developing and providing training deliverables internally. Having data available to support these possibilities based on current organizational constraints is an excellent starting point for these discussions. It also allows the PMO staff to intelligently discuss with management the constraints facing the PMO from a training development and delivery perspective.

The Role of Training in Project Management Career Path Development

Although developing job titles and career paths is primarily a human resources and line management function, the PMO may be influential in the development or support of a project management career path within the organization. Providing a clear career path for project managers, which includes growing their skills and providing progressively more challenging project management assignments, has significant benefits in terms of staff retention and job satisfaction. The PMO may assist in supporting the project management career path within the organization by aligning appropriate training opportunities with each level in the organization's project management career path, ensuring that members of the organization have access to appropriate training that will help them to be successful in their current project roles and gain the required skills to be successful in future, more senior roles. This alignment requires ensuring that an appropriate number of relevant training opportunities exist that are appropriate for each level within the career path and that progressively more advanced opportunities that build on past learning experiences are built into the PMO's training plans. Although each member of the organization will determine the training he or she will undertake, in consultation with his or her management and based on individual and organizational needs, providing a framework for allowing individuals to identify learning opportunities appropriate for their level within the organization provides an additional mechanism for guiding career development through education and training. It also assists individuals in determining appropriate learning opportunities deemed important for success within a particular project management position in the project management career path.

A NOTE ABOUT ALTERNATE TRAINING SOURCES

One area that has not been explored as part of this discussion on sources for training is alternate venues for gaining education and training on project management topics beyond traditional training courses. Conferences, seminars, and other experiences provided by professional organizations or other groups in the project management domain provide excellent opportunities to gain insight into project management tools, techniques, and trends. Often these seminars and conferences provide access to a variety of speakers who provide short, targeted presentations on topics of interest as well as panel discussions, keynote speeches from recognized experts, and informal networking opportunities to allow participants to learn from each other. Vendor exhibits and other activities may also be available as part of the agenda. Although they are not traditional forms of classroom training, these opportunities can be valuable learning experiences. The PMO likely cannot afford to send a large contingent to every project management conference that it becomes aware of in a particular year, but selecting a few high-quality and well-respected conferences that are produced by recognized professional organizations or vendors within the project and program management domains and permitting one or a few members of the PMO staff to attend can be a tremendously valuable experience. Participants will likely return with numerous ideas for new areas of focus for the PMO as well as ways to improve current operations from both the PMO operations and the project delivery perspective.

On a smaller scale, educational offerings and regular meetings of local project and program management groups (often chapters of larger organizations) provide a way to gain additional exposure to happenings in the domain of project and program management without spending a significant amount of money. These groups often host speakers on relevant topics, provide occasional short training courses, and encourage networking among project management peers to encourage sharing experiences and best practices. If these local organizations exist in locations convenient to members of the organization, members of the PMO staff and other members of the project management community within the organization should be encouraged to attend. If possible, the PMO may partially or fully fund participation in these activities for one or more members of the staff.

LINKING TRAINING AND EDUCATION

The introductory sections of this chapter have identified training as one component of the broader concept of educating the organization. Training provides formal opportunities to gain knowledge on a variety of topics, providing benefits to both the individual and the organization. In addition to training opportunities, providing resources, such as a project management knowledgebase or access to relevant articles, case studies, and other materials that contribute to gaining knowledge, represents educational opportunities beyond training itself. As the PMO staff considers the role of the PMO in providing education and training, it is important to ensure that an appropriate balance of educational and training resources is provided. Achieving this balance will require evaluating education and training needs on a regular basis and ensuring that appropriate plans are in place to meet the needs of the organization.

SUMMARY

This chapter has addressed two key domains of influence from a knowledge perspective—the project management knowledgebase as a foundation for formalizing project management knowledge within the organization and the role of the PMO in developing and providing relevant educational and training opportunities for members of the project and program management community within the organization. Building a foundation in these areas by "starting small and growing big" (a recurring theme within this text) is fundamental to achieving success in creating knowledge building and sharing opportunities within the organization. Because development of these areas progresses over time, the PMO will continue to grow as a knowledge "manager" and the organization will benefit from increased access to best practices, organizational know how, useful training opportunities, and enhanced knowledge sharing—all important components of a successful, knowledge building organization.

8

THE PMO AS A CONSULTING ORGANIZATION

INTRODUCTION

As the PMO begins to influence the organization and provide value, members of the project and program management community should begin to recognize the PMO as a center of excellence for project and program management within the organization. As time passes, members of the project and program management community will likely begin to come to the PMO with questions regarding project and program management practices and organizational standards as well as for assistance with project issues. This is clearly a desired outcome. The PMO should assume an active role in addressing these areas and as such should recognize itself as a consulting organization, albeit primarily as consultants to the internal staff rather than external organizations. In a consulting capacity, the PMO may operate in one or more of the following consulting domains:

- Project and process consulting
- Mentoring
- Project staff augmentation and active project management

Project and process consulting represents the traditional consulting role of providing advice and guidance to support others in the delivery of a relevant objective. This consulting role might include assisting with project workshops, assessing troubled projects and providing guidance to improve results, or answering questions from the PMO's constituents on PMO processes and standards or general questions in the realm of project and program management. Mentoring, an extremely powerful and often underutilized component of consulting, involves providing continuous guidance and coaching to members of the organization by pairing senior project or program managers with junior members in the organization. Mentoring gives junior members in the organization access to senior professionals for project guidance, career guidance, and general advice on topics of interest in the project management and professional development realms. Active project management relates to the role of the PMO in actively managing projects for the benefit of the organization. These PMO projects may be very complex efforts requiring guidance by the most-senior project management experts in the organization or they may be cross-functional efforts in which management does not logically rest within one group, division, or geography within the organization. In this capacity, the PMO will likely employ full-time PMO project managers and utilize resources from across the organization to accomplish project goals.

Each of these consulting domains will be discussed in this chapter, along with guidance on implementing an effective structure for achieving success in project and program consulting. Even if the PMO will not primarily serve as a consulting organization, some level of consulting will naturally occur. Therefore it is important to consider how the PMO should approach this consulting role. The consulting role offers the PMO an opportunity to further serve the project management community as a trusted expert and advisor, a role that will grow the credibility of the PMO and the effectiveness of its operations in achievement of its goal of improving project results.

PROJECT AND PROCESS CONSULTING

The range of project and process consulting activities that a PMO may choose to undertake can be significant. The following list categorizes the range of possible activities that a PMO may assist with and contains general areas of focus with examples of the types of activities that might take place within each:

- Overarching consulting
  - Consulting on organizational project and program management standards
  - Addressing general project management questions and concerns
- Project initiation and planning consulting
  - Proposal and business case development consulting
  - Project kickoff guidance/workshops
- Project execution consulting
  - Project tracking and reporting consulting
  - Troubled project recovery
- Project closeout consulting
  - Lessons-learned sessions

The areas in the list primarily represent explicit areas of focus in which the PMO may choose to develop and deliver *formal* consulting. However, a number of other areas may also exist within the consulting domain of the PMO. These other areas, such as addressing general questions and consulting needs, represent *ad hoc* consulting that the PMO may participate in for the benefit of projects undertaken within the organization. The PMO should address both formal and ad hoc consulting as part of project and process consulting planning and develop an appropriate scope of effort based on the organization's consulting needs.

Defining the scope of the PMO project and program consulting role first requires considering the structure of a PMO consulting organization. This organization may consist of a dedicated group within the PMO that primarily undertakes consulting activities or it may consist of one person or a portion of several persons' efforts, depending on the size and capacity of the PMO staff. There is no need, especially in smaller PMOs, to maintain dedicated consulting resources if the primary scope of the PMO is small from a consulting perspective. To determine if this is the case, the specific scope of the PMO's efforts from a consulting perspective must be defined. This definition should include the role of the PMO from a formal consulting perspective as well as from an ad hoc consulting perspective.

The Ad Hoc Consultant

The ad hoc consultant role addresses general questions, concerns, and issues from project managers and project team members throughout the organization served by the PMO. An ad hoc role is less concrete than the specific areas of project and process consulting that the PMO may have chosen to undertake as part of its formal consulting role. Yet, ad hoc consulting serves a critical role by assisting the organization with project management concerns as well as by providing a place to "get answers" or seek advice regarding project issues. Quantifying the ad hoc consulting needs of the organization and attempting to determine appropriate PMO resource needs from an ad hoc consulting perspective are not easy tasks. Ad hoc consulting requests are not likely be distributed uniformly over time. Additionally, depending on the nature of the request, the amount of time required to respond to a particular request could range from minutes to hours to days. Therefore, to determine PMO ad hoc consulting resource needs, approximate the number of expected requests based on the size of the constituency served by the PMO, the relative experience of the project management community, and other associated factors.

Another consideration is that the role of ad hoc consultant within the PMO does not have be filled by one person. Although designating a member of the PMO staff as the PMO consulting leader, whether full time or as part of a PMO staff member's other responsibilities, is desirable and supports management of the ad hoc consulting function, this individual will likely not have an answer to every question posed by members of the organization. Therefore, the PMO staff will be required to work collaboratively to serve in the ad hoc consultant role, with PMO staff members who have knowledge in particular domains of project or program management serving as consultants to address specific questions. The PMO consulting leader or a designated member of the PMO staff who is responsible for serving as the primary consulting contact should rely on various experts within the PMO (and potentially beyond) to address questions within their domains of expertise. Identifying these experts is a PMO task that should be included in planning for implementing the ad hoc consulting role.

The previous discussion has highlighted another important prerequisite for any ad hoc consulting activity. The PMO must develop a process for gathering consulting requests from the organization and tracking these requests to conclusion. A generic PMO consulting electronic mail address, a PMO consulting "hotline" phone number, or some other designated method of contact with the PMO should be communicated to the organization to ensure that members know how to request ad hoc consulting assistance from the PMO. The PMO must also ensure that requests received are managed and resolved in a timely fashion. If members of the organization submit requests for assistance and do not receive timely responses, the PMO will begin to develop a negative reputation, clearly contrary to the desire to have the PMO serve the project management community as a helpful resource. A simple tracking spreadsheet or database, which identifies requestors and requests as well as the member within the PMO who is responsible for responding to requests, can greatly assist with tracking the status of consulting requests. Communication to a requestor regarding the status of his or her request and an estimated response time will help ensure that requestors know that their requests are receiving attention and that a response will be forthcoming.

Formal PMO Consulting

The formal PMO consulting role should be defined by a list of areas of focus that the PMO will address from a consulting perspective. When determining the areas of primary focus from a formal consulting perspective, the detailed business case, strategic planning documents, or other relevant guiding documents of the PMO should be consulted. The formal areas of focus should still align with the key project management needs of the organization and should facilitate providing formal mechanisms to address areas of general concern. (*Note*: The list of general formal consulting categories and potential areas of focus within each that was included in a previous section is an example of some of the areas of formal consulting that a PMO might undertake. Many other potential areas exist.)

At the planning stage, the first task the PMO should undertake is to determine the specific areas of focus that will provide the most value to the organization. If the organization regularly faces project "false starts" or planning miscues that lead to issues with project delivery later in a project's life cycle, developing a consulting process to review project planning documents or conducting project kickoff workshops may be appropriate. If capturing knowledge at project closeout or continually making the same mistakes in a number of projects is a concern, PMO guidance in facilitating lessons-learned sessions or capturing and distributing project lessons for the benefit of the organization may be important. The areas of focus and the particular activities undertaken will largely be driven by organizational priorities and needs.

Providing an exhaustive list of all the possible formal consulting activities would be impossible. However, a few general comments in the sections that follow will provide perspective regarding several common areas of formal consulting.

Project Proposal Development

Developing project proposals may pose a particular challenge in organizations in which formal business case development is not typically undertaken in the project environment. If the organization has started developing detailed project proposals as part of the portfolio management and project chartering processes, some projects in the past were likely to have been undertaken without clear linkages to business priorities, potentially resulting in an unnecessary expenditure of funds and poor utilization of organizational resources.

Guiding project managers and other business leaders through a process of developing a project proposal or reviewing project proposal drafts and providing feedback can be valuable both from the perspective of the organization (in terms of the PMO providing a service to the organization) and from the perspective of the PMO (in terms of ensuring that quality proposals are developed before potential projects enter the project approval process). Even if the organization already has a defined a set of standards for proposal content and format (highly recommended), members of the organization who develop proposals may have to produce one or two drafts (or perhaps more) before a proposal is in a form that best represents the project proposal. Providing guidance and consulting throughout this process ensures that members of the organization sense that they are supported, especially during the development of their first or second proposal, when they may have a number of questions as part of the process of trying to "get it right."

Project Kickoff and Team Building

Providing consulting for a project kickoff or providing consulting for team building in a new project team also provides value to the organization and ensures that approved projects begin on a path to success. The role of the PMO may include directly facilitating project kickoff workshops or team building activities or it may involve providing project managers with the resources and best practices to allow them to facilitate their own sessions. However, an advantage of direct PMO involvement in these sessions is that the PMO will likely develop significantly more experience and expertise in facilitating effective workshops than an individual project manager can develop on his or her own. At most, a project manager might manage a few project efforts per year, but the PMO may conduct kickoff workshops and team building sessions for dozens of projects, thereby building PMO presentation skills and expertise in this area with each session. External guidance provided by the PMO also ensures that the project manager obtains the full benefit of the experience within the PMO, as well as allowing the project manager to participate rather than to be responsible for coordination of the session.

Troubled Project Recovery

Providing assistance to troubled projects is an important area of focus that should strongly be considered as part of the PMO's formal consulting plans. Even with the best practices and standards in place, projects may occasionally end up "off course." Although a project manager has made a best effort to correct project issues internally, doing so may not always lead to the project returning to a path to success. In this situation, by providing an external perspective, providing assistance with analyzing a troubled project, and developing plans to correct a troubled project, the PMO is well positioned to assist in these efforts. Senior project managers within the PMO staff can be made available to review troubled projects and to conduct detailed analysis of project issues. Senior PMO project managers can work together with the project manager and project team to determine an appropriate course of action to bring the project back on track and to monitor its progress to successful completion.

Having access to an external perspective from senior PMO project managers who are not directly involved with the project can also be extremely valuable. If necessary, proposing drastic actions such as canceling the project or instituting significant scope, schedule, or cost changes might be required. Having external validation of the need for these measures adds an additional level of credibility to any actions that may be proposed to management. Another consideration is that perhaps for reasons of personal pride or from having a commitment to the project or team, the project manager may not be willing to make the "tough call" of proposing drastic action or the project manager might be downplaying the magnitude of project issues. The PMO staff can provide a view of the issues that is neutral and propose possible remedies that are constructive. The PMO must act as a trusted partner rather than as an adversary in these situations. From a project-recovery perspective, the role of the PMO should not be to merely point out issues.

Recovering troubled projects involves becoming involved with the troubled project, identifying issues, proactively developing solutions, and working with the project manager to implement the proposed solutions and monitor project progress. For large projects, the project-recovery process can be long and time-consuming, but the benefits of seeing changes through and monitoring the efforts for further issues almost always outweighs the costs related to time and effort expended on project recovery efforts. The PMO manager may need to appoint one or more PMO staff members as primary project recovery consultants. These PMO staff members will be tasked with assisting troubled projects and providing regular reviews and updates to the PMO staff and management. In a smaller PMO or in an organization in which there are relatively few serious project issues at any one time, the project recovery consultant role may only be a part-time role within the broader responsibilities of one or more members of the PMO staff. In larger PMOs, the role could be a full-time job for one or more PMO staff members.

Project Tracking, Monitoring, and Reporting

Even if a project is not troubled, assistance may be needed with project tracking, monitoring, and reporting. This consulting role assists the organization by providing guidance in developing effective project tracking, monitoring, and reporting mechanisms for particular projects. Organizational standards may provide the framework for tracking and reporting projects to management, but the particular implementation of these standards may be a complex undertaking for managers of large projects. Given the vital importance of having accurate project data available, it is in the organization's best interests to ensure that mechanisms are in place within every project to facilitate timely and accurate tracking and reporting of project progress. The PMO may assist this effort by providing guidance about structuring project plans and schedules to support accurate reporting, assisting project managers with implementing systems to track project progress, and guiding project managers in understanding the project status reporting data collected and then using this data to better manage projects.

Project Auditing

In addition to assisting with project tracking, monitoring, and reporting, the PMO may serve in a project auditing capacity, consulting with project managers and management on issues related to inconsistencies in project reporting data or validating that effective systems are in place to track projects. Auditing may involve periodic reviews of project progress reports and project plans to validate that the progress reported accurately reflects the true state of the project or it may involve periodic data sampling from a variety of projects to validate that project tracking and reporting standards are being consistently followed. Based on audit results, project managers and project team members may be counseled about how to more effectively manage project tracking and reporting to ensure ongoing compliance with relevant standards. Data obtained from audits of frequently misunderstood or inappropriately executed standards practices may also be used to develop revised standards and best practices to ensure that more consistent results are obtained in the future.

Lessons Learned and Project Closeout

At the conclusion of a project's life cycle, an important part of project management best practices is to review the entire project from inception to completion and then to identify the lessons learned. This activity gathers knowledge assets that can assist in better management of future projects. The task is not a difficult undertaking, but issues will arise if the process of conducting lessons-learned sessions and documenting the results is inconsistent. (*Note*: The lessons learned themselves largely fall within the role of knowledge management, which involves gathering and disseminating the lessons learned from a variety of projects for the benefit of the organization.)

From a consulting perspective, facilitating the process to ensure uniform capture of lessons learned provides value. If the same team of PMO resources consistently conducts lessons-learned sessions with project managers and project teams, recurring themes related to project successes and challenges will likely emerge. These themes can be uniformly explored across a number of projects, and the lessons-learned can be captured for reuse. Knowing which areas to "dig into" within a particular project is based on experience that has been gained from conducting lessons-learned sessions with many projects. Expertise of this type is valuable, yet it is only easily applied if the experiences of a number of projects are available. The PMO has a much greater probability of achieving a breadth of experience that results from gathering information from many lessons-learned sessions than an individual project manager alone.

Finding the Right Mix

As the PMO staff undertakes planning of its formal consulting role, once again it is appropriate to remember the recurring theme of "start small, grow large." A number of the formal consulting areas of focus previously discussed may be of interest to the PMO staff. (Additional areas beyond those identified here may be beneficial to the organization as well.) Documenting which opportunities the PMO will take advantage of and developing the plans to implement these areas within the PMO are parts of the planning process that should be undertaken with the advice of management. Aligning these areas of opportunity to the PMO's strategy and ensuring that sufficient resources are available to undertake the activities chosen are critical success factors. If the PMO attempts to undertake a scope that is too large, the likely result in each area undertaken will be diluted effort, leading to mixed (at best) perceptions of the value of the PMO as a consultant to the project management community within the organization.

Within the process of finding the right mix, ensure that sufficient thought is given to the amount of ad hoc consulting that will be performed. Determining the appropriate amount of resources and time to devote to the consulting role must consider the formal and ad hoc perspectives and should ensure that each role receives appropriate focus by PMO resources. In the early stages of PMO operations, the focus may primarily be on "fire fighting" or responding to project crises in an ad hoc consulting manner. Although not preferred, this is an acceptable method of operation in the early life of the PMO, but a plan must be formulated to evolve the PMO's consulting role beyond being merely reactive and providing assistance in crisis situations. Developing a plan to provide consistent, ongoing consulting and ensuring that *proactive* consulting as well as *reactive* consulting are included in the PMO's consulting strategy are of critical importance. A time line, roadmap, plan, or some other guiding document may assist in this capacity by providing goals and assigning resources to lead the development of each consulting domain that the PMO intends to operate within.

The Consulting-Knowledge Link

Whether ad hoc or formalized, there is a significant link between the project and process consulting and knowledge roles within the PMO. Consulting requestors, whether requesting formal consulting in the form of a project review or ad hoc consulting in the form of asking a general project management question, are seeking knowledge. Members of the PMO staff provide knowledge to requestors in the form of consulting services, answers to questions, or insight into important issues facing projects. When a requestor comes to the PMO with a consulting request, his or her request will be responded to by an expert, likely via the request being directed to an expert through the PMO's consulting manager or coordinator, who tracks the status

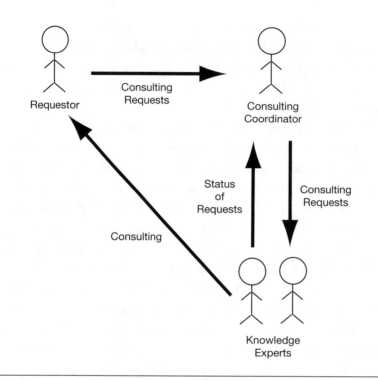

Figure 8.1 Requestor-knowledge expert relationship.

of requests and who may also provide consulting directly as well. This relationship is depicted in Figure 8.1.

Figure 8.1 illustrates this situation in many organizations, but a critical linkage is missing in this relationship. Although knowledge is being *shared* between the knowledge experts and the requestors, no corresponding knowledge *capture* is taking place to ensure that responses to consulting requests are recorded for reuse later. Ideally these knowledge assets would be available for general searching and use by members of the organization, lessening the need to rely on knowledge experts for answers to "common" questions over time. A revision of the requestor-knowledge expert relationship is depicted in Figure 8.2.

Figure 8.2 adds a project management knowledgebase (a key component of the PMO's knowledge strategy) to the requestor-knowledge expert relationship. In this relationship, requestors consult the project management knowl-

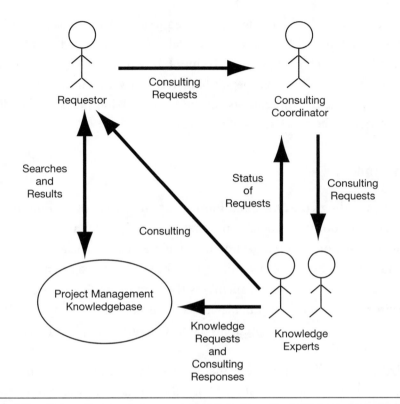

Figure 8.2   Requestor-knowledge expert relationship with project management knowledgebase.

edgebase to search for answers to questions (ideally before contacting the PMO for consulting) and the knowledge experts provide knowledge requests and responses as key inputs to the knowledgebase, making the knowledge broadly available to the organization.

If the PMO has already implemented a project management knowledgebase, feeding request and response information into the knowledgebase should be a fairly straightforward task. This task will require some additional effort on the part of knowledge experts, but it will pay significant dividends in terms of growing organizational knowledge. If the PMO has not yet implemented a project management knowledgebase or some other means of capturing organizational knowledge, this may be an appropriate time to consider doing so. At a minimum, consulting requests and responses, especially recurring ad hoc requests and responses, should be captured internally within the PMO. A catalog of requests and responses can be assembled that can subsequently be input into the knowledge management structure of the PMO when it begins to actively pursue a knowledge management strategy. Recurring requests can be identified and plans can be developed to address the root causes of recurring issues.

MENTORING

Beyond providing consulting for the project management community, the PMO has an opportunity to influence the growth of project management professionalism within the organization through mentoring. The general concept of mentoring involves pairing junior members of the project management organization with more senior members (beyond the individual's immediate supervisor) who guide and provide advice to junior members on a variety of issues related to project and program management, career planning, and general business skills.

Except in small organizations that have a limited number of junior project managers, it is unlikely that a PMO will itself have sufficient resources to facilitate mentoring for every junior member of the project management community. Additionally, mentoring may extend beyond the junior-to-senior project manager direct mentoring role to include junior project managers mentoring members of the project team staff who desire to assume project management roles as part of their career plans. Thus, senior project managers may mentor junior project managers who may eventually mentor project team members who want to assume more active project leadership roles. Clearly, the ideal role of a PMO would be to coordinate the mentoring process rather than to provide specific mentors to the organization at large. In a coordinating role, members of the PMO staff might be encouraged to serve as mentors on a limited basis in addition to coordinating the mentoring process.

Several important benefits are provided by a mentoring program. From the mentor's perspective, sharing knowledge and experience and guiding junior project managers has significant benefit in terms of personal satisfaction and contributing to the long-term growth of project management as a discipline within the organization. From the perspective of a member of the organization being mentored, advice from a more senior member of the project management community, beyond this individual's supervisor, can provide a unique perspective and guidance that can be extremely valuable. Having another member of the organization beyond the individual's immediate manager that can be sought for advice and guidance on project management and other general business issues can also be very valuable. A mentoring program can also provide value to the organization in general by further developing professional relationships within the organization and building greater collegiality within the project management community.

Developing a mentoring program involves identifying suitable members who are within the organization to serve as mentors, advertising the mentoring program to the organization, encouraging members with an interest in being mentored to participate in the mentoring program, and setting some general guidelines to facilitate the mentoring process. The PMO should have responsibility for coordinating these efforts and managing the mentoring program, but the PMO need not be regularly involved in interactions between mentors and the member of the organization being mentored. Observing a few general suggestions related to responsibilities of the PMO regarding mentoring will help ensure that the process developed by the PMO is successful and sustainable over time. These responsibilities include:

- Ensuring that participation in the mentoring program is optional (for mentors and members being mentored)
- Ensuring that potential mentors have the appropriate experience, expertise, and desire to participate in the mentoring program
- Requiring a commitment from mentors to participate in some minimal set of mentoring activities
- Monitoring the mentoring program and soliciting feedback from participants to assist with further development of the program over time

Perhaps the most critical responsibility of the PMO is to ensure that participation in a mentoring program is optional. It is essential that mentors and members of the organization proactively "opt in" to the program. Forcing members of the organization to serve as mentors or pairing mentors with individuals who do not wish to be mentored will not be a successful strategy. Any mentoring program should be designed to be strictly optional but generally available to members who have an interest in participating.

From a mentoring perspective, ensure that a mentor screening or selection process is in place to verify that potential mentors are suitably experienced and that they understand the commitment required to serve as mentors. The definition of "suitably experienced" may vary from organization to organization, but mentors should have enough experience in their current roles to provide expert guidance to members that they will mentor. Mentors should also have a more senior position in the organization than the member being mentored and be able to provide meaningful guidance and perspective. Of course, mentors should also possess a positive regard for the organization and its project management practices. Disgruntled or contrite mentors do little to encourage members who are being mentored.

As part of planning the mentoring process, also establish a set of minimal expectations for the mentor. These expectations need not be firm requirements that are regularly reported and tracked, but it is helpful if the mentor understands that some level of consistent, ongoing dialog should occur between the mentor and the individual being mentored. This could consist of a monthly phone call or lunch meeting or an occasional electronic mail communication. Although a mentor should generally be available to provide advice and guidance at any time, setting a minimal expectation of regular communication ensures that the mentoring relationship will be consistently maintained. Ideally communication will occur beyond these minimum expectations. As the mentoring relationship grows, quite likely more frequent communication will occur, an indication that the mentoring relationship is succeeding.

The PMO should also assume responsibility for gathering feedback from all participants in the mentoring program and for actively striving to improve the mentoring program. Occasional short surveys or other feedback mechanisms that allow participants to provide candid feedback on the mentoring program can be an excellent mechanism for gathering feedback. Feedback should then be incorporated into updates to appropriate areas of the mentoring program.

Locating Mentors and Mentoring Participants

When planning for the mentoring program has been completed, the next step involves finding mentors and mentoring participants for the program. To accomplish this, first solicit and identify suitable mentors. If the PMO regularly communicates with the organization via a PMO website, newsletter, electronic mail communications, or a regular meeting, these mechanisms provide an excellent opportunity to solicit mentors. The solicitation itself should provide some information on the general goals of the mentoring program, the requirements for mentors, and a means of expressing an interest in participating in the mentoring program. Contact information about where questions regarding the program can be directed should be included as well. If the goals and responsibilities of a mentor in the mentoring program are reasonable and clear, interested members of the organization will likely respond. Some amount of recruiting may be required to build a suitable group of mentors, but this recruiting must primarily be informational rather than giving an impression that participation in the mentoring program is mandatory or dictated by management. Some amount of screening of mentor candidates should be undertaken so that members who express an interest in mentoring are suitably qualified, understand the expectations of the program, and possess a genuine interest in participation.

Once suitable mentor candidates have been chosen, the process of identifying members of the organization who are interested in being paired with a mentor can begin. Ideally the number of mentors who have been chosen will exactly match the number of respondents who are interested in being paired with a mentor, resulting in an exact one-to-one relationship. Unfortunately, this will quite likely not be the case. If the number of mentors exceeds the number of interested mentoring participants, pairs may be established for as many of the mentors as possible, with the remaining mentors being placed on a "waiting list." As additional participants come forward, mentors can be selected from the waiting list to create matches with these new participants. If the number of mentoring participants exceeds the number of identified mentors, mentors should be polled to determine if they would be willing to mentor more than one individual. This situation might be acceptable to some mentors but not to others. In all cases, the wishes of the mentor should be observed. If mentoring participants remain after all mentors have been paired according to their wishes, a participants' waiting list should be established. As more mentors come forward, new pairings can be created from mentoring participants on the waiting list.

Matching mentors and mentoring participants appropriately can be a complex task. Although merely assigning pairs at random could be done, often some level of coordination is desirable. Creating pairs based on career interests, their work on similar types of projects, geographic location, or some other considerations may be appropriate. The PMO should determine any criteria to be observed in creating pairings and then consistently follow the process that is developed. A goal of mentoring is to create opportunities for gaining access to the benefits of mentoring for all members of the organization, not just members who meet a specific set of criteria. If the PMO determines that some methodology of selection for mentoring participants is necessary, the process should be clearly communicated and then undertaken in an unbiased manner. Avoid the appearance of certain groups within the organization receiving preferential assignment of mentors.

The Role of Junior Mentors

In addition to junior and senior project manager relationships, creating other mentoring relationships may also be desirable. Building the skills and knowledge of junior project managers is essential to ensure that sufficient resources are available to manage current and future project efforts. Yet, an additional area of focus is relevant. Senior project team members who have an interest in project management should also be encouraged to build the skills necessary to assume higher positions of project leadership within the organization in the future.

In most cases, junior project managers emerge from the ranks of senior project team members, project team members, subteam leaders, and similar roles. Over time they assume positions of greater leadership, eventually leading and managing entire project efforts. As these members of the organization assume project management roles, the next group of potential project managers must be provided with appropriate opportunities and guidance to allow them to gain the skills and experience required to assume junior project leadership positions. Mentoring can play a key role in encouraging members of the organization to become active project management students and to prepare them for project leadership positions in the future.

Mentoring project team members can also be a valuable component of a mentoring program. Junior project managers, who have already served in the capacity of team members and have succeeded in developing the skills and experience required to be promoted to project management roles, are ideal candidates to mentor senior project team contributors who have an interest in project management and have demonstrated a capacity to succeed as project managers.

In establishing this mentoring relationship, be selective with regard to which members of the organization are viable candidates for mentoring. Although many contributing members likely exist on project teams within the organization, not all contributors possess the desire and the skills to become successful project managers. Determining which members of the organization are ready for promotion to project management positions requires evaluation by management. Evaluation of candidates should be led by the management within the organization with advice from the PMO as needed. Once project management candidates have been identified, mentoring opportunities may be created to allow these individuals to grow their skills and knowledge in preparation for assuming project leadership roles.

Recently promoted project managers who have completed some level of detailed training and have gained some experience in leading projects within the organization are an ideal source of mentors for senior project team members. These project managers can provide guidance not only on project management practices within the organization, but they can also provide insight into lessons that they have learned as new project managers. This insight gained from experience is tremendously valuable and can help to encourage individuals who have the desire and skills to assume project management roles to further expand their skills and professional growth in preparation for assuming a project management position.

Managing the Mentoring Process

Over time, mentors will leave the organization, mentoring participants will move to different job functions, and other scenarios will arise that will leave mentoring participants with no mentor or mentors with no one to mentor. Managing the mentoring process should include periodically polling mentors and mentoring participants to validate that an active mentoring relationship still exists and, when necessary, reassigning mentors and mentoring participants. The process of recruiting mentors and mentoring participants should also be sustained, utilizing waiting lists as needed to deal with capacity constraints. A PMO staff member may be appointed to the role of mentoring coordinator to manage the monitoring process. Monitoring activities should not require a significant amount of effort on a regular basis. The coordinator function should oversee recruitment and retention of program participants and should also collect and act on participant feedback to improve mentoring program effectiveness.

Serving as a mentor will likely not result in any significant additional compensation, vacation time, or other tangible rewards. The personal satisfaction of contributing to the betterment of a professional colleague is a primary reward that mentors can expect to receive. Because a mentor's commitment of time and talent is worthy of recognition, the PMO may wish to consider providing modest recognition of mentors. An annual lunch or recognition reception attended by mentors, mentoring participants, and members of management is one possibility. A small token of appreciation could also be used as a gesture of thanks for participation in a mentoring program. Providing recognition, even if not elaborate, will go a long way toward ensuring that mentors will continue to be actively involved in the mentoring program and will help to facilitate growth of the program over time.

PROJECT STAFF AUGMENTATION AND ACTIVE PROJECT MANAGEMENT

Project staff augmentation and active project management are opportunities for the PMO to become more directly involved in day-to-day project work within the organization. Both require a commitment of PMO resources to work beyond the traditional consulting, knowledge, and standards roles of the PMO and therefore must be undertaken with a full staff of PMO resources so that appropriate focus is given to both roles—the traditional PMO roles and the additional project management roles. This section will provide an overview of the project staff augmentation role and the active project management role as well as suggestions for effective implementation in PMOs that will be assuming these roles.

Project Staff Augmentation

The project staff augmentation role involves the *temporary* allocation of PMO staff members to assist project teams with specific project issues or to fill project member roles in the event of resource constraints within the organization. Often, especially in a smaller PMO, the PMO does not maintain staff members who have no other PMO responsibilities than to serve as "on call" project managers. Therefore, assuming the role of staff augmentation or project support staff typically involves taking a PMO staff member away from other consulting, knowledge, or standards duties on a full-time basis for some period of time to fill a staffing gap, often at a relatively inopportune time for the PMO (realistically, there is seldom a convenient time for the PMO to be without resources).

In many organizations, the project staff augmentation role may formalize a role that will become an eventuality. As the organization undertakes projects and continues to face resource constraints, members of management may look to the PMO for assistance with relieving these resource constraints. Because the PMO staff has significant project management experience, the idea of "borrowing" members of the PMO staff for specific project tasks when resource constraints exist will undoubtedly occur to someone in the organization. Assisting with project efforts may not be a bad practice in all cases, but setting a precedent of regularly using PMO staff members to assist with project efforts rather than to advance PMO efforts is risky. If project staff augmentation is unavoidable, a few common-sense steps can ensure that an appropriate level of control is maintained over the staff augmentation function.

Defined scope. PMO engagement in project activities should not be undertaken without first having a clear understanding of the work to be performed and an expected time commitment. Essentially, the scope must be documented so that what is being requested in terms of services and for how long these services will be required is clearly understood. Discussing these details in advance allows the PMO manager to make informed decisions about whether or not PMO engagement is appropriate and, if so, to identify the appropriate resource within the PMO staff to provide assistance. This step ensures that the engagement is appropriately time-constrained so that the PMO staff members can understand the impact on existing PMO efforts and effectively reallocate resources. Additionally, expectations of the PMO will be aligned with expectations of the group requesting PMO staff augmentation services so there is a clear understanding of the required level of engagement.

Limited scope. Next, the scope of services provided under any staff augmentation arrangement should be limited to project or program management functions. PMO services should be *supporting* the project rather than *assuming* the project. PMO assistance in the form of project- or program management-related services could include temporarily assisting with specific project management deliverables, managing a small portion of a project, or filling-in for a project manager if some critical emergency takes the managerial resource away from normal project activities for a period of time. Yet, the PMO engagement cannot involve replacement of resources for long-term engagements. Although this situation may be unavoidable in the life of the PMO at times, regularly assuming project responsibilities due to staff turnover, changing organizational priorities, reassignment of resources, or other business-driven causes will create significant disruption of PMO operations.

Reimbursement. PMO resources should only be viewed as consulting resources. Therefore PMO services should be charged appropriately to the project effort using them. The notion of a PMO providing "free" staff to projects is contrary to the general principles of project cost management—resources have costs and the consumption of resources creates impacts to the project budget. The project utilizing PMO staff augmentation resources should provide reimbursement to the PMO for the time utilized, which represents the lost time or the reduction in available capacity for the PMO to undertake work. Replacing this lost capacity could require foregoing some PMO work, adjusting deliverable due dates, and requesting that PMO staff members work extended hours to meet deadlines, as well as other impacts. These impacts should be offset by a payment from the project utilizing PMO resources. Requiring payment for use of PMO resources also discourages members of the organization from considering the PMO to be a free labor pool.

Informed management. Appropriate members of management should be kept apprised of any situations that will divert PMO staff members from the work of the PMO to perform project staff augmentation activities. In all likelihood, requests to use PMO staff members for project staff augmentation activities will originate with a member of management rather than being directly from a project team, yet the point of origination might not be from the management that oversees the PMO. Because unplanned staff augmentation activities will likely affect PMO deliverables in some way, the appropriate level of management should address these impacts either as part of the process of approving staff augmentation activities (if management will be involved directly) or as part of normal PMO process reviews (if the PMO manager will authorize staff augmentation activities). The PMO should be a good "team player" and provide assistance when it makes good business sense to do so and does not cause excessive disruption to PMO activities, but requests for project staff augmentation should be brought to the attention of management so that members of management responsible for overseeing the PMO can understand the impact of any work undertaken.

Active Project Management

In the minds of many people, the most common role of a PMO is the role of an active project manager. Yet, in this text, a formal discussion of the role of a PMO as an active project manager has been left until last, not to diminish the role of the PMO in active project management, but rather to focus on the many other potentially valuable roles that a PMO, whether an enterprise, division, or group PMO, can play within an organization. The role of the PMO as an active project manager presents a unique opportunity for the PMO staff members to demonstrate their skills and expertise in the practice of project management.

Yet, the opportunity to demonstrate PMO skills and expertise should only be undertaken after appropriate thought and planning have been undertaken.

Often the roles of a PMO include developing the culture of project management, creating and maintaining standards and best practices, providing educational opportunities, and providing opportunities for the project management community within the organization to grow in terms of maturity and effectiveness. To effectively undertake these standards, knowledge, and consulting roles, a significant investment of time and resources will be required. Although adding the role of active project manager to the responsibilities of the PMO creates potential for the PMO to provide additional value to the organization, this added benefit must be balanced with the desire to focus on other priorities of the PMO such as knowledge, standards, and consulting. Therefore, give consideration to the impact on the effectiveness of the PMO in other areas for which it is responsible that will result from PMO staff members assuming operational responsibilities such as day-to-day management of projects. Dilution of effort across many PMO priorities is a dangerous practice. As with project staff augmentation, assuming an active project management role also requires due diligence.

When appropriate, potential benefits can be achieved through active project management. Because the PMO has a holistic view of the organization and maintains relationships with project managers and project team members across the organization, coordination of large, cross-functional efforts may be facilitated more easily via the PMO. Although effective coordination is certainly not a guarantee because the PMO will likely rely on matrixed resources for execution of project work, the cross-organizational perspective of the PMO and the PMO experience gained from working with diverse areas of the organization will provide benefits, in terms of establishing relationships with these different areas of the organization and achieving a broad understanding of the workings of the organization. Actively managing projects can be an additional opportunity for the PMO to gain firsthand knowledge and experience by using the standards and processes that the PMO has developed. Active management also provides an opportunity for the PMO staff members to test new processes and to gain direct exposure to the typical project challenges in the organization.

Because active project management requires a commitment of resources for an extended period of time and at a relatively high percentage rate of utilization (often 100%), the role of the PMO as an active project manager must be achieved through augmenting the PMO staff to include a group of dedicated PMO project managers who will focus exclusively on project execution. These dedicated PMO project managers represent a specific project management capacity within the PMO organization. They are resources who can be assigned to various projects and who, working with project team resources from within the organization as a whole, can execute complete project efforts on an as-needed basis. The scope of these efforts might be limited to only large or complex efforts that require coordination by well-trained professionals, but it could also include projects of less significant scope. In the case of large or complex projects, PMO project managers may be recruited from senior project managers within the organization or they may be hired externally by locating professionals with excellent project management credentials and broad industry experience.

Before undertaking the role of active project management, the PMO must consider the types of projects that will typically be managed and then ensure that persons recruited and asked to join the PMO staff in an active project management capacity have the skills and knowledge required to successfully implement the types of projects that will be undertaken. If the PMO regularly delivers projects that are late, are over budget, or have poor quality, word will undoubtedly "get around" and the value and effectiveness of the PMO could be called into question. The PMO must be adequately staffed to support the active project management role.

SUMMARY

A PMO can have an important role as a trusted consultant and advisor for an organization in matters of project and program management. This role may include a number of areas of focus, with each one representing an opportunity for the PMO to partner with the rest of the organization to ensure the success of project efforts. Providing advice and guidance, mentoring, growing the project culture within the organization, and assisting with the management of projects are important potential areas of focus within the consulting role. Each area should be considered as part of the consulting role definition for a

PMO. Over time, as a PMO matures and provides additional value to the organization, trust built between a PMO and the project and program community at large will likely develop and create a synergistic, partnering atmosphere that will enhance the relationship of a PMO within the organization and provide value to project managers, team members, organizational leaders, and the organization as a whole.

INDEX